Teradata Cookbook

Over 85 recipes to implement efficient data warehousing
solutions

Abhinav Khandelwal
Rajsekhar Bhamidipati

BIRMINGHAM - MUMBAI

Teradata Cookbook

Commissioning Editor: Amey Varangaonkar
Acquisition Editor: Varsha Shetty
Content Development Editor: Aaryaman Singh
Technical Editor: Dinesh Chaudhary
Copy Editor: Safis Editing
Project Coordinator: Manthan Patel
Proofreader: Safis Editing
Indexer: Aishwarya Gangawane
Graphics: Tania Dutta
Production Coordinator: Shantanu Zagade

First published: February 2018

Production reference: 1140218

Published by Packt Publishing Ltd.
Livery Place
35 Livery Street
Birmingham
B3 2PB, UK.

ISBN 978-1-78728-078-6

www.packtpub.com

`mapt.io`

Mapt is an online digital library that gives you full access to over 5,000 books and videos, as well as industry leading tools to help you plan your personal development and advance your career. For more information, please visit our website.

Why subscribe?

- Spend less time learning and more time coding with practical eBooks and Videos from over 4,000 industry professionals

- Improve your learning with Skill Plans built especially for you

- Get a free eBook or video every month

- Mapt is fully searchable

- Copy and paste, print, and bookmark content

PacktPub.com

Did you know that Packt offers eBook versions of every book published, with PDF and ePub files available? You can upgrade to the eBook version at `www.PacktPub.com` and as a print book customer, you are entitled to a discount on the eBook copy. Get in touch with us at `service@packtpub.com` for more details.

At `www.PacktPub.com`, you can also read a collection of free technical articles, sign up for a range of free newsletters, and receive exclusive discounts and offers on Packt books and eBooks.

Contributors

About the authors

Abhinav Khandelwal has 11 years of industry experience in BI, analytics, and data warehousing. He gained a BE from GIT Sitapura, Jaipur. He is pursuing his MBA at Welingkar, Mumbai and is currently based in Melbourne. He acts as a senior consultant on BI DWH projects. He has also been in the news for his award-winning projects. For more information, you can refer to his blogs called as anonymously rave and three of kind. Contact him on Twitter at @abhi_khandu.

Thanks Maa for persuading me to take this book, and Guds and Ravi for connecting me to Packt Publishing. Moni, I got this published before you; it's your turn now! Thanks to Teradata, the world's first data warehousing company. And to my all the editors, especially Aaryaman, for being a great help throughout.

Rajsekhar Bhamidipati has 13 years' industry experience in Teradata and DWH and gained his BTech from BPUT Rourkela. He is working in Pune with Teradata Corp as a Senior Teradata Specialist on Teradata DWH projects. He has been associated with Teradata for more than 8 years and has successfully led multiple projects in various roles, with notable success in service delivery. He leverages Teradata and related technologies in the areas of database administration, workload, performance and cloud.

About the reviewer

Viswanath Kasi is a decisive and results-driven professional with more than 12 years of experience in technology and management, with Teradata DBA expertise of 7 years. His experience with esteemed clients makes him unique and his passion for technology makes him technically stronger.

Packt is searching for authors like you

If you're interested in becoming an author for Packt, please visit `authors.packtpub.com` and apply today. We have worked with thousands of developers and tech professionals, just like you, to help them share their insight with the global tech community. You can make a general application, apply for a specific hot topic that we are recruiting an author for, or submit your own idea.

Table of Contents

Preface

Teradata is the world's leading provider of business analytics solutions, data and analytics solutions, and hybrid cloud products and services. Its eponymous **relational database management system (RDBMS)**, which is considered to be a leading data warehousing solution. It provides data management solutions for analytics. This book will help you get all the practical information you need to create and implement your data warehousing solution using Teradata.

The book begins with recipes on quickly setting up a development environment so that you can work with different types of data structuring and manipulation functions. You will tackle all the problems related to efficient querying, stored procedure searching, and navigation techniques. Additionally, you'll master administrative tasks such as user and security management, workload management, high availability, performance tuning, and monitoring.

This book is designed to take you through the best practices of performing real daily tasks no matter what role are you performing when dealing with Teradata. It will help you solve your problem and implement the best solution.

Who this book is for

This book is for database administrators and Teradata users who are looking for a practical, one-stop resource to solve all their problems while handling their Teradata solutions. If you are looking to learn the basics as well as advanced tasks involved in Teradata querying or administration, this book will be handy. Some knowledge of relational database concepts will be helpful to get the best out of this book.

What this book covers

Chapter 1, *Installation*, is about setting up the Teradata database and client utility to access the database.

Chapter 2, *SQLs*, teaches the basic SQL used to manage and process your data in a database.

`Chapter` 3, *Advanced SQL with Backup and Restore,* shows new and advanced SQL and explains how to back up your database.

`Chapter` 4, *All about Indexes,* resolves and improves our query performance using indexes.

`Chapter` 5, *Mixing Strategies – Joining of Tables,* shows how to improve join performance and explains how they work.

`Chapter` 6, *Building Loading Utility – Replication and Loading,* resolves utility issues and makes it work efficiently.

`Chapter` 7, Monitoring the better way, examines the best practices to catch and resolve performance issues on the database.

`Chapter` 8, Collect Statistics the Better Way, resolves query performance by collecting and managing statistics.

`Chapter` 9, *Applications and OPS DBA Insight,* identifies and resolves daily issues faced by application admins.

`Chapter` 10, *DBA Insight,* identifies and resolves daily issues faced by system admins.

`Chapter` 11, *Performance Tuning,* helps us identify, resolve, and improve query performance issues faced by database users.

`Chapter` 12, *Troubleshooting,* shows how to troubleshoot system-wide issues using database utilities.

To get the most out of this book

1. Readers of this book should have working knowledge of the Teradata database and SQL writing.
2. In order to install and connect to Teradata, readers have to download the software mentioned by creating a free account on the Teradata developer website.

Download the example code files

You can download the example code files for this book from your account at `www.packtpub.com`. If you purchased this book elsewhere, you can visit `www.packtpub.com/support` and register to have the files emailed directly to you.

You can download the code files by following these steps:

1. Log in or register at `www.packtpub.com`.
2. Select the **SUPPORT** tab.
3. Click on **Code Downloads & Errata**.
4. Enter the name of the book in the **Search** box and follow the onscreen instructions.

Once the file is downloaded, please make sure that you unzip or extract the folder using the latest version of:

- WinRAR/7-Zip for Windows
- Zipeg/iZip/UnRarX for Mac
- 7-Zip/PeaZip for Linux

The code bundle for the book is also hosted on GitHub at `https://github.com/PacktPublishing/Teradata-Cookbook`. We also have other code bundles from our rich catalog of books and videos available at `https://github.com/PacktPublishing/`. Check them out!

Download the color images

We also provide a PDF file that has color images of the screenshots/diagrams used in this book. You can download it here: `http://www.packtpub.com/sites/default/files/downloads/TeradataCookbook_ColorImages.pdf`.

Conventions used

There are a number of text conventions used throughout this book.

`CodeInText`: Indicates code words in text, database table names, folder names, filenames, file extensions, pathnames, dummy URLs, user input, and Twitter handles. Here is an example: "It went to the default `CASE` statement."

A block of code is set as follows:

```
/*Correlated query*/
SELECT Column1, Column2
FROM Table1 Tb1
WHERE Column1 IN
  (
```

When we wish to draw your attention to a particular part of a code block, the relevant lines or items are set in bold:

```
/*Aggregate CASE*/
SELECT SUM(
  CASE WHEN department='IT' THEN) AS SAL_IT
  SUM (
```

Any command-line input or output is written as follows:

```
tpareset -f testing the restart command
```

Bold: Indicates a new term, an important word, or words that you see onscreen. For example, words in menus or dialog boxes appear in the text like this. Here is an example: "**JavaScript Object Notation (JSON)** is a lightweight programming independent data interchange format."

Warnings or important notes appear like this.

Tips and tricks appear like this.

Get in touch

Feedback from our readers is always welcome.

General feedback: Email feedback@packtpub.com and mention the book title in the subject of your message. If you have questions about any aspect of this book, please email us at questions@packtpub.com.

Errata: Although we have taken every care to ensure the accuracy of our content, mistakes do happen. If you have found a mistake in this book, we would be grateful if you would report this to us. Please visit www.packtpub.com/submit-errata, selecting your book, clicking on the Errata Submission Form link, and entering the details.

Piracy: If you come across any illegal copies of our works in any form on the Internet, we would be grateful if you would provide us with the location address or website name. Please contact us at copyright@packtpub.com with a link to the material.

If you are interested in becoming an author: If there is a topic that you have expertise in and you are interested in either writing or contributing to a book, please visit authors.packtpub.com.

Reviews

Please leave a review. Once you have read and used this book, why not leave a review on the site that you purchased it from? Potential readers can then see and use your unbiased opinion to make purchase decisions, we at Packt can understand what you think about our products, and our authors can see your feedback on their book. Thank you!

For more information about Packt, please visit packtpub.com.

1
Installation

Teradata installation is easy and straightforward. This chapter will help you in the installation of Teradata 15.10.0.07 SLES 11 for VMware (40 GB), including the monitor tool Viewpoint on 64-bit Windows 7 with 8 GB RAM.

The following recipes will be covered in this chapter:

- Setting up Teradata 15.10
- Setting up Teradata Studio Express
- Teradata on Azure
- Defining a connection
- Connecting to the Teradata system
- Using studio tool options
- Setting up Teradata SQLA
- Configuring SQLA
- Building a query builder
- Importing data
- Exporting data

Go to `http://downloads.teradata.com/download/database`.

Setting up Teradata 15.10

Before we begin the installation process of our Teradata Database on a local machine, you need to install VMware workstation 12.x for Windows.

How to do it...

1. Fire up the installed VMware software:

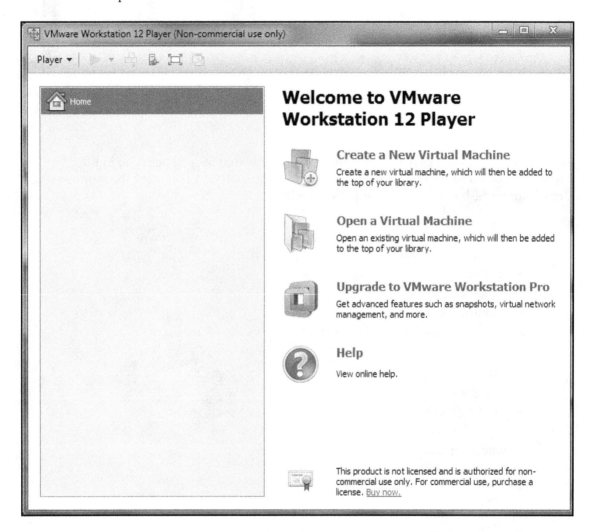

2. Click on **Open a Virtual Machine** and select the
   `TDExpress15.10.0.7_Sles11_40GB_vp.vmx` file from the open window
   prompt:

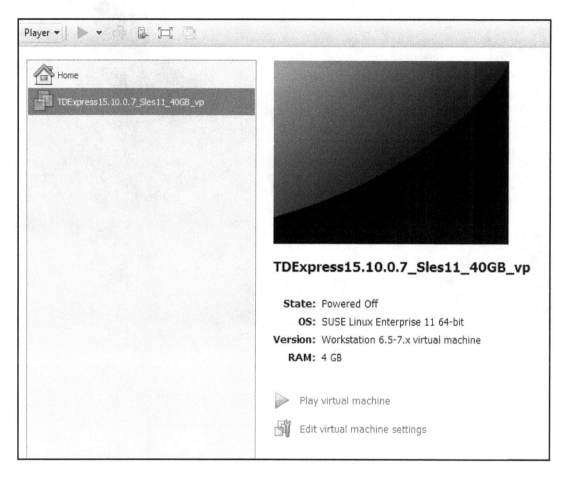

3. You are now ready to play the installed Teradata Database.

4. Click on the **Play Virtual machine** link. The setup will run its course and take you to the login screen:

```
bio: create slab <bio-0> at 0
Dquot-cache hash table entries: 512 (order 0, 4096 bytes)
registered taskstats version 1
  Magic number: 1:221:165
doing fast boot
Creating device nodes with udev
sd 0:0:0:0: [sda] Assuming drive cache: write through
sd 0:0:0:0: [sda] Assuming drive cache: write through
sd 0:0:1:0: [sdb] Assuming drive cache: write through
sd 0:0:1:0: [sdb] Assuming drive cache: write through
sd 0:0:1:0: [sdb] Assuming drive cache: write through
sd 0:0:2:0: [sdc] Assuming drive cache: write through
sd 0:0:2:0: [sdc] Assuming drive cache: write through
sd 0:0:2:0: [sdc] Assuming drive cache: write through
 sda6 sda7 >
sd 0:0:0:0: [sda] Assuming drive cache: write through
mount: devpts already mounted or /dev/pts busy
mount: according to mtab, devpts is already mounted on /dev/pts
Boot logging started on /dev/tty1(/dev/console) at Sat May 13 02:10:38 2017
Waiting for device /dev/disk/by-label/ROOT-BE1 to appear:  ok
fsck from util-linux-ng 2.16
[/sbin/fsck.ext3 (1) -- /] fsck.ext3 -a -C0 /dev/sda2
ROOT-BE1 has gone 633 days without being checked, check forced.
hrtimer: interrupt took 12123732 ns                         \ 17.1%
ROOT-BE1: |===================                              : 31.5%
```

5. **Login** with `root` as the username and password. Wait for the Teradata Lab log wallpaper to show up on the desktop in the bottom-right corner:

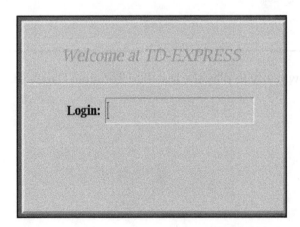

6. Voila! You have successfully installed the Teradata Database on your machine. The world's best analytical and data warehouse database is now up and running on your machine as the VM image:

7. Our next step will be to set up a client tool that connects to the existing database instance.

Setting up Teradata Studio Express

In the current version of VMware, we are already blessed with Teradata Studio Express. You will see an icon, **Teradata Studio Express**; all you need to do is click on this and it will fire up the client tool.

Getting ready

What if you want to install on your local machine/desktop without VMware? It's easy, all you need to do is create a login account at `http://developer.teradata.com/` and then go to the download link. Under tools, search for Teradata Studio Express.

How to do it...

For a Windows machine:

1. Unzip the client tool package to your local directory.
2. Run `setup.exe` to launch the Teradata Studio Express installation.
3. Teradata Studio Express is installed in the Program Files directory. For example, `C:\Program Files (x86)\Teradata\Client\16.00\Teradata Studio Express`.
4. Now, as the VMware machine is Linux OS-based, the installation file will be located in the `/opt/teradata` directory:

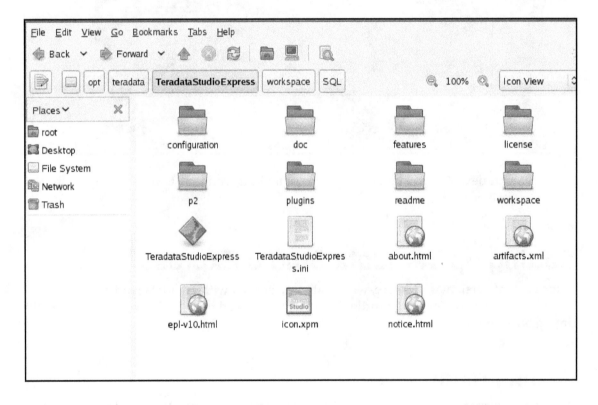

5. Teradata Studio Express requires a JDBC connection type; it does not support ODBC like the Teradata SQL assistant. You can connect to the following databases other than Teradata using studio. To add other databases to your preferred list of databases to connect to, go to the **Preference** tab and select from the list:

- Aster database
- Hadoop database
- DB2
- SQL
- Oracle

 Teradata Express also has a big brother, **Teradata Studio**; the main difference between Express and Studio is that the latter has an administrative window to it. The native Teradata administrator tool is integrated into Studio. So, if you are a DBA or power user, you will be needing Studio.

Here are some highlights of Studio and Express:

- Connection to variety of data databases
- Studio has an administrative window
- Copy and compare in Studio
- Hadoop data transfer in Studio
- Using load utilities in both
- Data lab feature in both

Teradata on Azure

With growing demand to increase its footprint, Teradata is now available on the cloud. This means that customers now don't have to worry about data centers and setting up the hardware.

Teradata has availability on the cloud as follows:

- Private cloud
- Public cloud
- Mixed cloud

With a proper subscription account, you can create your own Teradata Database on the cloud with all the capability and features you require.

With the current setup of Azure you can only deploy a 32 node system; if you require more nodes get in touch with Teradata sales personnel.

The thing you need to note is, many things in this recipe might change over time and some of them might not be valid. As the cloud platform is under continuous change, please check your subscription type before deploying a Teradata solution. Deploying Teradata on Azure is similar; you buy Teradata hardware on premises, you need to purchase the software with various available purchase methods.

 Deploying Teradata on cloud can cost you money, so be very vigilant when deploying database, as charges/fees can come as a surprise to you.

You can also deploy Teradata with all the additional products such as Viewpoint, datamover, and many others. Or you can buy these products individually; this gives you added advantages when you require flexibility.

There are many factors and parameters when you deploy the solution to the cloud, but in this recipe we will only cover how to create a Teradata Database and Viewpoint instance in Azure and make it available publicly.

Getting ready

You need to have an Azure subscription. Log in to the Azure marketplace and create a free account. It is recommended to have a subscription-based account to have enough cores available to you. Following are some prerequisites:

- Pay-as-you-go subscription on your Azure account
- Sufficiently high quota limits (recommended: 128 cores) in your Azure account

How to do it...

1. Once you are logged in to the Azure marketplace, search for Teradata, and as shown in the screenshot, select **Teradata Database** from the list:

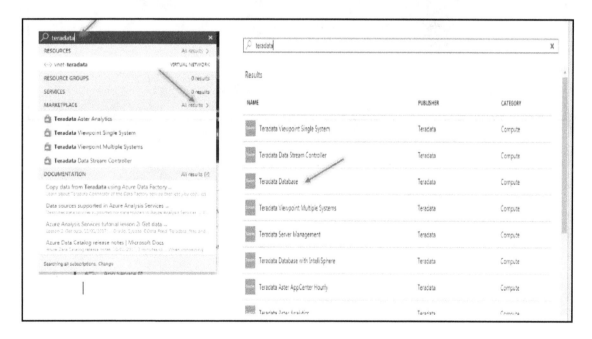

2. On next window, read the terms and conditions. And after that, click on **Create**, as shown in the screenshot:

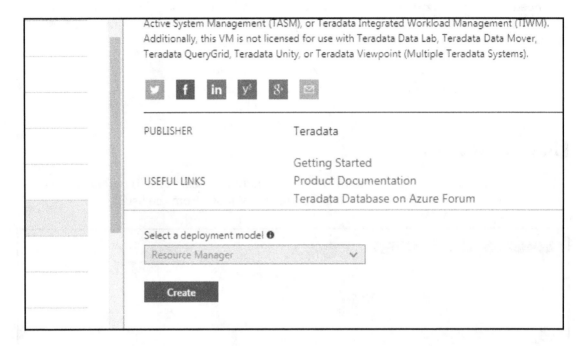

3. Next will be the window with the list of steps. In the first step, you need to provide a **User name**, a **Password**, and select a **Location** based on your requirements. Not all the **Locations** have products that you require. Click **OK** to move to step 2. Check the screenshot for details:

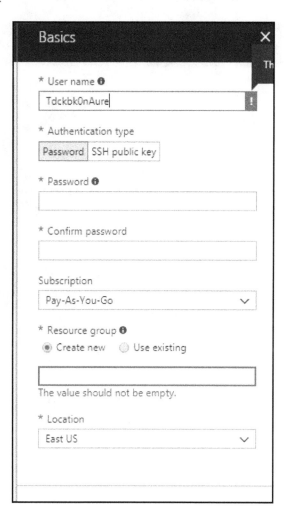

4. In step 2, select the name of your `database`, and provide the **DBC password** (keep it safe in a notepad). Also, select the flavor or **Database Tier** and **Version** of the database you want. Azure hosts the latest version Td 16.10. Click OK to move to the next step. Check the following screenshot:

5. The next step will be configuring your **Viewpoint**. To keep it simple, select only a single monitoring Viewpoint system. All the fields are self-explanatory. Password here will be used to log in to Viewpoint via an admin account. Check the following screenshot:

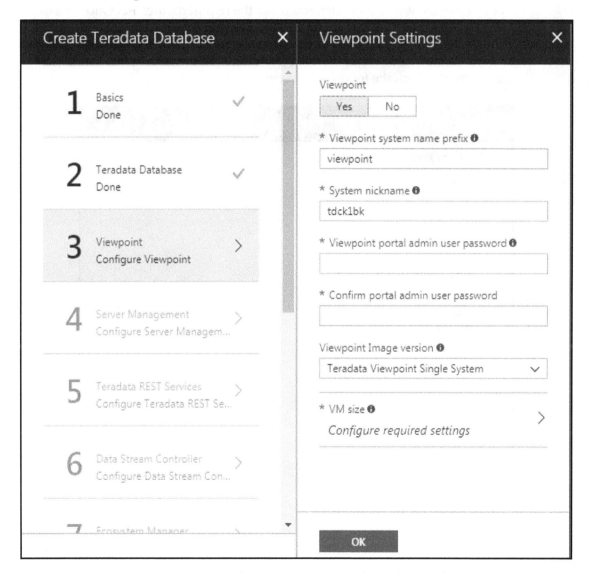

6. Options 4 to 8 are optional. You can either enable or disabled them as per your requirements.

7. In step 8, once all the configuration is done, a final validation is executed, which checks for all the parameters and cores available at your location. If all went fine, your deployment will start after you make the required purchase. Once finished with the configuration, a template will be prepared for future use. You can download the template from your database, which can be used afterwards if you want to create a same configuration system or want to use template based deployment. Check the following screenshot:

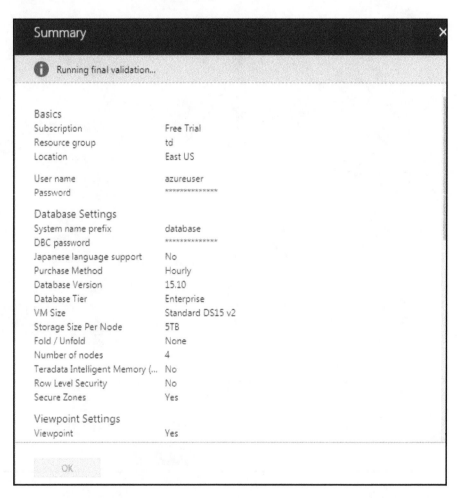

8. Your deployment will start, as shown in the following screenshot. It will take approximately 30 mins or so to get the system up and running. You can check the progress from the **Resource group** option from the left-hand side of the toolbar, and under the resource group you created while deploying the database. Check the following screenshot:

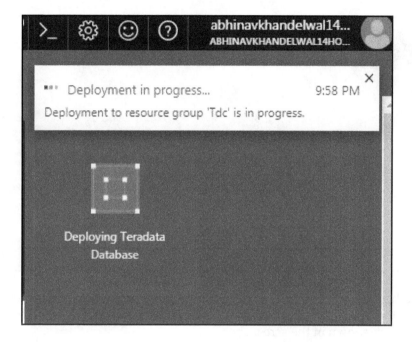

9. Now to connect our system on cloud with our local machine, we need to make system available publicly. To do this, once your system is up and running, go to **Resource groups** and select **search for database**. From the list, we will select network interface. In this option, we will enable the option to access this database publicly. Check the following screenshot:

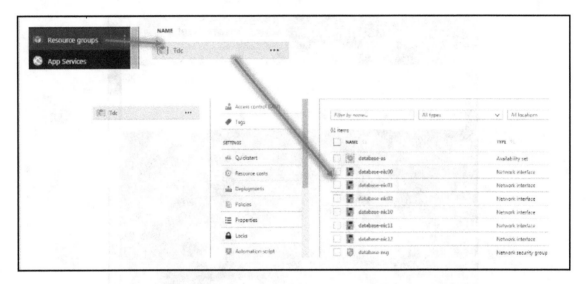

10. In the settings, click on IP configurations; next, click on the IP address in the bar. For the next option displayed, select **Enabled** under **Public IP address** and click **Save**, as shown in the screenshot:

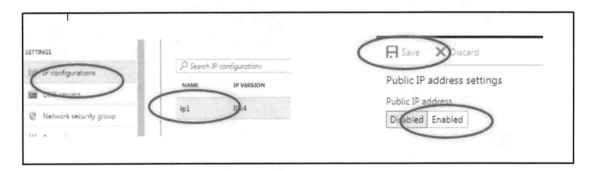

11. Once you have enabled the public IP, you can now give a DNS name to the IP for easy access. To enable this, search for public IP under the **type** column in your resource group. Under the **Configuration** tab, enter the **DNS name** as seems fit and save the settings. This can be seen in the following screenshot:

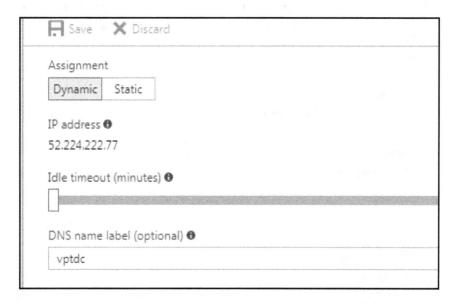

12. Repeat the same step for enabling a public IP and assigning a DNS name for accessing Viewpoint from your local machine.

13. Open your SQLA and enter the DNS name you grabbed from the settings, and enter the server name to create a DSN connection:

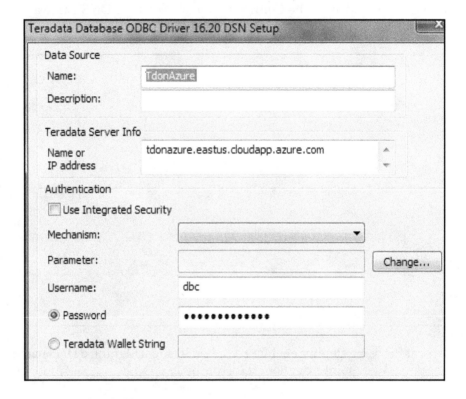

14. You can do the same for Viewpoint; grab the DNS as shown in the screenshot and enter it locally in your web browser. Log in using an admin account and enable the system to monitor your existing Teradata Database:

15. Welcome to Teradata on Azure.

How it works...

Teradata on Azure gives you the same performance as on premises. You can get same power of analytic database as you get from an on-premises database. Once on the cloud you can configure your system and can take advantage of the additional Azure applications, as well, to monitor and create system alerts.

If you are stuck with any of the issues when performing deployment, it is advisable to contact the Azure help desk via your dashboard. A ticket will be created and the issue will be resolved based on your subscription type:

```
SUPPORT REQUEST

118011317458754


STATUS

Closed


TITLE

Quota request - Cores
Location- EASTUS
DSv2 Ser


DESCRIPTION

Quota request - Cores
Location- EASTUS
DSv2 Series - 86
```

There's more...

Once you deploy your Teradata Database, from time to time you need to upgrade or apply patches to the database. You need to download these from the Teradata access portal and, based on your license tiers, Teradata engineering will help you.

There are four license tiers available as of now:

- **Developer**: With low performance
- **Base**: With simple and middle-level performance
- **Advance**: With high-performance workloads and better performance
- **Enterprise**: With full capability and enterprise-level performance

Defining a connection

Connect better! In this case, we will connect to the Teradata Express VMware machine, which is on the desktop PC, using Teradata Studio Express. However, in the real world, Teradata System(s) are located in safe data centers and you would need the IP address(es) of the system.

How to do it...

We will be establishing a JDBC data connection to a local database:

1. Click on **Database Connection, New...**:

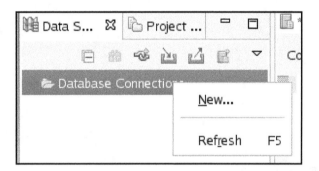

2. Select **Teradata Database** from the connection profile screen and provide a name for the connection:

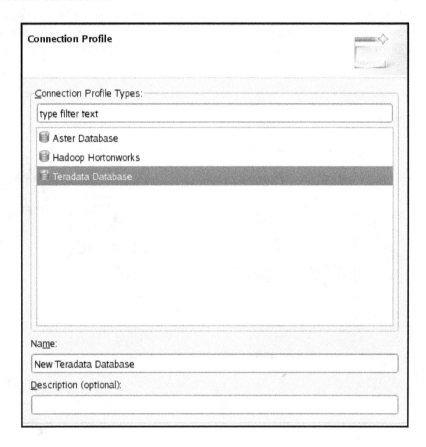

3. Enter `localhost` in the **Database Server Name**. When doing a connection to a real-world database, provide an IP or a hostname here. The **User Name** and **Password** will be `dbc`:

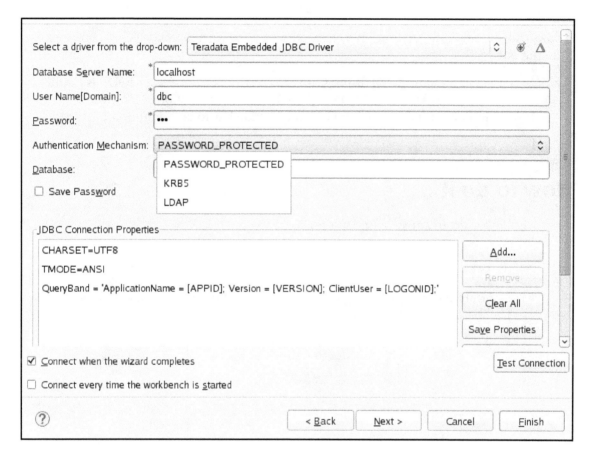

If your site/client is using an LDAP to log on, you need to choose an LDAP mechanism and enter your LDAP credentials.

4. Click on **Test Connection** to ensure connectivity.

   You are now connected to the **Teradata Database**; start firing up your queries using SLQ Editor.

Connecting to the Teradata system

Now, before starting up with our very first query, you need to know that express works in the ANSI TMODE. You need to change to TERA mode manually.

Additionally, you can have a multiple connections to the same database connection or a different one.

 TERADATA MODE is not Case sensitive, where as ANSI MODE is CASE sensitive. Also, in TERADATA MODE each transaction is committed implicitly and in ANSI MODE transaction has to be committed explicitly.

How to do it...

1. Let's execute our very first query:

```
/*Sample query*/
sel * from dbc.dbcinfo;
```

2. The output of the preceding query will give us the current version of the Teradata Database system. Yes, we are on 15.10.03.07:

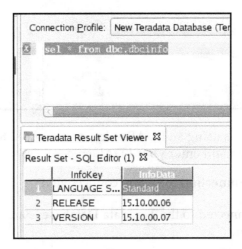

This is a heavy tool, so it will consume more resources from your PC compared to the handy and breezy SQL Assistant. We'll be exploring SQL Assistant in the later part of this chapter.

There's more...

Humans and software—we judge them on the basis of their characteristics. Let's explore some of the important options available with Teradata Studio Express.

Using Studio tool options

Here are some of the tool options that we will cover:

- **SQL compare**: Comparing two text documents is the basic necessity of the coding community. There are many tools for this job. However, when you have a built-in feature for it, you don't need to go anywhere else. You ask how to use it? Click on the **Project Explorer** tab (next to the **Data Explorer** tab). Right-click on the SQL tab and create SQL text files that you need to compare. Select both files and select the **Compare With | Each Other** option. The text that is different will be highlighted and shown:

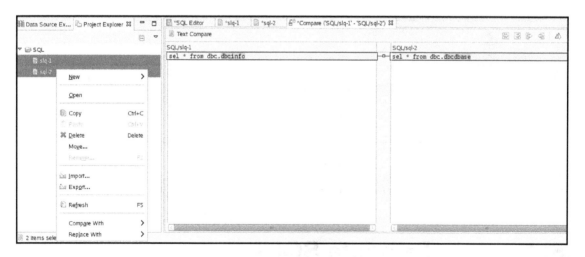

Different text highlighted in the Text Compare

- **Code assist and syntax checking:** Forgot the names of the tables in the database, a column name, or the syntax of your statement? Express will prompt as you type. Type EXEC for macro execution with the code assist ON and you will get a series of options that will go with the main command. Now, when you write a database name followed by a dot, it will give you a list of tables to choose from that database:

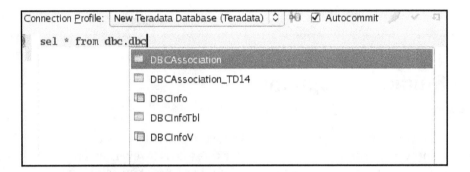

- **Object Viewer:** This works in a similar to the traditional tool SQL Assistant; however, it can help to get more details for your object of interest. If you have Studio, it will have even more options for admin use. Right-click on any object from the Explorer. You will see all the options affiliated with the object you need:

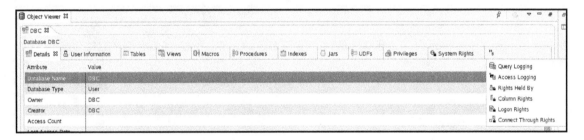

Options affiliated with the selected option

There are many other options at your disposal that you can explore.

Setting up Teradata SQLA

We will now turn our focus to the traditional but easy to use tool, **SQL Assistant** (**SQLA**). We now have a SQLA Java version just like Teradata Studio or Teradata Studio Express.

Getting ready

For SQLA to work, you need to download it from the `developer.teradata.com` website and download Teradata Tools and Utilities, also known as **TTU**. Once downloaded and installed, start making the connection using ODBC, .NET, or JDBC.

> SQLA can informally be referred to as a lightweight version of Studio or Express; you will find it easier to navigate and use.

Here, we will use SQLA 16.0. It is highly recommended that you use the TTU version that matches or is higher than the major release version number of the Teradata Database that you intend to connect with. So, if you are on Teradata Database 15.10, use TTU 15.10 or 16. TTU 13.10 is not recommended. Now that we have this covered, let's move on to the connection.

How to do it...

Use the following steps to establish a connection:

1. Click on the plug icon in the top-left corner; now you can either select file data source or machine data source.
2. Click on **New...** if you don't have a connection file. Select user or system data source:

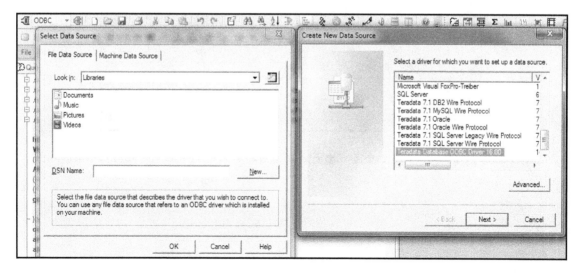

3. Then select the option of **Teradata Database ODBC driver 16.00**; after this, you will see the screen for providing the name of your data connection and source IP.

4. Enter your credentials; you have the option to save the password if you don't want to enter it every time you connect to the database:

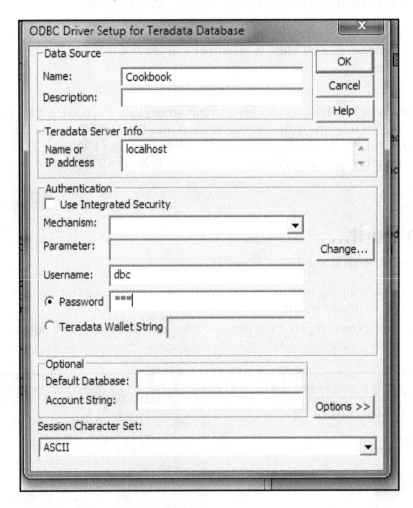

Wouldn't it be great to have an option to run SQL using the command-line interface with SQLA?

How it works...

Teradata SQLA allows you to connect to a data source using the ODBC and .NET framework. When you install SQLA from TTU toolkit, make sure to check all the options. You will have two executables:

- `TTU_BASE` has the following:
    - ODBC driver
    - BTEQ
    - All the loading tools, such as fastexport, fastload, and many others
    - Named pipe modules
    - Websphere access modules
    - .NET data provider
    - C preprocessor 2
    - Tearadata adminstrator
    - SQLA
    - Teradata Wallet and many more
- `TTU_DBM` has the following:
    - Index wizard
    - BTEQ
    - ODBC driver
    - Query scheduler admin, client, server
    - TSET
    - Workload analyzer
    - Visual explain
    - Teradata Wallet

There's more...

Here are some shortcuts to make your daily job easier:

- *F2*: It will open query builder, with syntax for all SQL queries
- *F5*: Execute SQL query
- *F6*: Explain plan for SQL query
- *F9*: Execute SQL queries in parallel
- *F10*: Abort SQL query
- *F11*: Display last error encountered
- *Ctrl + N*: New SQL query window
- *Ctrl + Q*: Format SQL query
- *Ctrl + U*: Convert to UPPERCASE
- *Ctrl + H*: Find and replace

Configuring SQLA

Once you have the SQLA all fired up, the next thing we want is to configure the settings. SQLA comes with some default settings that you might want to change. For example, every time you execute the query, you may want to preserve the previous ruleset. The default setting has a habit of closing the old ruleset.

In this recipe we will change the SQLA settings to better ones.

Getting ready

You need to open the SQLA.

How to do it...

1. Open SQLA.
2. To change the behavior of the `resultset`, click on **Tools** | **Options ...**, highlighted in the following screenshot:

3. From the pop-up window, click on the **Query** tab, as highlighted in the following screenshot:

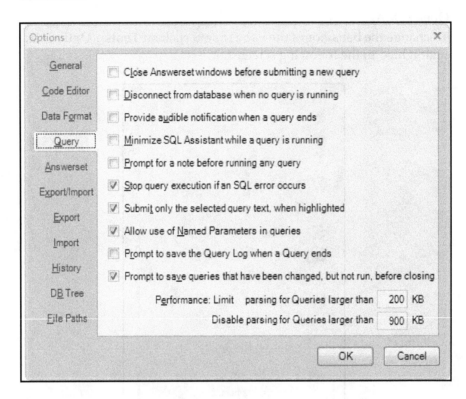

4. Next, uncheck the following boxes as shown in step 1; option 1 will make sure that your old answer set is not closed when you are submitting your query. Tick the 7; option will help you execute highlighted queries when you have multiple queries in your window:

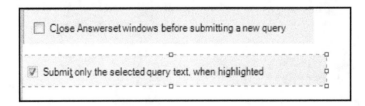

5. There are many other options that, if you want, you can check and uncheck.

How it works...

SQLA is a simple and efficient tool that helps users with their daily work. With better configuration, this tool can be used effectively.

SQLA also provides a way for you to automate your queries from a Windows machine. This recipe won't be covering the full process, but here are some commands that you can use to automate the scripts/jobs.

To execute SQLA from the command prompt, use the following:

Enter the following command on **Run**:

```
Sqla -c cookbook -f "c:\workbook\dbc.sql" -e "c:\workbook\resultset\dbc.log"
```

- The `-c` cookbook is used to establish a connection to the cookbook server
- `-f "c:\workbook\dbc.sql"` opens a file in the given path directly to SQL Assistant
- `-e "c:\workbook\resultset\dbc.log"` is used to export the `resultset` to the given file

This will open SQLA, execute the queries, and close it afterwards. This is useful to schedule your jobs/queries on Windows machines.

Building a query builder

Query builder is your quick reference guide to SQL syntax. It not only lets you use its own SQLs, but also provides you with the option to add your own along with editing the existing ones.

How to do it...

Query builder is available both in SQLA and Teradata Studio Express. Express query builder is more interactive and has drag-and-drop features. Let's first cover SQLA, followed by Studio Express.

Query builder in SQLA

Here is how you can proceed with query builder in SQLA:

1. Query builder in SQLA is under the **Help** tab, or you can press *F2*. Here, you can click on any existing command or browse for the one you need.

2. You can also add frequently used queries in query builder. Click on + as shown in the following screenshot and add the queries that you need most, so that you don't have to search for them:

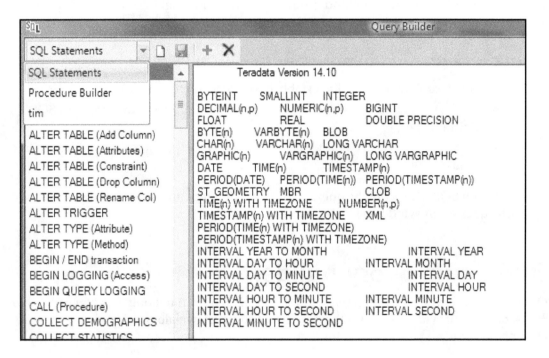

Query builder in Express

Here is how to proceed with query builder in Express:

1. In express, you can edit an existing query using the query builder. Selecting the query in the SQL Editor, right-click and select the **Edit in Query Builder** option:

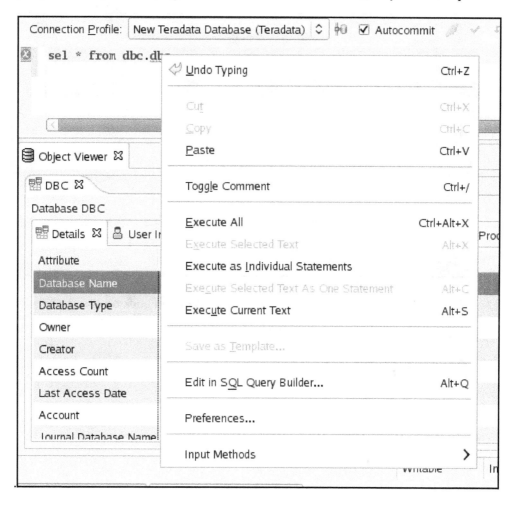

2. Once you click on the **Edit** option, your query will be opened in a new window with many other options. Here, you can add new tables to the existing query, creating a relationship between them. There is also a tab that gives you options to put conditions (where, or, and) in queries. You can also add the group by clause; refer to the screenshot for details:

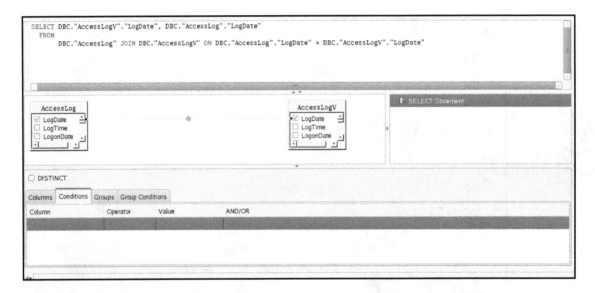

There is an option to change the statement type when you click on the statement box.

Importing data

Let's get the ball rolling now.

We have had Teradata Studio Express and SQLA up and running for a while now. It is time to load data into the Teradata Database.

Now, there are many ways to do this, but, for simplicity, I will be importing data via Excel using the **GUI** option in Teradata Studio Express. You can copy the table data from Teradata to a data lab just by dragging the source table from the data lab view. The datalab copy wizard helps you through step by step.

 A data lab is a separate dedicated work space, also known as a sandbox, sandpit or a test area.

You can get the dataset from various websites; there are tons of websites giving free datasets for analysis.

Getting started

The following are the prerequisites to import the data:

1. Create a new user, for example, `Mike`.
2. Create a new database, for example, `TestDb`.
3. Allocate space to the new database.
4. Grant appropriate access rights to the new database for the new user.

5. Create a table DDL under this database with the same column layout as the import file:

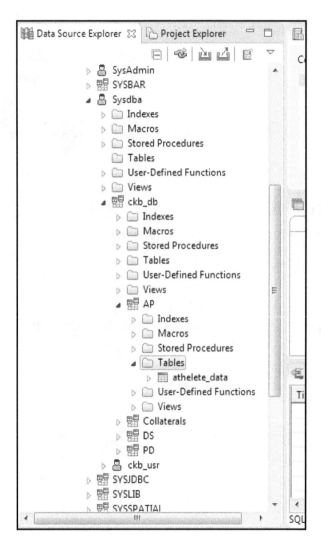

How to do it...

Let's begin with importing data using Studio first and then we will move on to SQLA. The following DDL was used to create the table in the new database. Now load the data from the external file. The following steps allow you to do so:

1. Go to data explorer.
2. Search for the database under which the required table is located:

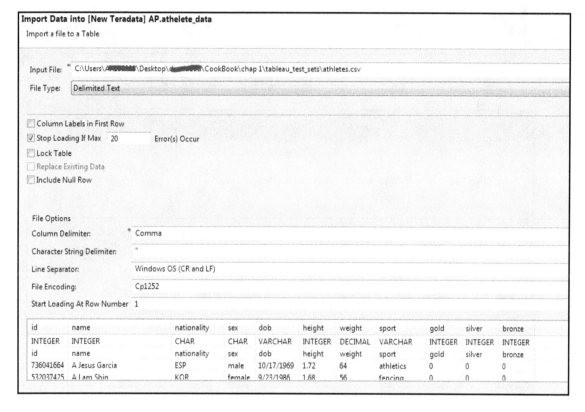

3. Explore the database.

4. Right-click on the table, **Name** | **Data** | **Load Data**:

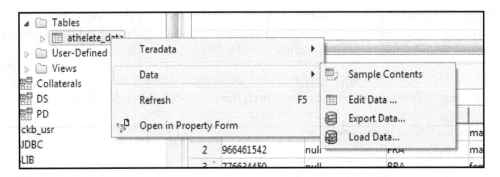

5. The Wizard will come up; select the source as **External File**:

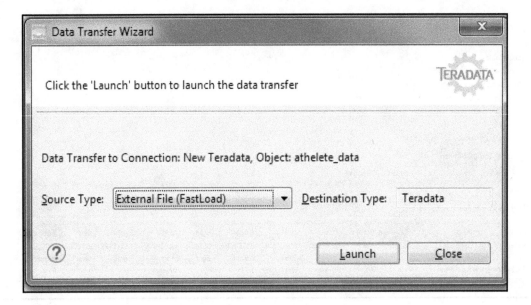

6. On the next screen, just browse to the CSV file you need to load the data from.
7. Once the data is loaded, you will get a success message.
8. To verify the data, right-click on the table, **Name** | **Data** | **Sample Data**; a few rows will pop up, showing that the data has been loaded.

In Express

This one is also as easy as Studio Express. The prerequisites are the same as Studio:

1. Select the Import data option from the **File** tab.
2. You need to write SQL to start importing the data.

```
ins into AP.countries (?,?)
```

3. `?` here defines the number of columns in your file.
4. Turn off the import function and execute `Sel *` from the table name to verify the data:

Use different formats to import files from **Tools** | **Options** | **Export/Import**.

To use the CSV file, select **Options**, as shown in the following screenshot:

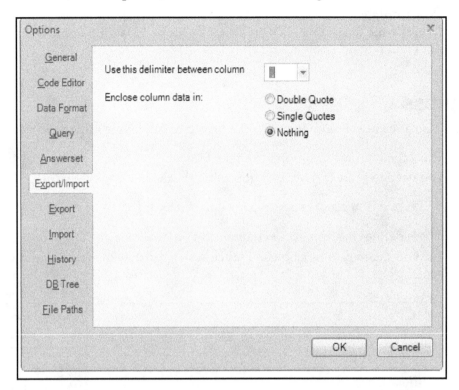

Data transfer is a two-way street. We sometimes also have requirements to export the data to a file.

Teradata Studio Express and SQL Assistant both can be used to export data as well.

Exporting data

The data that we imported can be exported back to a file.

How to do it

With Teradata Studio Express

Here is how we do it for Studio Express:

1. Go to data explorer.
2. Search for the database under which the required table is located.
3. Explore the database.
4. Right-click on the table, **Name** | **Data** | **Export Data**.
5. The Wizard will come up; select the destination file where the data needs to be written in.
6. Select the option of **Export Data Format** from **File** options.
7. Once the data is written to the file, you will get a success message.
8. Open the file to verify the data.

With Teradata SQLA

1. Select the **Export Data** option from the **File** tab.
2. Execute the select query from which you need to export the data.
3. As you hit *F5* for execution, a window prompt will appear. Save the file with the required name and format.
4. Your data will be written to the file.

If you have a date column in the table, use the data format from the **Options** tab to get the date format in the file.

To save the file in the Excel format, use `"filename.xlsx"` in double quotes:

```
"filename.xlsx"
```

How it works...

The export function of the tool let's you copy data from variety of files. This is useful when you want to copy a table data onto your local machine. This is fast and effective way to move data from table to any local file type that you want. It is however recommended not to copy large amount of data set as it might crash the local machine or the application.

There's more...

You can export data from a Teradata table (Source Type = Teradata):

- To another table in the same Teradata Database or in a different Teradata Database.
- To an external file in the file system, such as a text file or Microsoft Excel spreadsheet.
- To a Aster table.
- To a Hadoop table.

2
SQLs

In this chapter, we will learn techniques that will help in writing statements/SQL queries efficiently. Increasing the efficiency of DDL/DML/DCL statements/SQL queries will reduce the CPU/IO and runtime of a query.

The following topics will be covered:

- Writing queries
- Querying efficiently
- Explain before executing queries
- Decoding explain
- Resolving skewing data
- Resolving skew in databases
- Solving `insert` performance
- Solving `delete` performance
- Improving update performance
- Performing merge into

Introduction

Query writing is an art. When a painter starts on the canvas he has a clear understanding of what he is going to draw on the empty canvas; he can't just start with something and change his mind in the middle of the drawing. Imagine Leonardo da Vinci drawing Mona Lisa and half way in-between he changes his mind and starts drawing Medusa.

Data volumes are on the continuous rise and the size of the data warehouse has been increasing more than ever. In such a scenario, writing queries efficiently has become even more important. For a developer or a data scientist, using SQL still remains a very powerful method of analyzing data and building reports and trends.

Writing queries

Here we will assume that the reader is well versed with Teradata SQL syntax and has all the required tools to connect and execute the queries on Teradata.

Every SQL statement that executes on Teradata database consumes CPU, IO, AWT, and Spool.

Teradata's architecture is based on parallelism, which essentially means the efficiency of the query is based on how parallel efficient the query execution is, meaning how well it could leverage Teradata's parallelism. However, it also has an exception which will be covered in a later part of the chapter.

Getting ready

Teradata has many tools for writing the queries; you can use SQLA or a BTEQ for executing queries. There are also many third-party applications that connect to Teradata database using a data connector such as ODBC, JDBC, or .NET. Data loading utilities such as FastLoad, Multiload, or TPT can also be invoked using BTEQ or third-party apps. Here, we will use SQLA, the simplest of tools, to write a query, and show you how to use BTEQ.

How to do it...

There are two methods that can be used for writing queries, which are explained as follows.

Using SQLA

1. Start SQLA using the Run command or click on the **SQLA** icon:

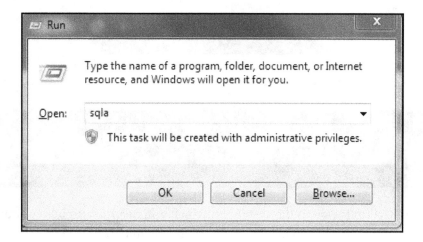

2. Connect to your data source.
3. Write a query in the **Query** window:

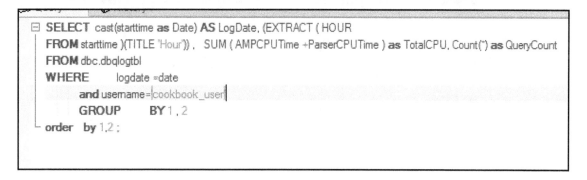

```
⊟ SELECT  cast(starttime as Date) AS LogDate, (EXTRACT ( HOUR
   FROM starttime )(TITLE 'Hour')) ,  SUM ( AMPCPUTime +ParserCPUTime ) as TotalCPU, Count(*) as QueryCount
   FROM dbc.dbqlogtbl
   WHERE        logdate =date
        and usemame = cookbook_user
        GROUP       BY 1 , 2
└ order  by 1,2 ;
```

4. You can execute it by hitting *F5* or clicking on the **Execute** button from the toolbar.

Using BTEQ in Windows

1. Open the command prompt and execute bteq:

```
C:\Users\abhi_ckbk\bteq
```

2. It will open up, and the BTEQ utility will prompt you to enter the bteq command:

```
Teradata BTEQ 16.00.00.02 for WIN32. PID: 10392
Copyright 1984-2016, Teradata Corporation. ALL RIGHTS RESERVED.
Enter your logon or BTEQ command:
.logon local/username,password
```

3. You need to log on to the system on which you need to execute your queries.
4. Alternatively, you can execute a script directly, incorporated with logon information followed by a query:

```
>
> C:\Users\abhi_ckbk\bteq < test_script > log.txt
```

5. Script output will be written in log.txt.

How it works...

When the user submits a query in a Teradata database, it follows a path from the origin to the data, as shown in the following figure:

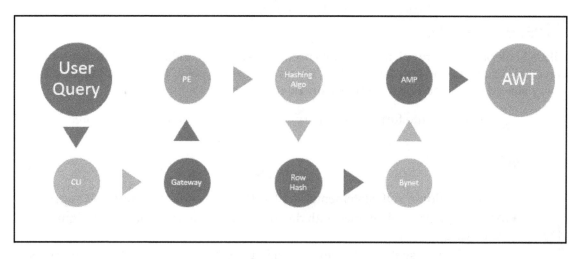

Flow of query from origin to data

Any query submitted to the Teradata system from a Teradata client, such as BTEQ or SQLA, goes through CLIv2 or ODBC to the **Parsing Engine** (**PE**), which parses the query to ensure syntax and generates an execution plan for the query. The execution steps are then passed on by the **PE** to **AMP**s over the **Bynet**; AMPs perform their operations and return the result set over the Bynet, back to PE, and PE delivers the result set to the Teradata client tool that submitted the query. It makes sense to mention the various modules of the PE here:

Syntaxer >> Resolver >> Security >> Optimizer >> Generator >> Dispatcher

Every module has its part to play.

There are three ways by which we can do data retrieval and insertion:

- **BTEQ**: It supports SELECT, INSERT, UPDATE, and DELETE. BTEQ also supports IMPORT/EXPORT protocols.
- **Utilities**: FastLoad, Multiload, and TPump transfer data from the host to Teradata.
- **Export:** FastExport performs high volume SELECTs to export data from Teradata to the host.

As a BI user/developer and admin, it is your responsibility to write queries in such a way that they utilize the resources such as CPU, IO, and Spool in an efficient way.

There's more...

Like a book or a beautiful picture, we also need to take care with how we write a query. We can either use SQLA or Teradata Studio Express for this purpose. The main thing is, our query should be readable and should easily be understood.

Ctrl + Q auto formats the query in SQLA and Teradata Studio Express.

- Keep individual SQL statements small as they are easier to debug and support.
- Always qualify table names with database names; default database assignments can change.
- Use ANSI join syntax with join criteria in the ON clause, not in the `WHERE` clause. Join the clause on one line, `tableA inner join tableB`, and use a separate line for each criteria.
- Use a separate line for each table in the form list.
- When using subqueries, indent the subqueries and ensure the parenthesis are aligned.
- If any third-party tool is used to generate the query, remove the additional formatting that comes along with it.
- Change keyword shortcuts (`sel`, `ins`, `upd`, `ct`, and so on) to their full word equivalents (`SELECT`, `INSERT`, `UPDATE`, `CREATE TABLE`, and so on).
- Use tabs and spaces to build a block structure where each item of a clause begins in the same column.
- Include an inline comment for any hard coded values. The proper use of the block comment `/**COMMENT USE**/`:

```
/** Query to get employee name and invoice sum**/
SELECT   oc.Employee_name
  , r.WEEK_YEAR
   , sum(oc.INVOICE)   Invc_Sum
  FROM   Test01.ORGANIZATION   oc INNER JOIN SALES.RETAIL_INVOICE_AGG
r
   AND   oc.start_dt = r.repo_dt
  WHERE   oc.Dept_no =   'RETAIL'
```

These are some tips that can be used to maintain the integrity of the SQL codes and make them more readable.

Querying efficiently

Have you been struggling with your queries running for a long time, have your queries been flagged on more than one occasion, or have you been reprimanded by your DBAs multiple times regarding high system resource consumption? Are these some situations you have been through? If yes, the queries you are running are not efficient and need to be looked at for performance improvement/optimization.

There are three types of typical users that use Teradata database:

- Business users
- Developers
- Administrators

The administrator community obviously wants the queries running on the Teradata system to be as efficient as possible.

Getting ready

Here, we will look at some basic rules that need to be kept in mind when executing queries:

- **Know your data**: Understand the relationships between tables, know your data, and fetch only the required columns.
- **Visualize the answer set**: Don't just keep on pulling the handle till you hit the jackpot; always try to know the count of possible rows expected.
- **Break your queries**: Use the various features of the database. Try volatile tables to do the calculations and then join it with the main query, or explore the option of breaking date range that turns YEARs queries into MONTHs.
- **JOINS**: Be reasonable with CROSS JOIN or LEFT joins. Bad joins with skew values result in high CPU and IO queries.
- **Data types**: Ensure appropriate data types for columns on the table(s). For example, don't define a Character data type for a Salary column.
- **Pre-aggregate data**: It's an old school technique. Do the aggregation in a volatile table and then you can join them to the main query. It avoids carrying large number of rows in joins.

- **Repeating queries**: The frequency of execution should be given consideration. A query executed thousands of times with 1,000 CPU seconds is a better tuning candidate than a 100,000 CPU second query which is only executed once.

How to do it...

The following are working points that will help you understand performance optimization from a Teradata database perspective, and how bad PI and `bad join` affects the performance of a database. Many a time, it only takes a single/few bad query(s) to bring database performance down:

1. **Check primary index (PI)**: What is a bad PI? When the table is skewed, mostly because of a large number of duplicate values on the column(s) that make the PI, a bad PI. PI is directly responsible for:
   - Row distribution
   - Access path
   - Join performance

2. **Check statistics**: Statistics can break and make a query. The Optimizer is more accurate when it has collected statistics. It is more conservative when it must rely on dynamic AMP sampling. Statistics or stats help the optimizer generate better execution plans. No stats or stale stats can lead the optimizer to create a bad plan, which means wrong joins and wrong estimations of rows to be processed/returned.

3. **Check partition primary index (PPI)**: Helps the user to reap the benefits of scalability inherent in the hash architecture of the Teradata database. How does it help? It helps reduce the I/Os of the system by providing an access path to the rows in the base table and an efficient join.

4. **Check secondary index (SI)**: Two indexes on tables? Wow! But why do you need SI? It offers an alternative path to access the data. Use SI when data distribution is done by a UPI and access is handled by SI.

5. **Check parallel efficiency, PE**: You can't define PE in a query, but you can calculate it. Remember, Teradata is a parallel architecture database. PE is simply defined as the Average Node CPU busy divided by the Maximum Node CPU busy. A high PE query means it's been executed on all AMPs.

6. **Verify SELECT ***: In a select * all of the columns are loaded into spool, which increase spool usage. Select columns that are required.

7. **Verify functions in joins**: Avoid using functions in joins and where clauses. The functions prevent the optimizer from seeing the data demographics, and the function must be executed for every row. Even if the column has collected stats, once the function is applied, the new manipulated column will not have stats, making the optimizer prone to wrong estimates of the data demographics.

8. Use `BETWEEN` rather than `IN` when possible.

9. **Use GROUP BY or Distinct**: Use group by instead of Select Distinct. Be cautious using count distinct. The distinct tends to skew and cause performance issues when dealing with large numbers or with large numbers of duplicates.

CPUSkew, IOSkew, product join indicator, unnecessary IO indicator, and ImpactCPU combine together to form a report, which can be called suspected queries. All of these can be useful for identifying high resource consumption and skewed queries for tuning opportunities.

How it works...

Let's take a look at how the parameters that are defined in the *How to to do it...* section affect the system and how you can correlate the steps to different areas of Teradata to measure the performance efficiency of a Teradata System:

Area	De-coding
User CPU	The difference between max and avg shows the overall parallel efficiency of the system. A big difference between the two indicates hot nodes or hot AMPs. Either or both hitting 100% means that the system is 100% CPU busy.
OS CPU	If the OS percent is very low (less than 5% when the CPU avg/max is high, then this is an indication of application problems – bad product joins in particular).
CPU and I/O wait	When the system is busy, the desired ratio of CPU to I/O wait should be 90%+ CPU to 10% or less I/O wait to be optimal. If I/O wait is rising while CPU busy is falling, it can mean that the system is not as busy as it was, and there are more CPU cycles available. But it could also mean that there is indeed an I/O bottleneck.

When you get a high CPU step in your query you might need to step on the preceding process chart to identify and rectify the step. The steps and the chart work hand in hand, and users must be able to identify the bottleneck in their query.

Explain before executing queries

Teradata gives you the benefit of checking the actual execution plan before executing the query. The English translation of the plan the Teradata optimizer develops to service the SQL. The terms execution plan and explain plan can be used interchangeably:

```
DIAGNOSTIC VERBOSEEXPLAIN ON FOR SESSION;
DIAGNOSTIC HELPSTATS ON FOR SESSION;
```

VERBOSEEXPLAIN adds information on the hash fields used to build intermediate spool files. This can be of significant value when diagnosing skewed redistribution.

HELPSTATS adds a list of RECOMMENDED STATISTICS to the end of the explain plan. A word of caution: do not blindly collect stats from this list of recommendations. The recommendation usually covers all joining columns with single as well as multi-column options and it may prove costly to collect them.

Getting ready

You can check the explain plan in SQLA or using Studio Express. The explain plan can also be generated in BTEQ but it would not be easy to read it. Explain is produced in plain simple English text.

It is a good practice to run an EXPLAIN of the query before submitting it for execution. In the explain plan we need to check the join type, execution time, and confidence level of the execution steps.

How to do it...

1. Hit *F6* by selecting the query to get the explain or write the EXPLAIN keyword before the query and press *F5*:

   ```
   Explain
   Insert  Into  test01.webclicks
   select * From   au.az_clicks;
   ```

2. First, we lock a distinct test01."pseudo table" for write on a RowHash to prevent global deadlock for test01.webclicks.

3. Next, we lock a distinct au."pseudo table" for read on a RowHash to prevent global deadlock for au.az_clicks.

4. We lock test01.webclicks for write, and we lock au.az_clicks for read.

5. We do an all-AMPs RETRIEVE step from au.az_clicks by way of an all-rows scan with no residual conditions into Spool 1 (all_AMPs), which is built locally on the AMPs. The input table will not be cached in memory, but it is eligible for synchronized scanning. The result spool file will not be cached in memory. The size of Spool 1 is estimated with low confidence to be 254,863 rows. The estimated time for this step is 4.53 seconds.

6. We do an all-AMPs MERGE into test01.webclicks from Spool 1 (last use).

7. We spoil the parser's dictionary cache for the table.

8. Finally, we send out an END TRANSACTION step to all AMPs involved in processing the request.

   No rows are returned to the user as the result of statement 1.

Press *F6* directly or write the EXPLAIN keyword before the query and press *F5* to generate an EXPLAIN plan in the SQLA tool.

Explain plan length varies as per the length of a query. Nested views tend to be more complex when written in an explain plan. You should copy explain plans into a separate notepad or a Word application to read it clearly, and always maintain a true copy of the original explain if you intend to modify the query and want to compare the explain plans afterwards.

How it works...

An explain plan is derived from the PE, steps, or so-called **optimized plans** given to AMPS to execute the query. Each highlighted part here represents an operation carried by the optimizer:

- **Estimations**: Big estimated times and row counts. This is usually due to missing/stale statistics.
- **Row Retrieval**: Check for partition elimination on large tables (most fact tables):
    - Mismatched data types and character sets (Unicode versus Latin) will prevent partition elimination
    - Using a function on a `partitioning` column may prevent partition elimination
    - An all-rows scan on big tables
    - Primary index retrieval **by way of the primary index**
- **Joins**: Steps with a translate in joins:
    - Mismatched data type or character set on join columns—rows hash to different AMPs causing costly joins
    - Product joins with a high number of estimated rows
    - Sliding window-based join, joining PPI and non-PPI tables
- **Statistics**: Steps with estimated row count = number of AMPs:
    - Prevents the optimizer from using statistics to create an optimal execution plan

There's more...

- You should run an EXPLAIN for a query with multiple Joins especially if joining columns are non-index columns
- Look for high estimated runtime's (more than one to three hours) or a large row count (several hundred million to billions in the case of large tables)
- If estimated rows don't match your expected row count, especially if they are exponentially high, don't execute a query before attempting to optimize it
- The explain plan of an executing query can be checked from the Viewpoint interface at the time of running

- The DBQLExplainTbl table in the DBC database holds the explain text of already executed queries. The DBQL ruleset to collect the execution plan needs to be enabled to store data in this table.
- Check for partition elimination on large tables (most fact tables) if the PPI column is used; mismatched data types, character sets (Unicode versus Latin), applying functions, or inequality on the PPI column will prevent partition elimination.
- If you see steps with estimated row count = number of AMPs on your system in a distributed or duplication step, it could mean that stats are missing or stale on that table.
- Product joins can be a problem, but can be the best option when one of the tables has very few rows (for example, a table with a number of rows less than the number of AMPs on the system).

Decoding explain

Even though the EXPLAIN plan is in plain English, it is not easy to understand the underlying meaning without understanding the main keywords. At first look, it possibly won't make any sense to you and you may not relate it to the query. We will decode the output into its pieces to carve out the relevant information behind it.

How to do it...

1. Identify the query for which you want to check the explain.
2. It is recommended to check the explain of all the queries before executing, as query plans get changed if table demographics are changed.
3. Hit *F6* by selecting the query to get the explain, or write the EXPLAIN keyword before the query and press *F5*:

```
Explain
Insert  Into  test01.webclicks
select * From    au.az_clicks;
```

4. The explain plan will be generated in the result set window.

How it works...

English text will be generated, showing the path of the query. Different queries have different keywords. It is the user who needs to understand based on the plan as it is optimized or not by looking at the keywords.

Pseudo table: Understand it like a conductor of a music concert. One of the AMPs from the all-AMP operation is declared as a **conductor**, who control other AMPs and acts as a gatekeeper. This helps in preventing the deadlocks when two users issue the same locks:

1. We lock a distinct test01."pseudo table" for write on a RowHash to prevent global deadlock for test01.webclicks:
   - **All-AMPs retrieve**: A full table scan is done and all the blocks on the tables are retrieved.

2. We do an all-AMPs RETRIEVE step from au.az_clicks by way of an all-rows scan with no residual conditions into Spool 1 (all_AMP):
   - **No residual conditions**: The condition in the where clause has been applied to the rows.
   - **Way of the unique primary index**: A single-AMP retrieve and UPI is used to access the row. web_page, being the following UPI column.

3. We do a single-AMP RETRIEVE step from oz.web_clicks by way of the unique primary index "oz.web_clicks.web_page = 70", with no residual conditions. The estimated time for this step is 0.04 seconds:
   - **By way of index #4**: Rows are read using the Secondary Index – the number from the **HELP INDEX**. If SI is unique then by way of unique index.

4. We do a two-AMP RETRIEVE step from oz.web_clicks by way of unique index #4, "oz.web_clicks.adv_number = 10", with no residual conditions. The estimated time for this step is 0.01 seconds. The row is sent directly back to the user as the result of statement 1. The total estimated time is 0.01 seconds:
   - **Eliminating duplicate rows**: Eliminating duplicates from SPOOL files. Retrieving only unique values, normally, as a result of DISTINCT, GROUP BY or a subquery.

5. Redistributed by hash code to all AMPs. The result rows are put into `Spool 1` `(all_AMPs)`, which is redistributed by hash code to all AMPs. Then we do a `SORT` to order Spool 1 by the sort key in spool field 1, eliminating duplicate rows. The size is estimated with index join confidence to be 1,732 rows (155,045 bytes), which is duplicated on all AMPs or is redistributed by hash code.

   - **Duplicating data from the table** (should be a smaller one) in preparation for a join: If you see a large table getting duplicated, try collecting stats.

6. We do an all-AMPs `RETRIEVE` step from Spool 10 by way of an all-rows scan into `Spool 3 (all_AMPs)`, compressed columns allowed, which is duplicated on all AMPs:

   - **STAT function**: A query with any order analytical functions such as `TOP`, `RANK`, `OVER`, and so on will result in a `STAT` function in the explain plan. Usually, you will see them at the end of the explain plan.

7. We do an all-AMPs `STAT FUNCTION` step from `test01.tbl1` by way of an all-rows scan with no residual conditions into Spool 2, which is built locally on the AMPs. The result rows are put into `Spool 1 (group_AMPs)`, which is built locally on the AMPs:

   - **Unmatched data types**: A `TRANSLATE` function in the explain plan identifies un-matched data types.

8. Spool 5 is left as outer joined using a merge join, with a join condition of `("(TR_DATE <= END_DT) AND ((TRANSLATE((ACCT_NUM )USING LATIN_TO_UNICODE)(FLOAT, FORMAT '-9.99999999999999E-999')) (ACCT_NUMBER ))")`:

   - Why are Translations bad? The `Translate` function, by itself, can be quite expensive when large volumes of data are involved. Demographics/collect stats cannot be used when the data types are not matched; the optimizer may not produce good estimates.

There's more...

By understanding the keywords of the explain and how the optimizer works internally in terms of how SQL statements are executed on a Teradata system, you can assess the quality of each query. This information allows you to track down performance issues. Here are more keywords; if this doesn't match with your query nature and you suspect that this should not be in your explain, you might need to work on alternatives:

- **JOINS**: The following table explains the different types of joins and their uses:

Type of join	Why this join?
Nested join	Least costly and fastest join. Happens on an equijoin with any index covering the join columns.
Merge join	Joining spool files are sorted normally by RowHash, with both have having the same PI or after redistribution.
Product join	Rows of one table are joined to all rows of another table with no concern for match.
ROWID join	It uses the ROWID of a UPI to retrieve a single row after using a UPI or a USI in the WHERE clause to reduce the join to a single row.

- **Confidences**: The following table explains the different types of confidences:

Type	Description
With high confidence	Stats collected on indexes or columns, available on where or joins or aggregation.
With low confidence	Sample stats available on indexes or columns available on where or joins or aggregation. Can be AND/OR'ed.
With no confidence	No stats available; based on Optimizer estimation.
With index join confidence	A join condition using a primary index

Resolving skewing data

In statistics, skewness is a measure of the asymmetry of the probability distribution of a real-valued random variable about its mean. And in Teradata, it is defined as imbalanced processing, caused by uneven distribution. Highly skewed means some AMPs have more rows and some much less, as in data is not properly/evenly distributed. We can have data skew, CPU skew, and IO skew.

Shared Nothing architecture – dividing the work

The shared nothing architecture ensures that each virtual processor is responsible for the storage and retrieval of its own unique data. Data is stored physically together on the node, but the virtual processors ensure parallelism. This is also the basis of Teradata scalability. Each AMP owns an equal slice of the disk:

We will now understand how we can detect skew in a table which has a bad PI and how we can resolve it. Then we will look at how skew can be resolved in joins.

Getting ready

Let's connect to our local database instance and create a table using SQLA. Remember, PI is the only index that is not only used for data distribution but for retrieval also. Choosing a PI is the most important task. Bad PI has a ripple effect on queries. The following are some pointers for choosing a better PI:

- Consider data distribution
- The more unique the PI, the better the distribution across all AMPs on Teradata
- Understand how will the table be joined to
- Using the most frequent join path will improve joins to the table
- However, this column may be highly skewed

Let say we have 850 AMPs on a 20 node system. A user creates the following table, to store approximately 100,000 rows per day.

How to do it...

1. Create a table with two columns.
2. Choose PI as a `date` column, which is skewed:

```
CREATE volatile MULTISET TABLE MY_SKEW_TABLE
(
 ITEM_ID DECIMAL(18,0) NOT NULL,
 Today_DT DATE NOT NULL
)
PRIMARY INDEX (Today_DT)
on commit preserve rows;
```

3. `Insert` the first day of data (100,000 rows).
4. Check the distribution of your PI; try this query:

```
/**Hash AMP which row query**/
LOCKING ROW FOR ACCESS
SELECT HASHAMP(HASHBUCKET(HASHROW(Today_DT))) AS WhichAMP
,COUNT(*) AS RowsPerAMP
    FROM MY_SKEW_DB.MY_SKEW_TABLE
GROUP BY 1
ORDER BY 2 DESC
;
```

5. Sort the data in the following format to check which AMP holds the most number of rows:

WhichAMP	RowsPerAMP
120	100,000
324	0
12	0
1	0
45	0
239	0

6. Now, to resolve this you can use the same query and use other columns of the table in composite form, or single, to get the better distribution:

```
CREATE MULTISET TABLE MY_NONSKEW_DB.MY_NONSKEW_TABLE
(
 ITEM_ID DECIMAL(18,0) NOT NULL,
 Today_DT DATE NOT NULL
) PRIMARY INDEX (Today_DT,ITEM_ID)
;
```

How it works...

The previous query will return the data distribution of PI, which is Today_DT. As we are loading daily data into this, it will only have one date, and that will be the current date. This means all the rows will be residing on only ONE AMP, which means SKEW:

- HASHROW(): Returns the RowHash number of the column(s)
- HASHBUCKET(): Returns the Hash Bucket number of the column(s)
- HASHAMP(): Returns the AMP that would store/process the column(s)

If you are wondering what these functions stand for.

There's more...

Here are some effects of skew PI:

- **Running out of space on a database:** Database space is equally distributed across all AMPs on a Teradata system. If your database runs out of space, it could be out of space on just one AMP because of a skewed table.
- **Running out of spool:** At runtime, if data is skewed on a join, one of the AMPs can run out of space, causing the query to fail.
- **High runtime:** Skew queries tend to run more, as one of the AMPs works more than the other.

See also

- **Skew CPU**: When a query for one AMP consumes more CPU compared to the other AMPs:

  ```
  1 - (AMPCPUTime /  (HASHAMP()+1))/NULLIFZERO(MaxAMPCPUTime)
  ```

- **I/O Skew**: When a query for one AMP does more I/O compared to the other AMPs:

  ```
  (1-(TotalIOCount /  (HASHAMP()+1))/NULLIFZERO(MaxAMPIO)
  ```

Resolving skew in database

A database can run out of space if it has excessive tables that are skewed. Skew in small tables is understandable and can't be controlled, whereas skew in big tables can be controlled and reduced.

`DBC.TableSize`: Provides space by AMP about table space usage for each AMP.

Getting ready

We will connect to our Teradata database instance and open SLQA to generate the list of tables with their space and skew details.

How to do it...

1. Pick the database on which you need to analyze the skew tables.
2. Execute this query to get the list of tables:

```
/**Skew table in a database query**/
Lock Dbc.TableSize For Access
Lock Dbc.tables For Access
SELECT B.databasename , B.TableName , A.LastAccessTimeStAMP , SUM (
currentperm ) ( NAMED CurrentPerm ) ,
 MAXIMUM ( currentperm ) ( NAMED MaxPerm ) , AVG ( currentperm ) (
NAMED AvgPerm ) ,
 ( ( MAXIMUM ( currentperm ) - AVG ( currentperm ) ) * 100.0 ) / (
MAXIMUM ( currentperm ) ) ( NAMED SkewPercent )
FROM dbc.tablesize B INNER JOIN DBC.TABLES A
 ON A.DATABASENAME = B.DATABASENAME
 AND A.TABLENAME = B.TABLENAME
WHERE B.DATABASENAME = <my_database>
GROUP BY 1 , 2 , 3
HAVING ( ( MAXIMUM ( currentperm ) - AVG ( currentperm ) ) * 100.0
) / ( MAXIMUM ( currentperm ) ) > 20
ORDER BY 1 , 2 ;
```

The following is the list of tables in the database `test_db` with their space in GB and skew percentage:

DB	Table Name	Current_Perm in GB	Avg. Perm in GB	Skew
test_db	clicks02	12,603	131.3	3.8
test_db	clicks07	2,372	24.7	3.8
test_db	clicks06	1,580	16.5	3.8
test_db	clicks09	1,506	15.7	3.8
test_db	clicks08	306	3.2	90.1
test_db	Sales_US	139	1.4	95.7

test_db	Sales_Canada	115	1.2	95.7
test_db	Sales_Japan	35	0.4	95.4
test_db	Sales_UK	22	0.2	95.4
test_db	Work_table	20	0.2	4.1
test_db	Sales_Australia	17	0.2	94.9
test_db	Sales_Mexico	14	0.1	93.4

3. Once you have identified a target table, you can display the detailed distribution with the following query:

```
/**Table distribution**/
Lock dbc.tablesize for Access
SELECT vproc, CurrentPerm FROM dbc.TableSize
WHERE DatabaseName = <my_database>
AND TableName = <my_table>
ORDER BY 1;
```

4. Once you identify the problematic tables you can check their PI distribution from the query shared.
5. Rebuild the tables with new PI columns with better distributions.

How it works...

The PI column is used to distribute the data across the AMPS. Same data values with lend on same AMPs, which will increase the skew in tables is distribution is more on one AMP then the others.

There's more...

With skew comes many performance issues, be it on space or at the query level. The following process flowchart will help you to reduce the skew and improve database performance:

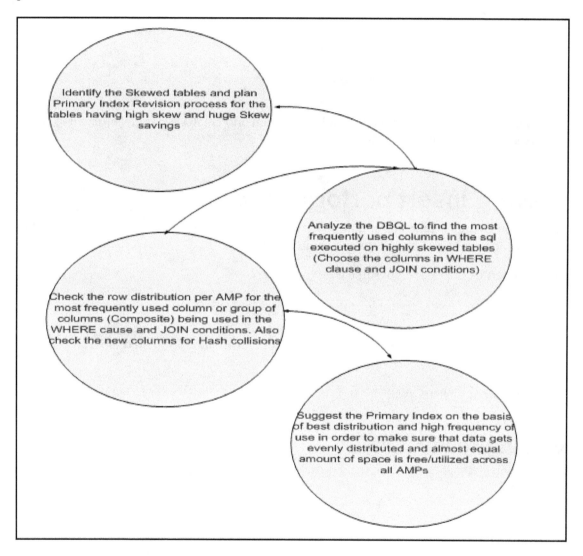

Flowchart to reduce skew and improve database performance

One more thing you can check is the amount of space you have wasted due to skew in the database. The skew formula, as seen previously, can be modified to get it. This will help you identify how efficiently you have utilized the space allocated to you. Every byte of space is important when you are on a space constraint system. It also reduces overall system skewness:

```
/**Waste space query**/
Lock dbc.tablesize for Access
select TableName, sum(CurrentPerm) as
ActualSpace,count(*)*(max(CurrentPerm)-avg(CurrentPerm)) as WastedSpace
  from dbc.TableSize where DatabaseName=<my_database> group by TableName
order by WastedSpace desc;
```

Shared nothing architecture makes Teradata efficient and creates a parallel efficient system and we should make the best of it.

Solving insert performance

`Insert` comes under data manipulation language. `Insert` means to place a new row into a table, which could be a duplicate or unique in itself.

The basic syntax of `insert` goes like this:

```
INSERT INTO table_name [(col_name [, ..., col_name])]
VALUES (expression [, ..., expression]);
```

A variation called `INSERT SELECT` takes data from an already populated table and inserts it into another one:

```
INSERT INTO table_name [(col_name [, ..., col_name])] SELECT statement;
```

Getting ready

To complete this recipe, you will need to connect to the Teradata database instance and open SQLA.

How to do it...

`Insert` is the topmost SQL statement that executes on the system. With a little tweak, we can optimize it to get better performance:

1. Create a source table:

```
/**Source Table**/
CREATE SET TABLE TEST01.web_clicks
  (Web_page_Number INTEGER,
   Location_Number INTEGER,
   Amount DECIMAL(10,2))
UNIQUE PRIMARY INDEX ( Web_page_Number );
```

2. Create a target table with the same PI as the source table:

```
/**Target Table**/
CREATE SET TABLE TEST01.Web_clicks_PI
  (Web_page_Number INTEGER,    Location_Number INTEGER,
      Salary_Amount DECIMAL(10,2))
UNIQUE PRIMARY INDEX (Web_page_Number);
```

3. Run the explain of the query:

```
/**Explain part**/
 1) First, we lock a distinct TEST01."pseudo table" for write on a
RowHash to prevent global deadlock for
TEST01.Web_clicks_Char_change_PI.
 2) Next, we lock a distinct TEST01."pseudo table" for read on a
RowHash to prevent global deadlock for TEST01.web_clicks.
 3) We lock TEST01.Web_clicks_Char_change_PI for write, and we lock
TEST01.web_clicks for read.
 4) We do an all-AMPs MERGE into TEST01.Web_clicks_Char_change_PI
from TFACT.web_clicks. The size is estimated with no confidence to
be 25,382 rows. The estimated time for this step is 2.29 seconds.
 5) We spoil the parser's dictionary cache for the table.
 6) Finally, we send out an END TRANSACTION step to all AMPs
involved in processing the request.
 -> No rows are returned to the user as the result of statement 1.
```

4. Now we will do a `insert.select` data from the older one to the newer one:

```
INSERT INTO TEST01.Web_clicks_PI SELECT * FROM TEST01.web_clicks;
```

How it works...

To `insert` data into the target table, the selected table, `TEST01.web_clicks`, has to be on the same AMP as the target table `TEST01.Web_clicks_CharPI`. In our case, as the PI of both the tables is different, the optimizer will prepare a plan to redistribute or duplicate the source table so that rows can be on the same AMP before the final `insert`.

If this extra step query runtime and other factors increase, this will drag the performance of the query.

This becomes `FAST PATH INSERT SELECT` when the target table is empty; having the same PI is an advantage as there's no redistribution necessary.

FASTPATH INSERT.SELECT:

- The target table must be empty
- All `INSERT` statements in the multistatement request must have the same target table
- Only `INSERT` statements can be included in the request

There's more...

This is the first method to optimize the `insert.select`. There are some due considerations that need to be acknowledged while changing the PI:

- Business needs
- Uniqueness of the PI column
- Usage of PI column in select

Following are some tasks that you need to do if you find issues with `insert.select` statements:

- **Problem**: Query stuck on `MERGE` step of a `INSERT.SELECT` statement. We do a `MERGE` into table `[TBId=0x1767]` from Spool 9.
- **Issue**: Bad primary index defined on target table (`SET` in nature). PI has multiple duplicate/skew values which are causing duplicate row check.

- **Solution**: Change the PI to the least skewed distribution values. Also, try creating a `MULTISET` table instead of a `SET` table.
- **Problem**: Secondary index on the target table.
- **Solution**: Due to secondary index on target table present `insert` into table becomes slow, drop and re create index after the `insert` is completed.

Improving delete performance

`Delete` is a data manipulation language, or DML operator for removing one or more rows from a table. You can also `delete` a user or a database:

```
DELETE FROM table_name [ALL | WHERE condition];
```

Getting ready

For this recipe to complete you need to connect to the Teradata instance and open SQLA.

How to do it...

1. Identify the table from which data needs to be deleted.
2. `Delete` full tables or only required rows:

   ```
   DELETE FROM test01.web_clicks ALL; -- All rows deleted
   DELETE FROM test01.web_clicks where site=01 and
   partition_date=date-1 -- Rows with Site=0 only deletes and use
   partition column to avoid full table scan.
   ```

How it works...

There are a few basic considerations that need to be taken into account while writing a `delete` query; access to the data needs to be optimized, which means the access path the optimizer chooses should be efficient:

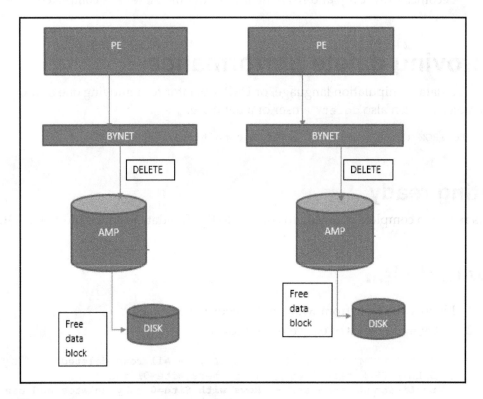

- **Full table scan:** Use primary index column, PPI, if available, when doing a `delete` of a million rows.
- **Index access:** Use index, if available; this helps the optimizer identify the ROWIDs. The number of rows qualified depends on the number of rows selected based on the index.

There's more...

If you have taken all due considerations and followed all performance recommendations and are still facing issues with DELETE, you might want to use utility tools for delete. MLOAD is the best option for this; the main reason is that MLOAD is more efficient than regular SQL delete:

- Less I/O as no TJ is required
- Uses less disk space and I/O
- Prevents lengthy rollbacks of aborted jobs

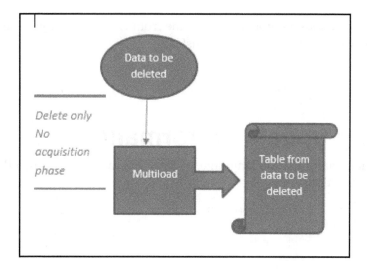

However, there are a few considerations when you use delete in MLOAD:

- As MLOAD DELETE does a full table scan, an equality of a UPI value is not permitted, but on NUPI this is allowed. But an inequality of a UPI value is permitted.
- Delete does not have an acquisition phase.
- Only a single DELETE statement is used.

- Only one target table is used and not `FIVE`:

```
LOGTABLE mld_test_delete;.
LOGON cookbook_td/testuser2,*****;
.BEGIN DELETE MLOAD TABLES web_clicks;
DELETE FROM web_clicks WHERE site_id > 1508;
.END MLOAD;
.LOGOFF;
```

`Delete` statement is more I/O intensive than the CPU. Always take due considerations when aborting a long-running `delete` statement; as said earlier, it may result in harmful rollback.

 Joined tables are not allowed in the from clause; they can't use the `JOIN` keyword. Use `FROM` *table-list* instead.

Improving update performance

An update is a data manipulation language, or DML operator. Updating a PI column causes performance degradation:

```
UPDATE table_name SET col_name=expression [, ..., col_name=expression]
[ALL | WHERE condition];
```

Getting ready

For this recipe to complete, you need to connect to the Teradata instance and open SQLA.

How to do it...

1. Identify the target table that needs to be updated.
2. Identify the source table from which the update is to be done:

```
update test01.web_clicks a -- Target update table
from test02.wed_address b -- Source update table
set acc_last_date= date -- Target column that's need to updated
where a.Rego_Start_Dt between '2016-12-25' and '2017-01-28' --
Partition column
```

How it works...

As we understand it, update is used to alter or change the values of existing rows of a table. The updating of the rows can be based on some where condition or full table if needed. You can use sub queries in update statements.

There is much to consider when it comes to updating rows in the table:

- **Index-based update**: Updating primary columns of the table if it is a very slow and high CPU/IO intensive job. Try to avoid it at all costs.
- **Abort update**: Huge update abort results in TJ. Avoid aborting long-running updates.
- **SI/JI**: If you find your update stuck at all-AMPs UPDATE in explain, check secondary or join indexes on the updating table. Drop them before updating and recreate them.
- **SET and updating column**: Always verify that columns that you are trying to update, which are in SET command, are not in your qualifier where clause.
- **NoPI**: SQL UPDATE requests cannot update a NoPI target table.
- **PPI considerations:** You need to reconsider the partition column when updating a table with the PPI column. The PPI helps in reducing I/O and also avoids full table scans. Not using the PPI results in performance degradation of the query.

There's more...

We not only have other alternatives to the update statement, but we can also write an update as an UPSERT, meaning, it executes an INSERT if not and performs the UPDATE if the row exists:

```
MERGE INTO
Table1 AS t1
USING
Table1_this AS t2
ON
t1.PK_Col=t2.PK_Col
WHEN MATCHED THEN UPDATE
SET
Col1=t1.Col1,
Col2=t1.Col2
WHEN NOT MATCHED THEN
INSERT
(
```

```
t1.PK_Col,
t1.Col1,
t1.Col2
)
;
```

You can update the data in a table not only using the update statement but using three other alternatives:

- **MERGE INTO:** Merges a source row set into a target table based on whether any target rows satisfy a specified matching condition with the source row. The MERGE statement combines the INSERT and UPDATE statements into a single conditional statement.
  What makes MERGE conditional is its two test clauses, called WHEN MATCHED and WHEN NOT MATCHED:

IF the source and target rows ...	THEN the merge operation is an ...
Satisfy the matching condition	update based on the specified WHEN MATCHED THEN UPDATE clause.
Do not satisfy the matching condition	insert based on the specified WHEN NOT MATCHED THEN INSERT clause.

  The step does a RowKey-based merge join internally, identifying source rows that qualify for updating target rows and

- Delete.Insert: This requires TJ space for each row until the transaction ends. This strategy is not optimal but can be efficient if you are updating a large number of rows with PI columns and no PPI is present on the target table. It is also the good choice when you have JI on the tables and you can't afford to drop and recreate them.
- Insert.Update, **also called UPSERT:** When the update operation fails, the INSERT statement executes, per upsert feature. Each record contains the primary key value of a row that is to be inserted successively into the target table whose columns are PI.

UPSERT on a PPI table: The INSERT portion must specify the same partition as the UPDATE portion.
The UPDATE must not modify any of the partitioning columns.
All values of the partitioning columns must be specified in the WHERE clause of the UPDATE portion.

- **Multiload update:** Replaces the whole block at a time, which helps in reducing I/O. It requires all transactions to be primary index operations when using the Update operator. UPSERT can also be performed using this. Also, it helps in TJ rollback as it has restart capabilities.

 Failure, 3538: A MultiLoad UPDATE Statement is Invalid:
Indicates that an UPDATE statement in a Multiload task that does not fully specify a primary index value. Use = for PI.

Based on your requirements and scenario, you need to choose which is the best strategy for you to update the rows.

See also

Resolving failure 7547: Target row updated by multiple source rows.

Performing MERGE INTO

MERGE statements can be used as an alternative to update statements. Updating rows is a CPU and I/O intensive operation, and, if you are updating PI on a big table which does not have a partition column, then updating columns becomes a challenge.

Getting ready

To complete this recipe you need to connect to the Teradata database and open SQLA.

How to do it...

1. Create a source table with the following definition and containing a million rows:

    ```
    CREATE volatile TABLE MergingTable_Source (
    ID DECIMAL(18,0),
    END_DT DATE,
    SOLD_AMT int
    )
    UNIQUE PRIMARY INDEX (ID) on commit preserve rows;
    ```

2. Create a target table with the following DDL:

    ```
    CREATE volatile TABLE MergingTable_Target (
    ID DECIMAL(18,0),
    END_DT DATE,
    SOLD_AMT int
    )
    UNIQUE PRIMARY INDEX (ID);
    ```

3. We will `insert` in the following `MergingTable_Target` table if the ID from `MergingTable_Source` does not exist. And if it does, we will update the `END_DT` and `SOLD_AMT` columns:

    ```
    MERGE INTO MergingTable_Target t
    USING MergingTable_Source        s
    ON T.ID = S.ID
    WHEN MATCHED THEN
    UPDATE SET END_DT = S.END_DT ,
    SOLD_AMT= S.SOLD_AMT
    WHEN NOT MATCHED THEN
    INSERT (S.ID,
    S.END_DT,
    S.SOLD_AMT);
    ```

How it works...

Merge statements combine update and `insert` statements into one; rows, when matched, can be deleted or updated, and non-matched rows are simply inserted.

Assume that both tables have the same unique primary index and contain 1 million rows.

An update is a very CPU or I/O intensive operator, as rows need to be modified, and if needed a table will be redistributed based on new values.

3
Advanced SQL with Backup and Restore

The following are the recipes we will be covering in this chapter:

- Exploring ordered analytic functions
- Using CASE statements
- Working with correlated subqueries
- Experimenting with JSON
- Partitioning tables column wise
- Archiving DD
- Archiving databases
- Archiving PPI tables
- Restoring a table
- Generating a unique row number

Introduction

This chapter will cover two broad areas of Teradata: one will be advanced SQL and the other will be backup and recovery.

Structured query language (**SQL**) is the relational database language used to store, retrieve, and manipulate data in databases. Teradata also uses SQL to work with datasets stored in the database.

Teradata SQL is basically divided into three parts:

- **Data definition language (DDL)**: These like CREATE and DROP
- **Data manipulation language (DML)**: These are like SELECT, INSERT, and DELETE
- **Data control language (DCL)**: These are like GRANT and REVOKE

Other than these basic SQL functions, Teradata Database has advanced SQL at its disposal. Advanced SQL helps users to execute complex cases and run more advanced data analytic functions.

Some of the advanced Teradata SQL features are:

- Windows aggregate function
- Ordered analytic function
- Extended time and date function
- Advanced ranking function
- Advanced sampling and random function
- Extended grouping function
- Merge into function
- Large binary object

In this chapter, we will cover some of the advanced features of Teradata. We will also cover some features of Teradata backup and recovery.

Backup and recovery

The purpose of the **ARC utility** is to allow for the archiving, restoring, and copying of database objects. To maintain data security and integrity, backing up data is a must. And when you damage or lose or want to restore the previous version of data, restore is required to be performed.

The following figure shows the high-level architecture of backup and recovery, or the BAR system:

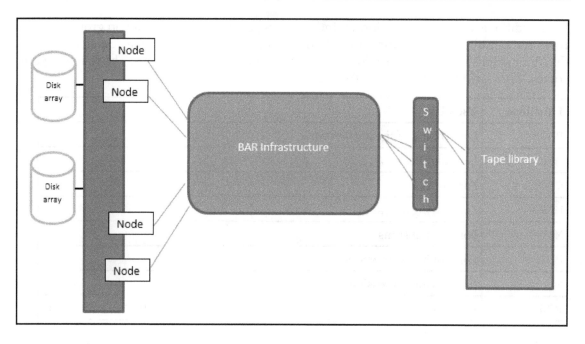

We will start with advanced SQL and then will cover some recipes on Teradata ARC.

Exploring ordered analytic functions

The **Online Analytical Processing (OLAP)** function, according to Wikipedia, is used to analyze multi-dimensional analytical queries quickly and efficiently. OLAP is part of the broader category of business intelligence, which also encompasses relational reporting and data mining. The typical applications of OLAP are business reporting for sales, marketing, management reporting, **business process management (BPM)**, budgeting and forecasting, financial reporting, and similar areas.

The term OLAP was created as a slight modification of the traditional database term **OLTP** (**Online Transaction Processing**). Databases configured for OLAP use a multidimensional data model, allowing for complex analytical and ad hoc queries with a rapid execution time.

Like traditional aggregate functions, window aggregate functions operate on groups of rows and permit the qualification and filtering of the group result. Unlike aggregations, OLAP functions also return individual detail rows, not just aggregations. The following are some OLAP functions available in Teradata:

Functions	Used For
RANK	For ranking of the answer set
QUANTILES	For quantiles
CSUM	For cumulation
MAVG	For moving averages
MSUM	For moving sums
MDIFF	For moving differences
MLINREG	For moving regression
ROW_NUMBER	Returns the sequential row number of a group starting with the number one

In this recipe, we will try to find the actual sales by each employee over the period of 3 months.

Getting ready

You need to connect to Teradata Database using SQLA or Studio. Let's create the following table and insert data into it:

```
CREATE Volatile TABLE EMP_SAL
(
EMP_ID INTEGER,
SAL_Months DATE,
DEPT_NAME CHAR (20),
sale_target INTEGER,
sale_done INTEGER)
PRIMARY INDEX ( EMP_ID );

INSERT INTO emp_sal values (10,'2017-01-01','IT',15000,13000);
INSERT INTO emp_sal values (20,'2017-02-01','HR',10000,11000);
INSERT INTO emp_sal values (30,'2017-03-01','HR',11000,10500);
INSERT INTO emp_sal values (40,'2017-04-01','LAW',12500,12500);
```

```
INSERT INTO emp_sal values (50,'2017-05-01','IT',15000,12500);
INSERT INTO emp_sal values (60,'2017-06-01','Sales',12000,11500);
INSERT INTO emp_sal values (70,'2017-07-01','Sales',15500,11500);
INSERT INTO emp_sal values (80,'2017-08-01','MKT',15000,15500);
```

How to do it...

1. Connect to Teradata Database using SQLA or Studio.
2. Execute the following query to get the result set:

```
/*OLAP select*/
SELECT EMP_ID,
SAL_Months,
sale_done,
sale_target,
min(sale_done)
OVER (
PARTITION BY EMP_ID ORDER BY
SAL_Months ROWS 2 PRECEDING) FROM EMP_SAL;
```

3. The result set will have the minimum amount of sales from employees in 3 months.
4. The RANK and ORDER BY functions will be used to sort rows in ascending and descending order as shown in code.

How it works...

We have used OLAP extensions in the query so that query can be manipulated by any size of dataset for OLAP and data mining processes. The OLAP extensions include the SQL expressions:

- RANK
- QUALIFY
- CSUM
- MAVG OR MSUM
- MDIFF

Here we have defined the window via:

- **PARTITION BY**: Clause defining the *grouping* of data
- **ORDER BY**: Clause defining the sequence of data
- **ROWS BETWEEN**: Defines the window used for calculation

All window aggregate functions broadly fall into four categories, which are used in connection with aggregate functions, as can be seen in the following figure:

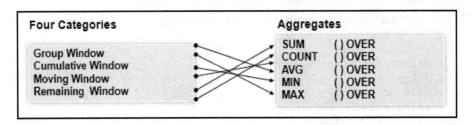

There's more...

There are some OLAP functions that we can use, such as:

- **Cumulative sum (CSUM)**: It computes a running or cumulative total of a column's value. Consider the following example code block:

```
/*CSUM select*/
SELECT EMP_ID , CSUM(SALARY,EMP_ID) FROM EMP_SAL;
```

CSUM(COLUMN_1) will result in an error as CSUM needs two columns as arguments. The first column is used for sorting the sequence and the second column is then used to perform the cumulative sum. Check the code for syntax for CSUM:

```
/*Syntax for CSUM*/
CSUM(columnname,sortlist)
```

- **Moving Average (MAVG)**: Used to calculate the moving average on a column. The number of rows used for the aggregation operation is called as query width, as shown in the code:

```
/*MAVG*/
SELECT EMP_ID,SAL, MAVG (SAL,2,EMP_ID) FROM EMP_SAL
```

- **RANK**: A function that assigns a ranking order to rows in a qualified answer set, as shown in the code:

```
/*RANK*/
SELECT str_id, prod_id, SAL,
RANK() OVER (ORDER BY SAL DESC) AS Rank_Sales
FROM SAL_TBL
QUALIFY rank_sales <= 5;
```

- **MDIFF**: Returns the moving difference between the current row-column value and the preceding *n*th value, as shown in the code:

```
/*MDIFF*/
SELECT str_id,
SAL_MONTH,Target_sale,mdiff(Target_sale,1,str_id)FROM SAL_TBL
```

- **Percent_Rank**: Its value represents the portion of rows in the answer set which precede any given row in the list. It is always a value between 0.0 and 1.0 inclusive, as shown in the code:

```
/*Percent_RANK*/
SELECT str_id, emp_name, sal,
RANK()   OVER (ORDER BY sal DESC) AS Rank_Sales,
PERCENT_RANK() OVER (ORDER BY sal DESC) AS Pct_Rank_Sales
FROM SAL_TBL
```

Using CASE statements

Like any other programming language, Teradata SQL provides if-then-else logic using the CASE statement. It helps in fetching alternate values for a column based on the condition specified in the expression. If any one of the values gets qualified as TRUE, its value gets captured and the counter goes on until all the rows have been processed.

Every CASE statement needs to have a pair of WHEN and THEN statements and to be closed using an END statement.

The syntax of CASE is as follows:

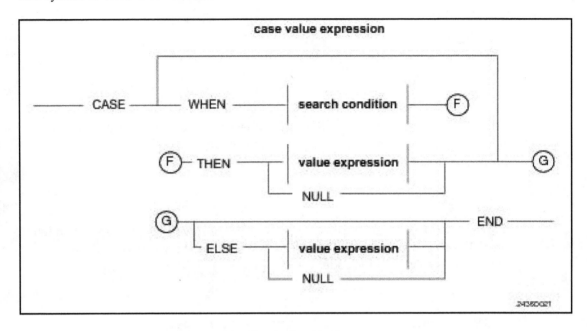

The syntax of case statement

Let's put this into a code statement as follows:

```
/*CASE SELECT*/
SELECT EMP_name, Month,
CASE WHEN MONTH = 'JUNE' THEN 'yes' ELSE NULL END AS SUMMER
FROM Table_CASE
```

Let's understand this by means of a flow chart:

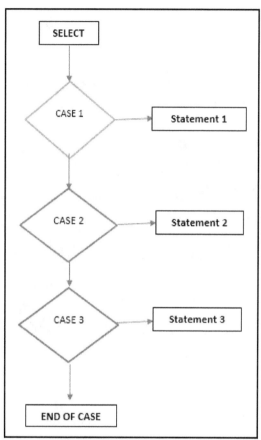

Decoding the statement:

1. The **CASE 1** statement checks each row to see if the conditional statement is met.
2. For any given row for **CASE 1**, if that conditional statement is true, the counter for the true condition is increased or the corresponding value gets stored.
3. In any row for which the conditional statement is false, nothing happens in that row, and the false statement is executed.
4. If the query has other **CASEs** involved, the flow will continue with another **CASE** statement.
5. Rows that don't qualify are executed by the default **CASE** statement.

In this recipe, we will write a **CASE** statement identifying customers who have pre-paid or post-paid connection.

Getting ready

You need to connect to the Teradata Database system using SQLA or Studio. Let's create the following table and insert rows into it:

```
/*Create table and insert for CASE*/
CREATE Volatile TABLE CUST_Type
(
Cust_ID INTEGER,
Connection_type INTEGER,
Cust_Add CHAR (20) CHARACTER SET LATIN NOT CASESPECIFIC,
PRIMARY INDEX ( Cust_ID );

INSERT INTO sales values (10,1,'212 bal');
INSERT INTO sales values (21,2,'86 court');
INSERT INTO sales values (31,2,'62 st');
INSERT INTO sales values (32,1,'21 rd');
INSERT INTO sales values (102,2,'271 main ');
INSERT INTO sales values (082,1,'10sroad');
INSERT INTO sales values (23,?,'jh1-0s');
```

How to do it...

1. Connect to Teradata Database using SQLA or Studio.
2. Let's try to find pre-paid and post-paid customers based on the `connection_type` code column; the `connection_type=1` would be `Pre-paid` and `connection_type=2` would be `post-paid`:

```
/*Select for CASE*/
SELECT
 cust_id,
 Cust_Add,
  CASE WHEN Connection_type=1 THEN 'Pre-paid'
       WHEN Connection_type=2 THEN 'Post-paid'
 ELSE 'Not Sure'
 END AS Connection_type
 FROM CUST_Type;
```

3. Let's check the output of the following:

```
cust_id          Cust_add          Connection_type
-----------      -----------       -----------
         10      bal                   Pre-paid
         21      86 court             Post-paid
         31      62 st                Post-paid
         32      21 rd                 Pre-paid
        102      271 main             Post-paid
        082      10sroad               Pre-paid
         23      jh1-0s                Not Sure
```

How it works...

As you saw, based on the `Connection_type` column we were able to classify pre-paid and post-paid customers. Both `CASE` statements get executed, as can be seen in the result set. You must have noticed that the last customer has a connection type of `Not Sure`; this is because the `Connection_type` for this customer is `NULL` and it was not able to get processed by both the `CASE` statements. Therefore, it went to the default `CASE` statement.

This is how we can use `CASE` statements in Teradata SQL to cater to the function of if-else statements.

A quick review:

- The `CASE` statement always has the `SELECT` clause.
- `CASE` must have the following identifiers: `WHEN`, `THEN`, and `END`. `ELSE` is an optional component.
- `WHERE` is used as conditional statement.
- Multiple `WHEN` statements are allowed; an `ELSE` statement is used to deal with any unaddressed conditions.

There's more...

`CASE` statements can also have aggregate functions. You can `COUNT` or `SUM` the column values based on conditions. Let's say you want to aggregate the `SUM` of all the employees' salaries in `DEPT=IT` and `DEPT=HR`. The following will help you aggregate the `SUM`:

```
/*Aggregate CASE*/
SELECT SUM(
```

```
   CASE WHEN department='IT' THEN) AS SAL_IT
SUM (
CASE WHEN department='HR' THEN) AS SAL_HR
   END)
FROM EMP_SAL;
```

How do you improve the performance of the CASE statement, you ask? Be sure to put the most commonly occurring condition FIRST in the CASE statements. Conditions will not be compared after the first "true" condition is met.

Working with correlated subqueries

A **correlated subquery (CS)** is a subquery whose outer query results are processed a row at a time, against the subquery result. The subquery result is computed for each row processed. The following are advantages of subqueries:

- Helps in eliminating the need for intermediate or temporary tables. Reduces user temp space and spool.
- Helps in minimizing joining costs.
- If used effectively, is significantly faster than the query using temporary tables.

Now, let's understand the workings of different types of queries in Teradata from the figure:

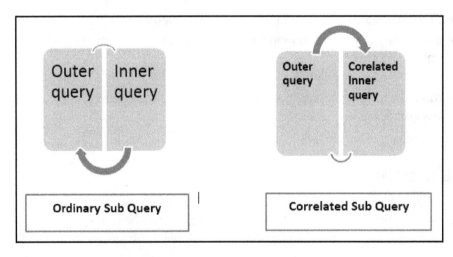

Ordinary Sub Query: In this case, the inner query is executed only once, and the output of the inner query is used by the outer query. The inner query is not dependent on the outer query:

```
/*Sub query*/
SELECT
Column1, Column2 FROM
Table1
WHERE Column1 IN (SELECT Column1 FROM Table1);
```

Correlated Sub Query: In this case, the outer query will be executed first, and for every row of the outer query, the inner query will be getting executed. This means the inner query will get executed as many times as the number of rows in the result of the outer query. The outer query output can use the inner query output for comparison. This maintains the dependency between inner and outer queries:

```
/*Correlated query*/
SELECT Column1, Column2
FROM Table1 Tb1
WHERE Column1 IN
(
SELECT Column1 FROM Table2 Tb2 WHERE
Tb1.Column2=Tb2.Column2
);
```

In this recipe, we will look at the workings of the correlated subquery.

Getting ready

You need to connect to Teradata Database using SQLA or Studio. Now, let's create two tables and insert data into them:

```
/* Table 1 for outer query*/
CREATE VOLATILE TABLE EMP_TBL1
(
EMP_ID INTEGER ,

EMP_NAME VARCHAR(25),

EMP_DEPT INTEGER

)
primary index(EMP_ID)
on commit preserve rows;
```

```
INSERT INTO EMP_TBL1 VALUES (1,'Rajesh',10);

INSERT INTO EMP_TBL1 VALUES (2,'Rob',11);

INSERT INTO EMP_TBL1 VALUES (3,'Joey',10);

INSERT INTO EMP_TBL1 VALUES (4,'Ross','21');

INSERT INTO EMP_TBL1 VALUES (5,'Rose','22');
```

Now, let's create table 2, which will be used for inner query:

```
CREATE VOLATILE TABLE DEPT_TBL2
(
DEPT_ID INTEGER,
DEPT_NAME VARCHAR(10),
DEPT_CNTRY VARCHAR(10)
)
PRIMARY INDEX(DEPT_ID, DEPT_CNTRY)
on commit preserve rows;

INSERT INTO DEPT_TBL2 VALUES (10,'IT','IN');
INSERT INTO DEPT_TBL2 VALUES (11,'HR','US');
INSERT INTO DEPT_TBL2 VALUES (21,'MKT','AUS');
```

Let's first check the relationship between the two tables:

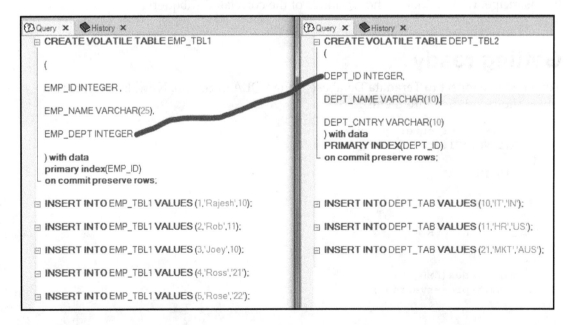

How to do it...

1. You need to connect to Teradata Database using SQLA or Studio.
2. Let's first collect the statistics of the joining column of both the tables:

   ```
   /*Collect stats on table*/
   Collect stats column EMP_DEPT on EMP_TBL1;
   Collect stats column DEPT_ID on EMP_TBL2;
   ```

3. Let's execute the following query:

   ```
   /*Correlated sub query*/
   SEL TB1.* FROM EMP_TBL1 TB1
   WHERE EXISTS /*Outer Query*/
   (SEL TB2.DEPT_ID FROM  /*Inner Query*/
   DEPT_TBL2 TB2
   WHERE TB1.EMP_DEPT = TB2.DEPT_ID ) ;
   ```

4. The following would be output of the query:

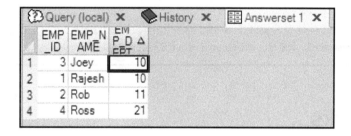

5. Now let's check the explain plan of the query:

```
1) First, we do an all-AMPs RETRIEVE step from DBC.TB1 by way of an
   all-rows scan with no residual conditions into Spool 2 (all_amps),
   which is redistributed by the hash code of (DBC.TB1.EMP_DEPT) to
   all AMPs. Then we do a SORT to order Spool 2 by row hash. The
   size of Spool 2 is estimated with high confidence to be 5 rows (
   155 bytes). The estimated time for this step is 0.01 seconds.
2) Next, we do an all-AMPs JOIN step from Spool 2 (Last Use) by way
   of an all-rows scan, which is joined to DBC.TB2 by way of an
   all-rows scan with a condition of ("NOT (DBC.TB2.DEPT_ID IS NULL)").
   Spool 2 and DBC.TB2 are joined using an inclusion merge join, with
   a join condition of ("(NOT (EMP_DEPT IS NULL )) AND (EMP_DEPT =
   DBC.TB2.DEPT_ID)"). The result goes into Spool 1 (group_amps),
   which is built locally on the AMPs. The size of Spool 1 is
   estimated with index join confidence to be 5 rows (195 bytes).
   The estimated time for this step is 0.05 seconds.
3) Finally, we send out an END TRANSACTION step to all AMPs involved
   in processing the request.
-> The contents of Spool 1 are sent back to the user as the result of
   statement 1. The total estimated time is 0.07 seconds.
```

How it works...

Our correlated subquery validates whether the values in the EMP_DEPT column exist or don't exist, and thereby it serves the filter to the result set for the outer query. Other than selecting the columns, it also lets you perform DML operations such as updating or deleting multiple rows in other tables. You should have unique indexes on these join columns because correlated subqueries run for each row returned by the outer query. Unique indexes let correlated queries perform faster with fewer computing resources.

If you are using the correlated sub query, it is recommended to use EXISTS, IN, and =, in that order to get better performance.

Let's insert following row and execute the query again:

```
/*Additional row insert*/
INSERT INTO DEPT_TBL2 VALUES (10,'IT','UK');
```

An error can be seen in the following figure:

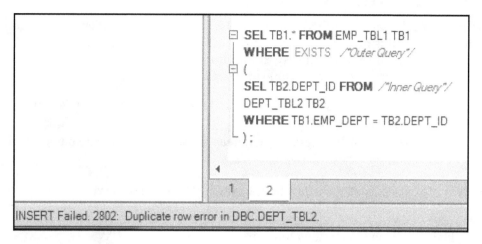

You can see in the preceding image that the query failed with an error, as there are multiple rows generated from the subquery.

There's more...

There are some rules to be followed when using a correlated sub query:

- Must be enclosed in parentheses
- Can be used with the IN or NOT IN clauses
- Can be used with the EXISTS or NOT EXISTS clauses
- Supports quantifiers such as ALL, ANY, and SOME
- Can use LIKE or NOT LIKE, used with a quantifier
- Can specify more than one column to match
- Gives a DISTINCT list of values
- ORDER BY can't be used
- Maximum of 64 tables/views can be specified in an SQL statement

Experimenting with JSON

JavaScript Object Notation (JSON) is a lightweight programming independent data interchange format. It is mainly used in web applications to transmit information. It is not only simple for humans to read but easy for machines to parse and generate. JSON has some advantages for traditional extensible markup language (XML):

- XML data is a typeless only string, whereas JSON data is typed like string, number, array, and boolean
- JSON data is readily accessible, whereas XML data needs to be parsed and assigned to variables

The JSON syntax is a subset of the JavaScript syntax. There are some rules when it comes to JSON syntax:

- Data is defined in name/value pairs
- Data is separated by commas
- Curly braces hold objects
- Square brackets hold arrays

```
{
"name":"Robert"
}
```

We can use JSON as we would use any other SQL data type:

- JSON content is stored in databases and optimized depending on the size of the data.
- The user is not responsible for executing the CREATE TYPE statement for the JSON data type. JSON data types do not need to be created via DDL by the user as the JSON data type exists in the database.
- The JSON data type cannot be created, dropped, or altered by the user.

JSON CHARACTER SET could be either UNICODE or LATIN.

The following is the syntax for the JSON data type:

```
JSON [integer] Character Set[Unicode/latin] Attribute
```

This table highlights the type integer length based on the character set chosen:

Character Set Type	Max Integer Length
Latin	16,776,192
Unicode	8,388,096

JSON also carries attributes like any other SQL datatype; it can be or have the following:

- Could be `NULL` and `NOT NULL`
- Can have `FORMAT`
- Can have `TITLE`
- Could be `NAMED`
- Could be `DEFAULT NULL`
- Could be `COMPRESS USING` and `DECOMPRESS USING`

JSON data is stored inline and in LOB subtables depending on the size of the data.

In this recipe, we will create a JSON table, insert values into it, and select and collect statistics on the JSON column.

Getting ready

You need to connect to Teradata Database using SQLA or Studio.

How to do it...

1. Connect to Teradata using SQLA or Studio.
2. Create the following JSON table in your database:

    ```
    CREATE VOLATILE TABLE JSON_TBL
    (
    EMP_id INTEGER, J1 JSON(1000)
    )on commit preserve rows
    ;
    ```

3. Let's insert values into it:

    ```
    INSERT INTO JSON_TBL VALUES
    (1, NEW JSON('{"name" : "Roberts", "Month" : 1}'));
    ```

4. Let's see the snippet from SQLA:

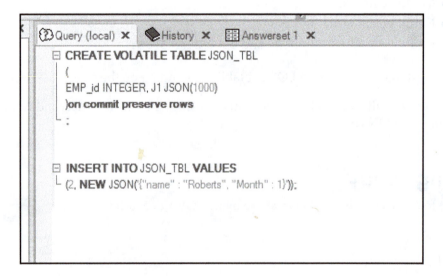

5. Now we will SELECT data from table we have created. The output will be written to the file on your desktop, as JSON data is stored in LOB. The following would be the output. Press **Cancel** to display the result in the result set in SQLA:

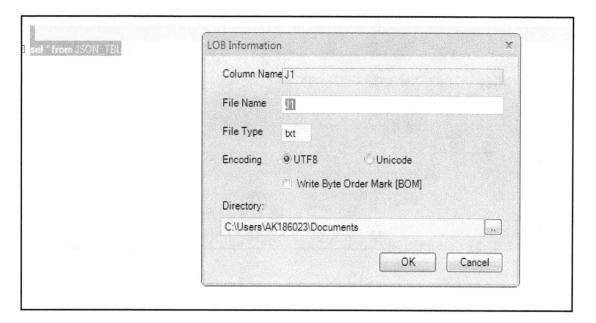

6. Following would be the result set, when you press **Cancel**:

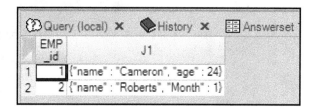

7. Let's collect statistics on the JSON column using the following code:

```
/*Collect stats on JSON column*/
COLLECT STATISTICS COLUMN J1.name AS json_name_stats ON JSON_TBL
```

8. Let's do a help statistics as follows and check the output:

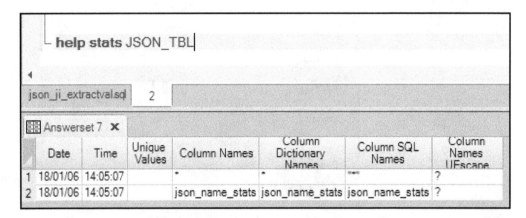

How it works...

We can see that a JSON data type can be used in the same way as any other datatype in Teradata Database. This feature brings power of **Information of Things (IoT)** into Teradata Database with ease.

We can perform the following DML operations with the JSON datatype defined in a table:

- INSERT
- INSERT-SELECT
- MERGE
- UPDATE (UPSERT)

Moreover, if you try to insert the following row in an existing JSON table, it will return a duplicate error:

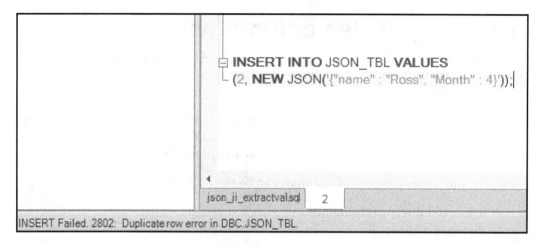

```
INSERT INTO JSON_TBL VALUES
(2, NEW JSON('{"name" : "Ross", "Month" : 4}'));
```

json_ji_extractval.sql   2

INSERT Failed. 2802: Duplicate row error in DBC.JSON_TBL.

If a SET table has a JSON column defined, the JSON column is not used in the determination of uniqueness of the row or table. For that reason, all other columns in a row are equivalent to another row; the two rows are deemed equivalent.

There's more...

The following are some disadvantages of JSON with the current version of the database. Teradata engineering must be working to resolve these disadvantages:

- GROUP BY, ORDER BY, PARTITION BY, WHERE, ON, SET, DISTINCT, HAVING, QUALIFY, IN, CUBE, GROUPING SETS, or ROLLUP are not allowed with a JSON column.
- Indexes (UPI/NUPI/USI/NUSI) cannot be defined in JSON.
- You can only update the JSON column, not individual portions of the JSON instance.

But the following are the advantages of JSON:

- Can be used to create a join index
- Statistics can be collected on the JSON column
- Functions can be defined using JSON
- ARRAY can be used

Partitioning tables column wise

Starting with Teradata 14.0, a new feature was introduced called **Columnar**. Using a **partition primary index** (**PPI**), Teradata partitions tables into rows. But now you can also partition tables column wise.

Columnar provides you with this feature. You can now partition tables with a high number of columns into smaller tables. This not only reduces the I/O, but space too, by auto compressing column containers. Tables can be row partitioned plus column partitioned.

Advantages of using the Teradata Columnar can be the following:

- Improved query performance
- Reduced disk space
- Reduced I/O
- Ease of use

Please note there are certain features of Columnar that are not available in later versions of the database but are in Teradata 15.10:

- Has the primary index (from version 15.10)
- Has the primary AMP index (from version 15.10)
- Joins index column-based partitions (previous version also)
- NOPI table column-based partitions (previous version also)
- No SET tables (previous version also)
- No Temp tables (previous version also)
- Fastload/Mload/Merge not allowed (previous version also)

These features of Teradata need to be enabled separately and, before implementing any design changes, the Teradata engineering team needs to be consulted.

In this recipe, we will create a column-based partition on a table.

Getting ready

Connect to Teradata Database using SQLA or Studio.

How to do it...

1. Connect to Teradata Database using SQLA or Studio.

2. Create a columnar table using the following DDL:

```
/*Columnar table DDL*/
CREATE MULTISET TABLE cookbook_td.columnarTbl
(
COL1 INTEGER,
DOB DATE
) PRIMARY AMP INDEX (COL1)
PARTITION BY COLUMN, RANGE_N (DATE BETWEEN '2017-01-01' AND
'2017-12-31' EACH INTERVALL '1' MONTH));
```

3. Insert data into the columnar table as follows:

```
/*Insert into columnar table*/
INSERT into cookbook_td.columnarTbl VALUES (1001,'2017-09-01');
INSERT into cookbook_td.columnarTbl VALUES (1002,'2017-02-01');
INSERT into cookbook_td.columnarTbl VALUES (1003,'2017-01-01');
INSERT into cookbook_td.columnarTbl VALUES (1004,'2017-12-05');
```

4. The columnar table is ready.

How it works...

The columnar table is ready, with rows on AMP vertically stored. Partitioning a table helps to reduce I/O by accessing only subsets of columns from a table. It is like creating mini tables from one big table.

To understand this, check the following figure:

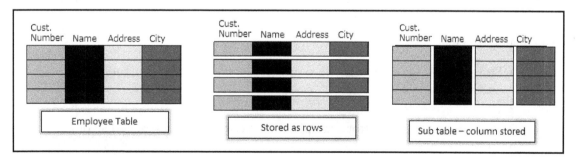

The Employee table is stored in a row, so if we need to query a request, all the rows will be read. But if you select particular columns with table partitioned as columnar only, a subset of the table will be read and hence less I/O.

This means that if you select all the columns or more columns from the column partitioned table, it will have lower performance than a normal table.

There's more...

An alter can be executed on an empty columnar partitioned table; a table with data needs to be rebuilt.

In the explain of the query, look for the following when dealing with column level partitioned tables:

```
/*explain of column partitioned table*/
We do an all-AMPs RETRIEVE step from X column partitions (XX
contexts) of <columnartable> using covering CP merge Spool 2 (2 subrow
partitions and Last Use)
```

Archiving data dictionary

A **dictionary**'s actual meaning is a resource of words for a particular language, which provides their meaning. Similarly, we have this feature in Teradata Database.

The Teradata **data dictionary** (**DD**) is a complete database composed of system tables, views, and macros that reside in the Teradata system, called **DBC**. Data dictionary tables are dumped when you install the system. Users reference some of these tables with SQL requests, while others are used for system or data recovery only. Data dictionary views reference data dictionary tables. Views and macros are created by running **Database Initialization Program** (**DIP**) scripts.

Data dictionary tables are used to:

- Store definitions of objects you create (for example, databases, tables, indexes, and so on)
- Control access to data
- Record system events (for example, logon, console messages, and so on)

- Hold system message texts
- Record and control system restarts
- Accumulate accounting information

As we saw, DD tables include current definitions, control information, and general information about the following:

- Databases
- Character sets
- Users
- Accounts
- Tables
- Views
- Columns
- Indices
- Sessions and session attributes
- Triggers
- Access rights
- Journal tables
- Disk space
- Events
- Resource usage
- Macros
- Stored procedures

In this recipe, we will back up the data dictionary.

Getting ready

You need to be connected to the Teradata `arcmain` utility. To archive database DBC, the user must be User DBC or be granted the `ARCHIVE` and `SELECT` privileges by User DBC, as shown in the following code:

```
/*ARC grant to archive user*/
GRANT DUMP, SELECT ON DBC TO ARC_USR_ROLE;
GRANT ARC_USR_ROLE to ARCH01;
```

How to do it...

1. Connect to the Teradata `arcmain` utility:

```
                                    Terminal                              _ □ ×
 File  Edit  View  Terminal  Help
Your use is subject to the terms and conditions of
        the click through agreement that brought you to this
        screen ("TERADATA EXPRESS") EVALUATION AND DEVELOPMENT
        LICENSE AGREEMENT), including the restriction that this
        evaluation copy is not for production use.
TD-EXPRESS:~ # arcmain
01/06/2018 21:06:43   Copyright 1989-2015, Teradata Corporation.
01/06/2018 21:06:43   All Rights Reserved.
01/06/2018 21:06:43
01/06/2018 21:06:43    ***   ****    ****
01/06/2018 21:06:43    *   *   *   *   *        PROGRAM: ARCMAIN
01/06/2018 21:06:43    *****  ****   *          RELEASE: 15.10.00.02
01/06/2018 21:06:43    *   *   *   *   *         BUILD:   150152eLX64 (Sep  2 2015)
01/06/2018 21:06:43    *   *   *   *    ****
01/06/2018 21:06:43
01/06/2018 21:06:43   RESTARTLOG = ARCLOG180106_210643_11734.rlg
01/06/2018 21:06:43
01/06/2018 21:06:43   PARAMETERS IN USE:
01/06/2018 21:06:43
01/06/2018 21:06:43
01/06/2018 21:06:43
01/06/2018 21:06:44   CHARACTER SET IN USE: ASCII
[]
```

2. Log in using the archive user to execute the backup job.
3. Copy the following statement and execute it in the `arcmain` window. Save the file with the `DBC_ARC.arc` name:

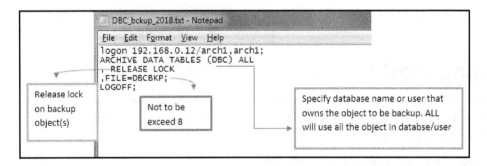

Parameters to keep in mind

4. The log will be saved in the `DBC_BKP_2018`. Check the log file for the status and ensure the completion of the job.

How it works...

Teradata ARC does not record most of the modifications it makes to a database in the transient journal. Instead, Teradata ARC uses a file called *restart log* to maintain the operation status of the job being run.

The restart log catalogs the effects of utility operations on a database or table. Teradata ARC writes restart entries in the log at the beginning and end of each significant step (and at intermediate points in a long running task). If a job is interrupted for some reason, Teradata ARC uses this log to restart the archive or restore an operation that was being performed.

When Teradata ARC is started, it first places markers into the restart log to keep track of the current input and logon statements. Then Teradata ARC copies the command stream to the restart log. Teradata ARC uses these commands during restart to continue with the most recent activity using the same logon user originally entered.

It is recommended to use separate user(s), role(s), and profiles(s) for backup and archive work, as backup users require different permissions from regular database users. Also, backup jobs execute in separate workloads on the system. There are many reasons for choosing Concurrent Users to make backups.

To reduce the archive window time, you might need to choose concurrent archive jobs with different archive users to make backups of databases or groups of databases. This is done to reduce the archive window compared to an archive window using a single user:

```
/*Archive database and user*/
Create Database ARC_Usr as PERM=0;
Create User Cookbook_ARCUSER from ARC_Usr as PERM=0, PASSWORD=password;
```

There's more...

Do not forget to place a `RELEASE LOCK` statement in the archive script. When backups are performed, a utility read lock is invoked; therefore, a release lock is required to allow access to the database. A release lock occurs after a backup is finished, right before logoff. If backup is killed in-between or aborted for any reason, the lock needs to be removed manually to avoid blocking all the other jobs on the system.

Archiving databases

To provide security and data integrity, Teradata Database provides the backup and archive facility. The backup and recovery of data is very critical in case of system crush, which leads to data corruption, or when developers want to rebuild a table with new columns or definitions. Backup and recovery comes to the rescue in many cases.

The ARCHIVE command allows you to back up objects in a database to media (tape). The following diagram shows the syntax for ARCHIVE command:

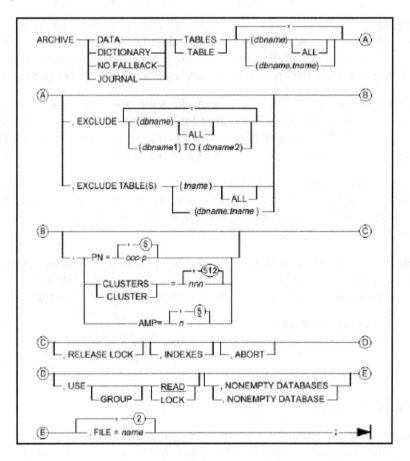

Teradata ARC orange book

In this recipe, we will back up one of the databases along with all the object in that database.

Getting ready

You need to be connected to the Teradata `arcmain` utility. To archive the database, the user must be granted the `ARCHIVE` and `SELECT` privileges on the database to be archived. This can be checked in the following code:

```
/*GRANT Archive to archive role*/
GRANT RESTORE, DUMP ON DATABASENAME TO ARCH_ROLE;
GRANT ARCH_ROLE to ARCH01
```

How to do it...

1. Connect to the Teradata `arcmain` utility:

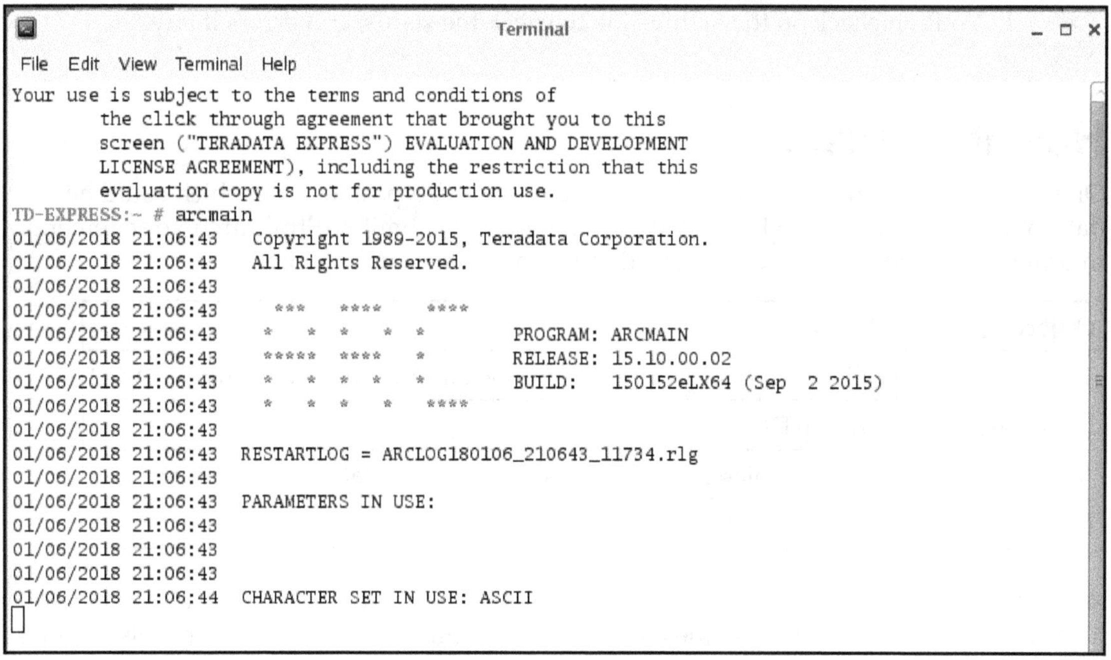
Terminal
File Edit View Terminal Help
Your use is subject to the terms and conditions of
the click through agreement that brought you to this
screen ("TERADATA EXPRESS") EVALUATION AND DEVELOPMENT
LICENSE AGREEMENT), including the restriction that this
evaluation copy is not for production use.
TD-EXPRESS:~ # arcmain
01/06/2018 21:06:43 Copyright 1989-2015, Teradata Corporation.
01/06/2018 21:06:43 All Rights Reserved.
01/06/2018 21:06:43
01/06/2018 21:06:43
01/06/2018 21:06:43 PROGRAM: ARCMAIN
01/06/2018 21:06:43 RELEASE: 15.10.00.02
01/06/2018 21:06:43 BUILD: 150152eLX64 (Sep 2 2015)
01/06/2018 21:06:43
01/06/2018 21:06:43
01/06/2018 21:06:43 RESTARTLOG = ARCLOG180106_210643_11734.rlg
01/06/2018 21:06:43
01/06/2018 21:06:43 PARAMETERS IN USE:
01/06/2018 21:06:43
01/06/2018 21:06:43
01/06/2018 21:06:43
01/06/2018 21:06:44 CHARACTER SET IN USE: ASCII

2. Log in using the archive user to execute the backup job.

3. Execute the statement as show in the figure, and execute in the `arcmain` window. Save the file with the `DB_Bckup_2018.arc` name:

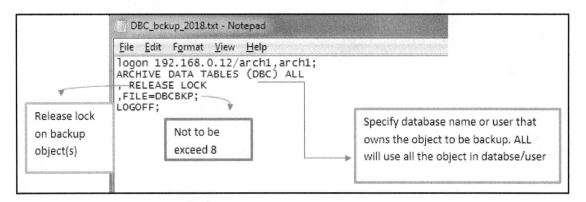

4. You can check on the archive job to check the status, and errors if any.

How it works...

One archive statement can only back up one table/object type at a time, which could be data, a dictionary, no fallback, or a journal. Users must submit multiple archive statements in order to archive each. Following is a description of each archive type:

Object type	Description
Tables	Fallback-non fallback, partition-non partition, all AMP-multiple AMP
Dictionary table	Back up DD
No fallback table	Back up tables on AMP that is down during data table archiving
Journal table	DD tables and journal tables

An object is backed up based on the option you have specified in your ARCHIVE statement. You can specify all the objects in the database to be archived or select specific tables/objects from database to be archived.

There's more...

Local AMP is the feature where ARC will, as best it can, use local sessions connected to the same node as an AMP to archive the data for that AMP. This reduces the BYNET traffic considerably during the `BAR` operation, and can provide a substantial improvement in archive and restore performance, in some cases up to double the throughput.

An ARC user on the system must be granted the `MONITOR` privilege so that it can query the necessary AMP location information. Any of the monitor privileges will work, so the site can choose which is best to grant from a security standpoint.

To execute the BAR process at its maximum speed, there are a few tuning processes that can be performed:

- **Network tuning**: This can be achieved by increasing the frame size, and increasing the device buffer to connect to a large number of sessions. Also, COP entries determine how the BAR server will connect to Teradata nodes.
- **Software tuning**: Session count used by ARC. This is dependent on the number of AMPs, number of streams, and tape drive.

 It is recommended to use a session count equal to the number of AMPs per node.

It is important to know and understand the importance of data availability while backup is in progress, and the impact of resource usage of the backup, both of which can impact performance of other operations during the backup window.

Archiving PPI tables

Teradata provides various indexing mechanisms, and **Partitioned Primary Index** (PPI) is one of them. PPU tables are useful in improving the performance of queries that utilize range-based data. It helps to restrict data retrieval to the partitions in which rows are present. In normal cases, rows are inserted into a table, they are stored in an AMP, and arranged by their row hash order. With the table defined with PPI, the rows are sorted by their partition number and are stored in a collective manner in their partitions. Within each partition, they are arranged by their row hash. Rows are assigned to a partition based on the partition expression defined.

Teradata provides two types of partitions on tables as show in the following figure:

- Row level partition
- Column level partition

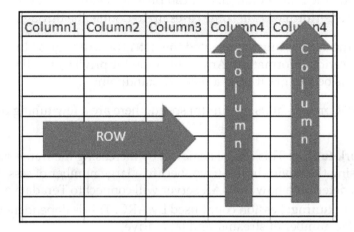

You can perform an all-AMPs archive on one or more partitions of a table rather than performing a full-table backup. The ability to select partitions from PPI tables is limited to all-AMP archives. Dictionary, cluster, and journal archives are not supported.

Use archive partitioning to accomplish the following tasks:

- Archive only a subset of data (this can minimize the size of the archive and improve performance)
- Restore data in a table that is partially damaged
- Copy a limited set of data to a disaster recovery machine or to a test system

In this recipe, we will create a PPI table and take a backup of a specified partition using the ARCHIVE command.

Getting ready

You need to connect to Teradata Database using SQLA or Studio to create the following partitioned table and insert data into it:

```
/*Create a PPI table and insert rows*/
CREATE TABLE cookbook_td.EMP_SAL_PPI
(
```

```
id INT,
Sal int,
dob date,
o_total int
) primary index( id)
PARTITION BY RANGE_N (dob BETWEEN DATE '2017-01-01'
    AND DATE '2017-12-01' EACH INTERVAL '1' DAY)

INSERT into cookbook_td.EMP_SAL_PPI VALUES (1001,2500,'2017-09-01',890);
INSERT into cookbook_td.EMP_SAL_PPI VALUES (1002,5500,'2017-09-10',890);
INSERT into cookbook_td.EMP_SAL_PPI VALUES (1003,500,'2017-09-02',890);
INSERT into cookbook_td.EMP_SAL_PPI VALUES (1004,54500,'2017-09-05',890);
INSERT into cookbook_td.EMP_SAL_PPI VALUES (1005,900,'2017-09-23',890);
INSERT into cookbook_td.EMP_SAL_PPI VALUES (1006,8900,'2017-08-03',890);
INSERT into cookbook_td.EMP_SAL_PPI VALUES (1007,8200,'2017-08-21',890);
INSERT into cookbook_td.EMP_SAL_PPI VALUES (1008,6200,'2017-08-06',890);
INSERT into cookbook_td.EMP_SAL_PPI VALUES (1009,2300,'2017-08-12',890);
INSERT into cookbook_td.EMP_SAL_PPI VALUES (1010,9200,'2017-08-15',890);
```

The snippet of SQLA shows the following code upon execution:

```
CREATE TABLE cookbook_td.EMP_SAL_PPI
(
id INT,
Sal int,
dob date,
o_total int
) primary index( id)
PARTITION BY RANGE_N (dob BETWEEN DATE '2017-01-01'
  AND DATE '2017-12-01' EACH INTERVAL '1' DAY);


INSERT into cookbook_td.EMP_SAL_PPI VALUES (1001,2500,'2017-09-01',890);
INSERT into cookbook_td.EMP_SAL_PPI VALUES (1002,5500,'2017-09-10',890);
INSERT into cookbook_td.EMP_SAL_PPI VALUES (1003,500,'2017-09-02',890);
INSERT into cookbook_td.EMP_SAL_PPI VALUES (1004,54500,'2017-09-05',890);
INSERT into cookbook_td.EMP_SAL_PPI VALUES (1005,900,'2017-09-23',890);
INSERT into cookbook_td.EMP_SAL_PPI VALUES (1006,8900,'2017-08-03',890);
INSERT into cookbook_td.EMP_SAL_PPI VALUES (1007,8200,'2017-08-21',890);
INSERT into cookbook_td.EMP_SAL_PPI VALUES (1008,6200,'2017-08-06',890);
INSERT into cookbook_td.EMP_SAL_PPI VALUES (1009,2300,'2017-08-12',890);
INSERT into cookbook_td.EMP_SAL_PPI VALUES (1010,9200,'2017-08-15',890);
```

How to do it...

1. Connect to the Teradata `arcmain` utility:

```
Terminal                                                          _ □ ×

File  Edit  View  Terminal  Help

Your use is subject to the terms and conditions of
        the click through agreement that brought you to this
        screen ("TERADATA EXPRESS") EVALUATION AND DEVELOPMENT
        LICENSE AGREEMENT), including the restriction that this
        evaluation copy is not for production use.
TD-EXPRESS:~ # arcmain
01/06/2018 21:06:43   Copyright 1989-2015, Teradata Corporation.
01/06/2018 21:06:43   All Rights Reserved.
01/06/2018 21:06:43
01/06/2018 21:06:43      ***    ****    ****
01/06/2018 21:06:43     *  *   *   *   *         PROGRAM: ARCMAIN
01/06/2018 21:06:43     *****  ****    *         RELEASE: 15.10.00.02
01/06/2018 21:06:43     *  *   *   *   *         BUILD:   150152eLX64 (Sep  2 2015)
01/06/2018 21:06:43     *  *   *   *   ****
01/06/2018 21:06:43
01/06/2018 21:06:43   RESTARTLOG = ARCLOG180106_210643_11734.rlg
01/06/2018 21:06:43
01/06/2018 21:06:43   PARAMETERS IN USE:
01/06/2018 21:06:43
01/06/2018 21:06:43
01/06/2018 21:06:43
01/06/2018 21:06:44   CHARACTER SET IN USE: ASCII
```

2. Log in using the archive user to execute the backup job.
3. Copy the following statement and execute it in the `arcmain` window. Save the file with the `PPITBL_Bckup_2018.arc` name:

```
PPITBL_Bckup_2018.arc.txt - Notepad

File  Edit  Format  View  Help

.logon 192.168.0.12/arch1,arch1;
ARCHIVE DATA TABLES
(cookbook_td.EMP_SAL_PPI)
(PARTITIONS WHERE (!dob Between DATE '2017-01-01'
    AND DATE '2017-12-01'!))
,RELEASE LOCK, FILE=BKPPPI;
LOGOFF;
```

4. Execute the file using the following command. This command needs to be executed from the `arcmain` window and not from `bteq` or the command prompt:

```
/*Execute arcmain*/
arcmain < ppitbl.bckup_2018.arc.txt
```

5. You can check the log to check the progress of the job.

How it works...

`PARTITION WHERE` is the option that specifies the conditional expression for selecting partitions. If the condition selects a partial partition, the entire partition is archived.

We need to consider the following when archiving the partition table using `ARCHIVE`:

- A restore operation always deletes the selected partitions of the target table before restoring the rows that are stored in the archive
- Use the `EXCLUDE TABLES` option to manage both PPI and non-PPI tables in a single command
- Locks are placed on the table and not on the partition getting archived
- Statistics on the table need to be re-collected after the table has been restored
- A change in table definition will make the restore fail

There's more...

You need to use `PARTITION WHERE` with caution; if the range of the partition is missed or not defined clearly in the archive script, unwanted backup could occur. This option not only helps in archiving the partition of the table but is also used when restoring the table. Before restoring the archived partition to the selected table, it will delete the rows in that partition. And clean, fresh rows will be added to the partition as shown in this code:

```
RESTORE DATA TABLES
(PPITABLE)
(PARTITIONS WHERE
(!DOB BETWEEN DATE '2017-07-01' AND DATE '2017-12-31' !)
```

The following options are allowed when restoring the partition:

- ERRORDB/ERRORTABLES
- PARTITIONS WHERE
- ALL PARTITIONS
- LOG WHERE
- QUALIFIED PARTITIONS

Restoring a table

Proper management of the backup process is a critical step in maintaining the integrity and security of a Teradata system. It helps in verifying that the data warehouse is properly protected against unexpected data loss and data availability is maintained. In addition, it is important to know the requirements for data availability while the backup is in progress, and the impact of resource usage of the backup, both of which can impact performance of other operations during the backup window. It is important to know these requirements at the time the BAR solution is designed, to ensure that the solution that is provided will meet the needs of the customer. The BAR window should not be exceeding the time given to it, or else other users or jobs on the system could be hampered.

When designing the BAR solution, the first requirement that should be considered is the frequency at which backups will be executing. This defines your recovery point objective, or the point at which a system must be restorable back to in the event of data loss. You can compare this to your windows recovery point; you create a restore point in your PC to the point you want to return to in the event your system crashes. Do the same for Teradata Database, for example, a site may have requirements for nightly backup to ensure that at most one day's worth of data must be reloaded or regenerated in the event of a system failure. Note that this recovery point may vary for different databases and tables on the same system; some may need more frequent backups, up to many times daily, while other less-critical tables may only need to be backed up once a week or month.

The benefit of more frequent backups is a direct improvement in data protection; less data will be lost in the event of a failure. However, this comes at a higher operational cost, and additional impact on the Teradata system from the additional backups, in which case a larger BAR solution may be needed to minimize the impact of the more frequent backups on the system's availability:

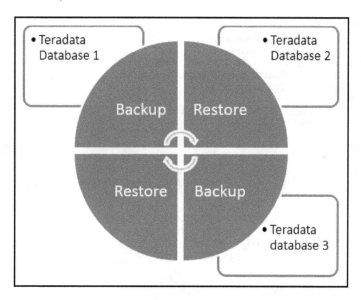

The figure exhibits that data or objects backed up on one Teradata system can be restored to any other Teradata system with ease. But, there are some precautions that we might need to take when restoring the object/user to another Teradata system.

In this recipe, we will check how to use the RESTORE command to restitute the database and all the objects under it.

Getting ready

You need to connect to the arcmain utility to restore the database.

How to do it...

1. Connect to the Teradata `arcmain` utility:

```
┌──────────────────────────────────────────────────────────────────────────┐
│  ▣                              Terminal                         _ ▢ ✕    │
├──────────────────────────────────────────────────────────────────────────┤
│  File  Edit  View  Terminal  Help                                         │
│  Your use is subject to the terms and conditions of                       │
│          the click through agreement that brought you to this             │
│          screen ("TERADATA EXPRESS") EVALUATION AND DEVELOPMENT            │
│          LICENSE AGREEMENT), including the restriction that this           │
│          evaluation copy is not for production use.                       │
│  TD-EXPRESS:~ # arcmain                                                    │
│  01/06/2018 21:06:43   Copyright 1989-2015, Teradata Corporation.         │
│  01/06/2018 21:06:43   All Rights Reserved.                               │
│  01/06/2018 21:06:43                                                      │
│  01/06/2018 21:06:43     ***    ****    ****                              │
│  01/06/2018 21:06:43    *  *  *  *  *           PROGRAM: ARCMAIN           │
│  01/06/2018 21:06:43    ****  ****    *          RELEASE: 15.10.00.02      │
│  01/06/2018 21:06:43    *  *  *  *    *          BUILD:   150152eLX64 (Sep  2 2015) │
│  01/06/2018 21:06:43    *   *   *   *   ****                               │
│  01/06/2018 21:06:43                                                      │
│  01/06/2018 21:06:43   RESTARTLOG = ARCLOG180106_210643_11734.rlg         │
│  01/06/2018 21:06:43                                                      │
│  01/06/2018 21:06:43   PARAMETERS IN USE:                                 │
│  01/06/2018 21:06:43                                                      │
│  01/06/2018 21:06:43                                                      │
│  01/06/2018 21:06:43                                                      │
│  01/06/2018 21:06:44   CHARACTER SET IN USE: ASCII                        │
│  ▯                                                                         │
└──────────────────────────────────────────────────────────────────────────┘
```

2. Log in to the utility using the archive user.
3. Execute the following command to restore the database:

```
RESTORE DATA TABLES (restore_DB)
, release lock
, file = RETBL;
logoff;
```

4. Check the log to see the progress of objects being restored, as follows:

```
restore data tables (restore_db)
, release lock
, file = RETBL;
UTILITY EVENT NUMBER - 69
LOGGED ON 8 SESSIONS
STARTING TO RESTORE DATABASE "restore_db"
DICTIONARY RESTORE COMPLETED
"EMP" - 16 BYTES, 2 ROWS RESTORED
"EMP_SAL" - 20 BYTES, 4 ROWS RESTORED

"restore_db"- LOCK RELEASED

STATEMENT COMPLETED


logoff;
LOGGED OFF 8 SESSIONS
```

How it works...

`Restore` is done from media or tape to Teradata AMPs, meaning archive data is transferred to AMPs again. The target system could be different to that in which data is archived.

The following is the pictorial representation of the restore process:

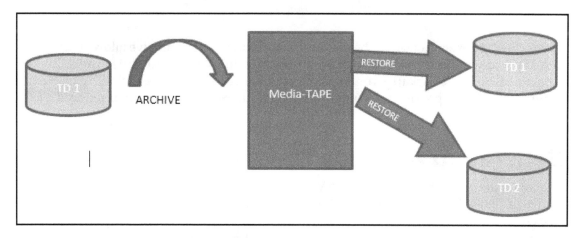

There are a few things that we need to consider when doing a restore:

- Do not drop the database after you archive the object you want to restore. Use `COPY` if this occurs.
- Restore will drop any new object created since archiving.
- Space on targeted machines should be more or similar to the restoring object.
- `JOIN INDEXES` all need to be dropped and recreated if it's on any restored object

There's more...

Restore also presents us with the option of `COPY` when you need to replicate the data or duplicate it to another database or system. Unlike restore, it doesn't delete the data and just makes another copy of the rows in the target system. And it is not dependent on DBC tables like restore.

Copy creates a new table if one does not already exist on the target database. In case of copying a partition, the table must exist and be a table that was previously copied as a full-table copy.

Use the following code to use the copying object:

```
copy data tables (To_database) (from(Source_table))
, release lock
, file = CPY;
```

Some other features to consider: the first is online archive. Online archive allows backups to be performed without placing read locks on the tables; this means that write availability is maintained while the backup is running. You should use this if the availability requirements do not provide for a window where updates can be stopped or reduced.

Generating a unique row number

Teradata Database distributes rows to AMPs based on the hash values generated by the hash map algorithm. This data distribution algorithm is easy and efficient. The primary index of the table defines where the data will reside in which AMP. The uniqueness of this primary index becomes very important when distributing rows to AMPs.

If data is skewed, meaning residing on one or few AMPs, a query using the index becomes slow in processing and also causes space issues in the database:

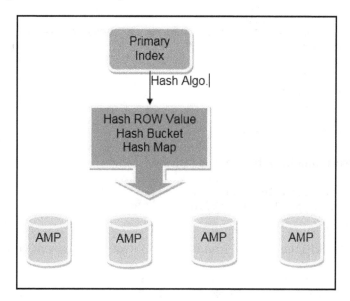

This uniqueness of rows can be generated using the following methods:

- Based on original data
- ETL process, outside Teradata

The third method that we will be using is the identity column. The identity column feature allows for generating unique numbers for each row and inserting values into a column defined in the table. It is like generating sequence numbers automatically, which helps in preserving the uniqueness of the table.

Getting ready

You need to connect to Teradata Database using SQLA or Studio.

How to do it...

1. Connect to Teradata Database using SQLA or Studio.

2. Execute the following CREATE table statement with an identity column defined:

```
/* Create Identity table*/
CREATE TABLE Idn_EMP_TBL
(EMP_ID INTEGER GENERATED ALWAYS AS IDENTITY -- Identity column
(START WITH 1
INCREMENT BY 1
MINVALUE 0
MAXVALUE 1000000
NO CYCLE),
Name VARCHAR(20),
Phone VARCHAR(10));
```

3. Let's insert data into the table as follows:

```
/*Insert data into identity table*/
insert into td_cookbook.Idn_EMP_TBL values (1,'Rob',2500);
insert into td_cookbook.Idn_EMP_TBL values (2,'Moss',2322);
```

4. Now let's skip the first column value and insert the rows as show in code again:

```
/*Insert data into identity table*/
insert into td_cookbook.Idn_EMP_TBL values (,'Andrew',250);
insert into td_cookbook.Idn_EMP_TBL values (,'Rose',232);
```

5. Let's check the content of the table we have created. The select statement is as follows:

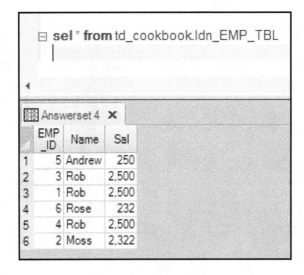

6. We can see that the `EMP_ID 5` and `EMP_ID 6` values are sequential and generated automatically.

How it works...

The identity column helps in generating sequence numbers, keeping uniqueness in place without manual intervention. This is also called a database generated unique primary index, as we are forcing the system to generate a row value for us.

Identity columns save ETL overhead and maintenance by generating unique values if rows are not naturally unique. Identity columns can also help in even data distribution.

`DBC.idcol` is a dictionary table, and a row is written to it whenever a identity column is created. Following is the DDL of the table:

```
CREATE SET TABLE DBC.idcol ,FALLBACK ,
    NO BEFORE JOURNAL,
    NO AFTER JOURNAL,
    CHECKSUM = DEFAULT,
    DEFAULT MERGEBLOCKRATIO
    (
    TableId BYTE(6) NOT NULL,
    DatabaseId BYTE(4) NOT NULL,
    AvailValue DECIMAL(18,0) FORMAT '---,---,---,---,-9' NOT NULL,
    StartValue DECIMAL(18,0) FORMAT '---,---,---,---,-9' NOT NULL,
    MinValue DECIMAL(18,0) FORMAT '---,---,---,---,-9' NOT NULL,
    MaxValue DECIMAL(18,0) FORMAT '---,---,---,---,-9' NOT NULL,
    Increment INTEGER FORMAT '-,---,---,-9' NOT NULL,
    Cyc CHAR(1) CHARACTER SET LATIN UPPERCASE NOT CASESPECIFIC NOT NULL)
UNIQUE PRIMARY INDEX ( TableId );
```

As we have just created an identity column table, let's check the content of this dictionary table. It will list all the tables in the system that have the identity column:

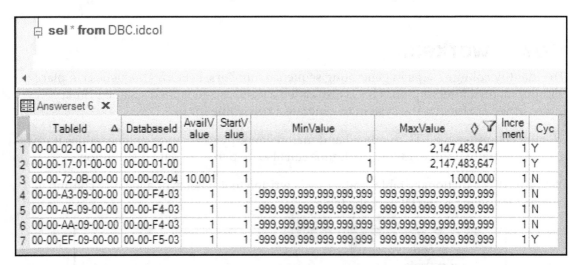

```
sel * from DBC.idcol
```

	TableId ▲	DatabaseId	AvailValue	StartValue	MinValue	MaxValue ◇ ▽	Increment	Cyc
1	00-00-02-01-00-00	00-00-01-00	1	1	1	2,147,483,647	1	Y
2	00-00-17-01-00-00	00-00-01-00	1	1	1	2,147,483,647	1	Y
3	00-00-72-0B-00-00	00-00-02-04	10,001	1	0	1,000,000	1	N
4	00-00-A3-09-00-00	00-00-F4-03	1	1	-999,999,999,999,999,999	999,999,999,999,999,999	1	N
5	00-00-A5-09-00-00	00-00-F4-03	1	1	-999,999,999,999,999,999	999,999,999,999,999,999	1	N
6	00-00-AA-09-00-00	00-00-F4-03	1	1	-999,999,999,999,999,999	999,999,999,999,999,999	1	N
7	00-00-EF-09-00-00	00-00-F5-03	1	1	-999,999,999,999,999,999	999,999,999,999,999,999	1	Y

Remember we can only have one identity column per table.

There's more...

DBS control has a parameter known as **IdColBatchSize** in general option of DBS control, which indicates the size of the spool of numbers to be reserved for generating numbers for a batch of rows that are to be bulk-inserted with an identity column.

If the system is over utilized in terms of AWT and the identity table is accessed, it can cause a system restart, as the sequence number generation is waiting on AWT. In this case, you might need to get in touch with your Teradata site engineer and reserve AWT for the identity column. But before that, you might need to check for an alternative way to generate unique sequence numbers.

4
All about Indexes

In this chapter, we will cover:

- Creating a partitioned primary index to improve performance
- Creating a join index to improve performance
- Creating a secondary index to improve performance
- Creating a value ordered index to improve performance

Introduction

The Teradata database provides various effective ways to improve the performance of a query. Indexes are the most important part of designing the database structure. Indexes not only provide an effective way to store data, but also help in determining effective access paths to data.

The commonly used indexes in Teradata are:

- Unique/non-unique primary index (UPI/NUPI)
- Unique/non-unique secondary index (USI/NUSI)
- Partitioned primary index (PPI)
- Join index (JI)

Think of an index as a two-field table: one contains a value, and the other a pointer to instances of that value in a data table:

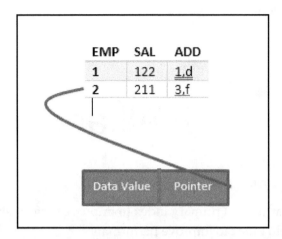

Teradata is the relation database management system, RDBMS, which uses hashing to distribute rows across the AMPs; the value is added into an entity called a row hash, which is used as the pointer. The row hash is addressed to the value in the table. The Teradata RDBMS uses this row hash address as a retrieval index.

The following are characteristics of indexes:

- An index is used not only to distribute, but also to retrieve rows in a table. It can be a single column or multiple columns of the table.
- A table can have a number of indexes, like a PI, SI, or JI, up to 32 secondary indexes.
- An index on a table may be primary or secondary, which in turn may be unique or non-unique. Each kind of index affects system performance and can be important to data integrity.
- An index is usually chosen based upon a table column whose values are frequently used in specifying WHERE constraints or join conditions.

Let's break indexes down into three parts:

- **Primary indexes (PI)**: To distribute and retrieve data rows in a table. Storage and maintenance are free.
- **Partitioned primary index (PPI)**: A table organization to optimize the physical database design for range constraint queries. Storage is 2 bytes per row.

- **Raw data extensions**: Any structure that duplicates or points to primary data for purposes of better performance. These are like secondary indexes (SI) or join indexes (JI). Storage and maintenance are not free.

In this chapter, we will cover recipes to design indexes and see how they can help in improving query performance.

Creating a partitioned primary index to improve performance

A PPI is a type of index that enables users to set up databases that provide performance benefits from a data locality, while retaining the benefits of scalability inherent in the hash architecture of the Teradata database. This is achieved by hashing rows to different virtual AMPs, as is done with a normal PI, but also by creating local partitions within each virtual AMP.

Normal PI access remains unchanged, but in the case of a range query for example, each virtual AMP is able to immediately focus its search on specific partitions within its workspace.

If the PPI column is specified in the join condition, the system knows the range of values in a query and it scans only the portions of the table that correspond to those dates. Table can be or have:

Non-partitioned primary index: A traditional non-partitioned PI allows the data rows of a table to be:

- Hash partitioned (that is, distributed) to the AMPs by the hash value of the primary index columns
- Ordered by the hash value of the primary index columns on each AMP

Partitioned primary index: A partitioned primary index allows the data rows of a table to be:

- Hash partitioned to the AMPs by the hash of the primary index columns
- Partitioned on some set of columns on each AMP
- Ordered by the hash of the primary index columns within that partition

The following image shows the different types of partitioning:

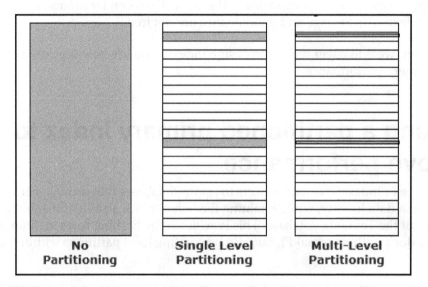

Multi-level partitioned primary index: Extends the existing PPI capability to support and allow for the creation of a table or non-compressed join index with a **multi-level partitioned primary index (ML-PPI)**. As shown in the preceding figure, a multi-level partition has many levels, unlike a single-level partition. The use of ML-PPI on tables affords an opportunity for the Teradata optimizer to achieve a greater degree of partition elimination at a more granular level, which results in achieving a greater level of query performance.

In this recipe, we will see how PPIs will improve the performance of a query.

Getting ready

You need to connect to the Teradata database. Let's create a table and insert data into it using the following DDL. This will be a non-partitioned table, as follows:

```
/*NON PPI TABLE DDL*/
CREATE volatile TABLE EMP_SAL_NONPPI
(
id INT,
Sal INT,
dob DATE,
o_total INT
) primary index( id)
```

```
on commit preserve rows;

INSERT into EMP_SAL_NONPPI VALUES (1001,2500,'2017-09-01',890);
INSERT into EMP_SAL_NONPPI VALUES (1002,5500,'2017-09-10',890);
INSERT into EMP_SAL_NONPPI VALUES (1003,500,'2017-09-02',890);
INSERT into EMP_SAL_NONPPI VALUES (1004,54500,'2017-09-05',890);
INSERT into EMP_SAL_NONPPI VALUES (1005,900,'2017-09-23',890);
INSERT into EMP_SAL_NONPPI VALUES (1006,8900,'2017-08-03',890);
INSERT into EMP_SAL_NONPPI VALUES (1007,8200,'2017-08-21',890);
INSERT into EMP_SAL_NONPPI VALUES (1008,6200,'2017-08-06',890);
INSERT into EMP_SAL_NONPPI VALUES (1009,2300,'2017-08-12',890);
INSERT into EMP_SAL_NONPPI VALUES (1010,9200,'2017-08-15',890);
```

Let's check the explain plan of the following query; we are selecting data based on the DOB column using the following code:

```
/*Select on NONPPI table*/
SELECT * from EMP_SAL_NONPPI
where dob <= 2017-08-01
```

Following is the snippet from SQLA showing explain plan of the query:

As seen in the following explain plan, an `all-rows scan` can be costly in terms of CPU and I/O if the table has millions of rows:

```
Explain SELECT * from EMP_SAL_NONPPI
 where dob <= 2017-08-01;

/*EXPLAIN PLAN of SELECT*/
1) First, we do an all-AMPs RETRIEVE step from DBC.EMP_SAL_NONPPI by
way of an all-rows scan with a condition of (
"DBC.EMP_SAL_NONPPI.dob <= DATE '1900-12-31'") into Spool 1
(group_amps), which is built locally on the AMPs. The size of
Spool 1 is estimated with no confidence to be 4 rows (148 bytes).
The estimated time for this step is 0.04 seconds.
2) Finally, we send out an END TRANSACTION step to all AMPs involved
in processing the request.
-> The contents of Spool 1 are sent back to the user as the result of
statement 1. The total estimated time is 0.04 seconds.
```

Let's see how we can enable partition retrieval in the same query.

How to do it...

1. Connect to the Teradata database using SQLA or Studio.
2. Create the following table with the data. We will define a PPI on the column DOB:

```
/*Partition table*/
CREATE volatile TABLE EMP_SAL_PPI
(
id INT,
Sal int,
dob date,
o_total int
) primary index( id)
PARTITION BY RANGE_N (dob BETWEEN DATE '2017-01-01'
    AND DATE '2017-12-01' EACH INTERVAL '1' DAY)
on commit preserve rows;

INSERT into EMP_SAL_PPI VALUES (1001,2500,'2017-09-01',890);
INSERT into EMP_SAL_PPI VALUES (1002,5500,'2017-09-10',890);
INSERT into EMP_SAL_PPI VALUES (1003,500,'2017-09-02',890);
INSERT into EMP_SAL_PPI VALUES (1004,54500,'2017-09-05',890);
INSERT into EMP_SAL_PPI VALUES (1005,900,'2017-09-23',890);
INSERT into EMP_SAL_PPI VALUES (1006,8900,'2017-08-03',890);
```

```
INSERT into EMP_SAL_PPI VALUES (1007,8200,'2017-08-21',890);
INSERT into EMP_SAL_PPI VALUES (1008,6200,'2017-08-06',890);
INSERT into EMP_SAL_PPI VALUES (1009,2300,'2017-08-12',890);
INSERT into EMP_SAL_PPI VALUES (1010,9200,'2017-08-15',890);
```

3. Let's execute the same query on a new partition table:

```
/*SELECT on PPI table*/
sel * from EMP_SAL_PPI
where dob <= 2017-08-01
```

Following snippet from SQLA shows query and explain plan of the query:

1) First, we do an all-AMPs RETRIEVE step from a single partition of **SYSDBA.EMP_SAL_PPI** with a condition of ("SYSDBA.EMP_SAL_PPI.dob = DATE '2017-08-01'") with a residual condition of ("SYSDBA.EMP_SAL_PPI.dob = DATE '2017-08-01'") into **Spool 1** (group_amps), which is **built locally** on the AMPs. The size of **Spool 1** is estimated with **no confidence** to be **1 row** (37 bytes). The estimated time for this step is 0.04 seconds.
-> The contents of **Spool 1** are sent back to the user as the result of statement 1. The total estimated time is 0.04 seconds.

4. The data is being accessed using only a single partition, as shown in the following block:

```
/*EXPLAIN PLAN*/
 1) First, we do an all-AMPs RETRIEVE step from a single partition
of
     SYSDBA.EMP_SAL_PPI with a condition of
("SYSDBA.EMP_SAL_PPI.dob =
     DATE '2017-08-01'") with a residual condition of (
     "SYSDBA.EMP_SAL_PPI.dob = DATE '2017-08-01'") into Spool 1
     (group_amps), which is built locally on the AMPs. The size of
     Spool 1 is estimated with no confidence to be 1 row (37
bytes).
```

```
      The estimated time for this step is 0.04 seconds.
   -> The contents of Spool 1 are sent back to the user as the
result of
      statement 1. The total estimated time is 0.04 seconds.
```

How it works...

A partitioned PI helps in improving the performance of a query by avoiding a full table scan elimination. A PPI works the same as a primary index for data distribution, but creates partitions according to ranges or cases, as specified in the table.

There are four types of PPI that can be created in a table:

- **Case partitioning**:

  ```
  /*CASE partition*/
  CREATE TABLE SALES_CASEPPI
  (
      ORDER_ID INTEGER,
      CUST_ID INTERGER,
      ORDER_DT DATE,
  )
  PRIMARY INDEX(ORDER_ID)
  PARTITION BY CASE_N(ORDER_ID < 101,
      ORDER_ ID < 201,
      ORDER_ID < 501,
      NO CASE,UNKNOWN);
  ```

- **Range-based partitioning**:

  ```
  /*Range Partition table*/
  CREATE volatile TABLE EMP_SAL_PPI
  (
  id INT,
  Sal int,
  dob date,
  o_total int
  ) primary index( id)
  PARTITION BY RANGE_N (dob BETWEEN DATE '2017-01-01'
      AND DATE '2017-12-01' EACH INTERVAL '1' DAY)
  on commit preserve rows
  ```

- **Multi-level partitioning**:

```
CREATE TABLE SALES_MLPPI_TABLE
(
    ORDER_ID INTEGER NOT NULL,
    CUST_ID INTERGER,
    ORDER_DT DATE,
)
PRIMARY INDEX(ORDER_ID)
PARTITION BY (RANGE_N(ORDER_DT BETWEEN DATE '2017-08-01' AND DATE
'2017-12-31'
    EACH INTERVAL '1' DAY)
    CASE_N (ORDER_ID < 1001,
        ORDER_ID < 2001,
        ORDER_ID < 3001,
        NO CASE, UNKNOWN));
```

- **Character-based partitioning**:

```
/*CHAR Partition*/
CREATE TABLE SALES_CHAR_PPI (
    ORDR_ID INTEGER,
    EMP_NAME VARCHAR (30) CHARACTER,
    PRIMARY INDEX (ORDR_ID)
  PARTITION BY CASE_N (
                        EMP_NAME LIKE 'A%', EMP_NAME LIKE 'B%',
                        EMP_NAME LIKE 'C%', EMP_NAME LIKE 'D%',
                        EMP_NAME LIKE 'E%', EMP_NAME LIKE 'F%',
                        NO CASE, UNKNOWN);
```

PPI not only helps in improving the performance of queries, but also helps in table maintenance. But there are certain performance considerations that you might need to keep in mind when creating a PPI on a table, and they are:

- If partition column criteria is not present in the WHERE clause while selecting primary indexes, it can slow the query
- The partitioning of the column must be carefully chosen in order to gain maximum benefits
- Drop unneeded secondary indexes or value-ordered join indexes

There's more...

A partitioned PI not only helps in retrieval from a single table, but it also helps when joining PPI tables. Direct merge joins of two PPI tables are available as an optimizer choice when the tables have:

- The same PI and identical partitioning expressions
- All PI columns and all partitioning columns specified as equality join terms
- A row-key based merge join
- Identical performance characteristics for row-key based merge joins and traditional merge joins
- A direct merge join, in the traditional sense, is not available when one table is partitioned and the other table is not, or when both tables are partitioned, but not in the same manner

 Delayed partition elimination is when the partitioning column values are not known until the query execution time. You won't see it in an explain plan, but it will occur when a query is executing.

The optimizer has three general avenues of approach when joining a PPI table to a non-PPI table, or two PPI tables with dissimilar partitions (day versus month, and so on):

- One option is to spool the PPI table (or both PPI tables) into a non-PPI spool file in preparation for a traditional merge join.
- A second option (not always available) is to spool the non-PPI table (or one of the two PPI tables) into a PPI spool file, with identical partitioning, in preparation for a row-key based merge join.
- The third approach is to use a **sliding window** join of the tables without spooling either one. If the optimizer cannot create a partitioned spool, it will have no choice but to create a standard spool table out of the PPI table in order to join to the non-PPI table.

When checking the explain plan, look for the following when PPI tables are involved:

- **"a single partition of" or "n partitions of"**: Indicates that an AMP or group of AMPs only needs to access a single partition, or there may be **n** number of partitions of a table. This is an indication that partition elimination occurred. Partition elimination can occur for SELECT, UPDATE, and DELETE. For a DELETE, the optimizer recognizes partitions in which all rows are deleted. Rows in such partitions are deleted without using the transient journal, thus making them very fast and with less impact on the system.

- **"SORT to partition Spool m by rowkey"**: The spool is to be sorted by row-key (partition and hash of the PRIMARY INDEX). Partitioning the spool file in this way allows for a faster join with another partitioned table.

- **"rowkey-based merge join"**: It indicates an equality join on the row key. Both partitioned primary and partitioned columns have equality constraints. It is always best to have this in your explain plan.

- **"enhanced by dynamic partition"**: It indicates a join condition on a partitioned table and a non-partitioned table are joined with an equality condition on the partitioning column set of the partitioned table. It is important to have statistics collected on joining columns.

You can also add or drop partitions to/from the existing partitioned table. This can be done by either:

- Rebuilding the table
- Using the ALTER statement

To understand how to use ALTER, let's suppose we have the following table with the partition defined:

```
CREATE TABLE td_cookbook.PPI_part1
(
COLA INTEGER NOT NULL,
DOB Date
) PRIMARY INDEX (COLA)
PARTITION BY (RANGE_N
(DOB BETWEEN DATE '1900-01-01' AND DATE'2017-12-31' EACH INTERVAL '1' DAY,
NO RANGE));
```

To add a 2016 partition for the first six months to this, we use the following ALTER statement:

```
ALTER TABLE td_cookbook.PPI_part1
MODIFY PRIMARY INDEX ADD RANGE BETWEEN DATE '2016-01-01' AND DATE '2016-06-30'
EACH INTERVAL '1' DAY;
```

Before using ALTER to add partitions, we need to consider the performance impact of ALTER. As the ALTER statement tends to hold an exclusive lock on the table, it can block other jobs on the system. Also, big tables going under ALTER can run longer than anticipated.

Creating a join index to improve performance

A join index is a data structure that contains data from one or more tables, with or without aggregation:

- The columns of two or more tables
- Two or more columns of a single table

The guidelines for creating a join index are the same as those for defining any regular join query that is frequently executed or whose performance is critical. The only difference is that, for a join index, the join result is persistently stored and automatically maintained.

Join indexes are used in Teradata to:

- Pre-join tables that are often joined in queries.
- Pre-aggregate summary data.
- Create *materialized views* of data. In Teradata, it is described as a link between view and index.
- Create a sparse data set.

A join index helps in increasing the efficiency and performance of the queries containing joins:

- A join index is accessed repeatedly when called by queries
- A new join index sub-table is created and automatically updated when the base tables change
- A join index can have a different PI than the base table

There are certain rules when it comes to creating join indexes:

- Cannot include **CLOB (Character Large Object** > 4000 char), **LOB (Large Object** <= 1000 char), or **UDT (User Defined Type)** data type columns
- No system-derived columns (SESSION, CURRENT_DATE, and so on) allowed
- ROWID may be specified (for joins back to the main table), but it must be aliased
- Aggregation is allowed, but be sure to cast the column as a large enough data type to ensure that the aggregate values will fit (CAST(IntegerCol as Decimal (18,0))
- Cannot define a join index to include queue tables, any form of temporary table, or other join indexes

It is important to note that we don't want to *ever* do a SELECT * when building a JOIN INDEX.

Let's check the syntax for creating a multi-table join index:

```
/*MULTI TABLE JOIN INDEX*/
CREATE JOIN INDEX IDX_NAME
AS
SELECT COLUMN_NAME
FROM TABLE_NAME A
INNER JOIN TABLE_NAME B
ON A.JOIN_COLUMN = B.JOIN_COLUMN
UNIQUE PRIMARY INDEX (COLUMN);
```

Statistics are important if you need an optimizer to use a join index in a query. A base table having current statistics is different than having stats collected on an index.

A join index is most useful when its columns can satisfy, or cover, most or all of the requirements in a query.

For example, the optimizer may consider using a covering index instead of performing a merge join.

Covering indexes improve the speed of join queries. The extent of improvement can be dramatic, especially for queries involving complex, large-table, and multiple-table joins. The extent of such improvement depends on how often an index is appropriate to a query.

In this recipe, we will see how join indexes help in improving the performance of queries.

Getting ready

You need to connect to the Teradata database using SQLA or Studio. Let's create a table and insert the following code into it:

```
CREATE TABLE td_cookbook.EMP_SAL
(
id INT,
DEPT varchar(25),
emp_Fname varchar(25),
emp_Lname varchar(25),
emp_Mname varchar(25),
status INT
)primary index(id);


INSERT into td_cookbook.EMP_SAL VALUES (1,'HR','Anikta','lal','kumar',1);
INSERT into td_cookbook.EMP_SAL VALUES (2,'HR','Anik','kumar','kumar',2);
INSERT into td_cookbook.EMP_SAL VALUES (3,'IT','Arjun','sharma','lal',1);
INSERT into td_cookbook.EMP_SAL VALUES (4,'SALES','Billa','Suti','raj',2);
INSERT into td_cookbook.EMP_SAL VALUES (4,'IT','Koyd','Loud','harlod',1);
INSERT into td_cookbook.EMP_SAL VALUES (2,'HR','Harlod','lal','kumar',1);
```

Further, we will create a single table join index with a different primary index of the table.

How to do it...

The following are the steps to create a join index to improve performance:

1. Connect to the Teradata database using SQLA or Studio.
2. Check the explain plan for the following query:

```
/*SELECT on base table*/
EXPLAIN SELECT id,dept,emp_Fname,emp_Lname,status from
```

```
td_cookbook.EMP_SAL
where id=4;

1) First, we do a single-AMP RETRIEVE step from td_cookbook.EMP_SAL
     by way of the primary index "td_cookbook.EMP_SAL.id = 4" with
no
     residual conditions into Spool 1 (one-amp), which is built
locally
     on that AMP. The size of Spool 1 is estimated with low
confidence
     to be 2 rows (118 bytes). The estimated time for this step is
     0.02 seconds.
  -> The contents of Spool 1 are sent back to the user as the
result of
     statement 1. The total estimated time is 0.02 seconds.
```

3. Query with a WHERE clause on id; then the system will query the EMP table using the primary index of the base table, which is id.

4. Now, if a user wants to query a table on column emp_Fname, an all row scan will occur, which will degrade the performance of the query, as shown in the following screenshot:

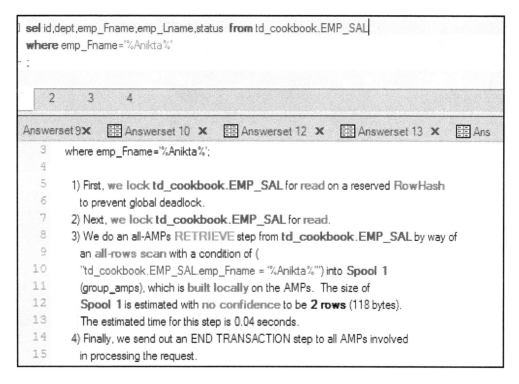

5. Now, we will create a JOIN INDEX using emp_Fname as the primary index:

```
/*Join Index*/
CREATE JOIN INDEX td_cookbook.EMP_JI
AS
SELECT id,emp_Fname,emp_Lname,status,emp_Mname,dept
FROM td_cookbook.EMP_SAL
PRIMARY INDEX(emp_Fname);
```

6. Let's collect statistics on the join index:

```
/*Collect stats on JI*/
collect stats td_cookbook.EMP_JI  column emp_Fname
```

7. Now, we will check the explain plan query on the WHERE clause using the column emp_Fname:

```
Explain sel id,dept,emp_Fname,emp_Lname,status  from
td_cookbook.EMP_SAL
where emp_Fname='ankita';

  1) First, we do a single-AMP RETRIEVE step from
td_cookbooK.EMP_JI by
     way of the primary index "td_cookbooK.EMP_JI.emp_Fname =
'ankita'"
     with no residual conditions into Spool 1 (one-amp), which is
built
     locally on that AMP.  The size of Spool 1 is estimated with
low
     confidence to be 2 rows (118 bytes).  The estimated time for
this
     step is 0.02 seconds.
  -> The contents of Spool 1 are sent back to the user as the
result of
     statement 1.  The total estimated time is 0.02 seconds.
```

8. In EXPLAIN, you can see that the optimizer is using the join index instead of the base table when the table queries are using the Emp_Fname column.

How it works...

Query performance improves any time a join index can be used instead of the base tables. A join index is most useful when its columns can satisfy, or cover, most or all of the requirements in a query.

For example, the optimizer may consider using a covering index instead of performing a merge join.

When we are able to cover all the queried columns that can be satisfied by a join index, then it is called a **cover query**.

Covering indexes improve the speed of join queries. The extent of improvement can be dramatic, especially for queries involving complex, large-table, and multiple-table joins. The extent of such improvement depends on how often an index is appropriate to a query.

There are a few more join indexes that can be used in Teradata:

- **Aggregate-table join index**: A type of join index which pre-joins and summarizes aggregated tables without requiring any physical summary tables. It refreshes automatically whenever the base table changes. Only COUNT and SUM are permitted, and DISTINCT is not permitted:

    ```
    /*AG JOIN INDEX*/
    CREATE JOIN INDEX Agg_Join_Index AS
    SELECT Cust_ID,
    Order_ID,
    SUM(Sales_north) -- Aggregate column
    FROM
    sales_table
    GROUP BY 1,2
    Primary Index(Cust_ID)
    ```

    Use FLOAT as a data type for COUNT and SUM to avoid overflow.

- **Sparse join index**: When a WHERE clause is applied in a JOIN INDEX, it is know as a **sparse join index**. By limiting the number of rows retrieved in a join, it reduces the size of the join index. It is also useful for UPDATE statements where the index is highly selective:

```
/*SP JOIN INDEX*/
CREATE JOIN INDEX Sparse_Join_Index AS
SELECT Cust_ID,
Order_ID,
SUM(Sales_north) -- Aggregate column
FROM
sales_table
where Order_id = 1 -- WHERE CLAUSE
GROUP BY 1,2
Primary Index(Cust_ID)
```

There's more...

We have seen the benefits of join indexes, but they are not good all of the time. As a join index needs maintenance and use space, it becomes important to check its validity from time to time. It can happen that the **join index** (**JI**), you have defined some time back is now no longer getting used by the query. Also, the loading utility tends to degrade when JIs are in use on the loading table.

The following points need to be considered when manipulating join indexes:

- **Load utilities**: Not supported by MultiLoad and FastLoad utilities, they must be dropped and recreated after the table has been loaded.
- **Archive and restore**: Cannot be used on a join index itself to back up and restore. During a restore of a base table or database, the join index is marked as invalid. The join index must be dropped and recreated before it can be used again in the execution of queries.
- **Fallback protection**: Cannot be fallback-protected.
- **Permanent journal recovery**: Needs manual intervention to create the join index during the recovery process. The join indexes are marked as invalid and must be dropped and recreated manually.
- **Triggers**: Cannot be defined on a table with triggers.
- **Collecting statistics**: Need to have collected statistics on the primary index columns of each join index. Column statistics for join indexes and their underlying base tables are not interrelated.

Creating a secondary index to improve performance

What if you need an index other than a primary index? You can only have one primary index on a table, but what if you have a requirement to have multiple indexes on a table? Teradata gives you the secondary index (SI) to satisfy that requirement. You can use a primary index for distribution and access, but to have a secondary access path, you can use SI:

```
CREATE UNIQUE INDEX (Coulumn_Name) on TABLE_NAME; -- UNIQUE INDEX, USI
CREATE INDEX (Coulumn_Name) on TABLE_NAME; -- NON UNIQUE INDEX, NUSI
```

Secondary indexes supply alternate access paths. As we know, primary indexes are used for the distribution of rows, and sometimes, to reduce the skewness of tables, we might need to choose columns based on even distribution instead of selectivity. So, to rescue and provide the alternative approach, Teradata has a feature known as the secondary index.

This increases performance. For best results, base secondary indexes on frequently used set selections and on an equality searches. The optimizer may not use a secondary index if it is too weakly selective. Statistics play an important part in optimizing access when NUSIs define conditions for the following:

- Joining tables
- Satisfying WHERE constraints that specify comparisons, string matching, or complex conditions
- Satisfying a LIKE expression
- Processing aggregates

Because of the additional overhead for index maintenance, index values should not be subject to frequent changes. When you change a secondary index, the system:

- Deletes any secondary index references to the current value (AMP-local for NUSIs, and across AMPs for USIs)
- Generates new secondary index references to the new value (AMP-local for NUSIs, and across AMPs for USIs)

SIs allow access to information in a table by alternate, less frequently used paths, and improve performance by avoiding full table scans. Although SIs add to table overhead, in terms of disk space and maintenance, you can drop and recreate SIs as needed. SIs have the following properties:

- Do not affect the distribution of rows across AMPs
- Can be unique or non-unique
- Are used by the optimizer when the indexes can improve query performance

There are other types of secondary indexes available:

- Ordered Secondary Index:
    - Used when ranges of values are desired
    - Order can be by HASH or VALUE

Use ORDER BY HASH when you expect a lot of JOIN operations using the indexed column. Use ORDER BY VALUE when you expect a lot of queries against the indexed column requiring a range (such as MYDATE BETWEEN '2010-10-01' AND CURRENT_DATE).

Getting ready

You need to connect to the Teradata database using SQLA or Studio. Let's create a table and insert the following code into it:

```
CREATE TABLE td_cookbook.EMP_SAL
(
id INT,
DEPT varchar(25),
emp_Fname varchar(25),
emp_Lname varchar(25),
emp_Mname varchar(25),
status INT
)primary index(id);

INSERT into td_cookbook.EMP_SAL VALUES (1,'HR','Anikta','lal','kumar',1);
INSERT into td_cookbook.EMP_SAL VALUES (2,'HR','Anik','kumar','kumar',2);
INSERT into td_cookbook.EMP_SAL VALUES (3,'IT','Arjun','sharma','lal',1);
INSERT into td_cookbook.EMP_SAL VALUES (4,'SALES','Billa','Suti','raj',2);
INSERT into td_cookbook.EMP_SAL VALUES (4,'IT','Koyd','Loud','harlod',1);
INSERT into td_cookbook.EMP_SAL VALUES (2,'HR','Harlod','lal','kumar',1);
```

Further, we will create a secondary index with different primary index on the table.

How to do it...

The steps to create a secondary index to improve performance are as follows:

1. Connect to the Teradata database using SQLA or Studio.
2. Check the explain plan in the following query:

```
/*Explain of Select*/
EXPLAIN SELECT id,dept,emp_Fname,emp_Lname,status from
td_cookbook.EMP_SAL
where dept='IT';

1) First, we lock td_cookbook.EMP_SAL for read on a reserved
RowHash
to prevent global deadlock.
2) Next, we lock td_cookbook.EMP_SAL for read.
3) We do an all-AMPs RETRIEVE step from td_cookbook.EMP_SAL by way
of
an all-rows scan with a condition of ("td_cookbook.EMP_SAL.DEPT =
'IT'") into Spool 1 (group_amps), which is built locally on the
AMPs. The size of Spool 1 is estimated with no confidence to be 2
rows (118 bytes). The estimated time for this step is 0.04
seconds.
4) Finally, we send out an END TRANSACTION step to all AMPs
involved
in processing the request.
-> The contents of Spool 1 are sent back to the user as the result
of
statement 1. The total estimated time is 0.04 seconds.
```

3. Now let's create an SI on the table as the following:

```
/*SI on table*/
CREATE  INDEX(emp_Fname) on td_cookbook.EMP_SAL;
```

4. Let's check the explain plan of the following query:

```
We do an all-AMPs RETRIEVE step from  td_cookbook.EMP_SAL by way of
index # 4
of ("td_cookbook.EMP_SAL.emp_Fname = 'ankita'") with no residual
conditions into Spool 2
```

5. The explain plan on the query shows the use of the SI with a phrase similar to `by way of index # 4`. Secondary and join indexes will increment by four if you have more than one on a particular table.

How it works...

Teradata follows these guidelines for index access:

Teradata uses...	To...
Primary Index (PI)	satisfy an equality on an IN condition in a join.
Unique Primary Index (UPI)	ensure fastest access to table data.
Non-Unique Primary Index (NUPI)	• Perform a single-disk row selection or join process • Avoid sorting or redistributing rows.
Unique Secondary Index (USI)	process requests that employ equality constraints.
UPIs to match values in one table with index values in another	ensure optimal join performance.
information from a single AMP	estimate the cost of using an index when statistics are not available. This assumes an even distribution of index values (an uneven distribution affects performance).
index based on more than one column (a composite index) only	process requests that employ equality constraints for all fields that comprise the index. You can define an index on a column that is also part of a multi-column index.

Reference from Teradata orange book

Secondary indexes come with pros and cons:

Pros:

- Queries execute quickly when the index is accessed
- Ordered indexes allow fast range scans
- Hashed indexes are very useful when joining to the non-PI column

Cons:

- Whenever data is inserted, updated, or deleted from the base table, the index must also be maintained, thus affecting ETL time
- Sometimes it is difficult to *force* the optimizer to use the secondary index

Smaller tactical queries, where the predicate for the indexed column is used in the query, are proven to be effective and improve tactical query performance.

 Tactical queries are characterized by single row access, or the access to a limited number of rows, or faster response time. They are usually the fastest responsive queries on the database.

For SIs, Teradata database computes a hash value using the hash of the values of the SI columns. This value is used for access when an SI value is specified in the SQL. The SI subtable records the hash value for the SI, the actual value of the index columns (for synonym resolution), and a list of primary index row identifiers for the table being indexed, as shown in the following figure:

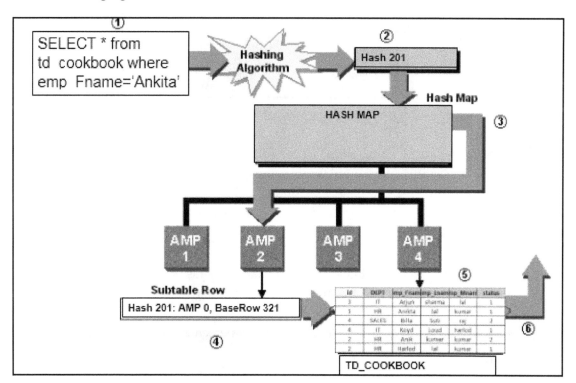

Query hits the parser, it goes through following path:

1. The query is legal, so off to the optimizer.
2. The optimizer recognizes that there is a USI for the column in question. So, it hashes the predicate.
3. Once the row hash is determined from the hash map, the appropriate AMPs, and only the appropriate AMPs, are queried via the sub-table.
4. Using the ROWID, the primary row is returned.

There's more...

A secondary index helps in reducing the full table scan on the table. Full table scans read every data block, whereas a non-unique SI does not read every data block, but its usefulness depends on the percentage of rows qualifying and the number of rows in the data block:

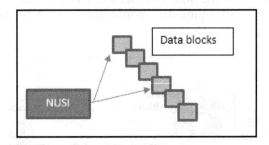

A full table scan is faster when:

- >= 1 row per block qualifies, THEN a full table scan of the base table is faster than NUSI access, and NUSI is not used
- > If 100 rows/block and 1% of the data qualifies, then every block will be read
- A full table scan is done for values that represent a large percent of the table

NUSI is used when:

- < 1 row per block qualifies, THEN NUSI access is faster than a full table scan
- > If 100 rows/block and 1 in 1000 rows qualify, then one in every 10 blocks will be read. NUSI will be used.
- NUSI is used for values that represent a tiny percentage of the table.

You can drop indexes using the following command:

```
/*Drop SI*/
DROP INDEX index_name ON tablename
```

Creating a hash index to improve performance

Hash indexes are designed to improve query performance like join indexes, especially single table join indexes, and in addition, they enable you to avoid accessing the base table. The syntax for the hash index is as follows:

```
/*Hash index syntax*/
CREATE HASH INDEX <hash-index-name>
[, <fallback-option>]
(<column-name-list1>) ON <base-table>
[BY (<partition-column-name-list2>)]
[ORDER BY <index-sort-spec>] ;
```

The partition column name list acts as the primary index for the hash index. This is comparable to having a secondary index defined as the partition column name list, but having additional data columns defined together with the index columns. The hash index is similar to a NUSI, in that it allows referring back to the primary data row. The hash index has the additional capability of doing index covering where a query can be satisfied by the columns of the hash index, plus the capability of doing partial index covering where rows can be qualified by the columns in the hash index, and then the primary data row can be accessed to get other columns to satisfy the query.

The benefit of a hash index is the hash index automatically provides the pointer back to the native data row.

Hash indexes can be value ordered.

Hash join is not the same thing as a hash index. A hash join is a join strategy that the optimizer chooses instead of a MERGE JOIN:

- It can be chosen when the join columns are not indexed (at least one of the join tables is redistributed)

- The primary benefit of a hash join is it saves the sorting of one or both of the join tables
- Can provide a 10-40% performance improvement for the join step

Getting ready

You need to connect to the Teradata database. Let's create a table and insert data into it using the following DDL:

```
/*Create table with data*/
CREATE TABLE td_cookbook.EMP_SAL
(
id INT,
DEPT varchar(25),
emp_Fname varchar(25),
emp_Lname varchar(25),
emp_Mname varchar(25),
status INT
)primary index(id);

INSERT into td_cookbook.EMP_SAL VALUES (1,'HR','Anikta','lal','kumar',1);
INSERT into td_cookbook.EMP_SAL VALUES (2,'HR','Anik','kumar','kumar',2);
INSERT into td_cookbook.EMP_SAL VALUES (3,'IT','Arjun','sharma','lal',1);
INSERT into td_cookbook.EMP_SAL VALUES (4,'SALES','Billa','Suti','raj',2);
INSERT into td_cookbook.EMP_SAL VALUES (4,'IT','Koyd','Loud','harlod',1);
INSERT into td_cookbook.EMP_SAL VALUES (2,'HR','Harlod','lal','kumar',1);
```

How to do it...

1. You need to connect to the Teradata database using SQLA or Studio.
2. Let's check the explain plan of the following query shown in the figure:

```
/*EXPLAIN of SELECT*/
Explain sel id,emp_Fname from td_cookbook.EMP_SAL;

1) First, we lock td_cookbook.EMP_SAL for read on a reserved
```

```
RowHash
 to prevent global deadlock.
 2) Next, we lock td_cookbook.EMP_SAL for read.
 3) We do an all-AMPs RETRIEVE step from td_cookbook.EMP_SAL by way
of
 an all-rows scan with no residual conditions into Spool 1
 (group_amps), which is built locally on the AMPs. The size of
 Spool 1 is estimated with high confidence to be 6 rows (210
bytes).
 The estimated time for this step is 0.04 seconds.
 4) Finally, we send out an END TRANSACTION step to all AMPs
involved
 in processing the request.
 -> The contents of Spool 1 are sent back to the user as the result
of
 statement 1. The total estimated time is 0.04 seconds.
```

3. Now let's create a hash join index on the EMP_SAL table:

```
/*Hash Indx*/
CREATE HASH INDEX td_cookbook.EMP_HASH_inx
(id, DEPT) ON td_cookbook.EMP_SAL
BY (id)
ORDER BY HASH (id);
```

4. Let's now check the explain plan on the select query after the hash index creation:

```
/*Select after hash idx*/

EXPLAIN SELCT id,dept from td_cookbook.EMP_SAL

1) First, we lock td_cookbooK.EMP_HASH_INX for read on a reserved
 RowHash to prevent global deadlock.
 2) Next, we lock td_cookbooK.EMP_HASH_INX for read.
 3) We do an all-AMPs RETRIEVE step from td_cookbooK.EMP_HASH_INX
by
 way of an all-rows scan with no residual conditions into Spool 1
 (group_amps), which is built locally on the AMPs. The size of
 Spool 1 is estimated with high confidence to be 6 rows (210
bytes).
 The estimated time for this step is 0.04 seconds.
 4) Finally, we send out an END TRANSACTION step to all AMPs
involved
 in processing the request.
```

```
-> The contents of Spool 1 are sent back to the user as the result
of
   statement 1. The total estimated time is 0.04 seconds.
```

Explain plan can be see in the snippet from SQLA:

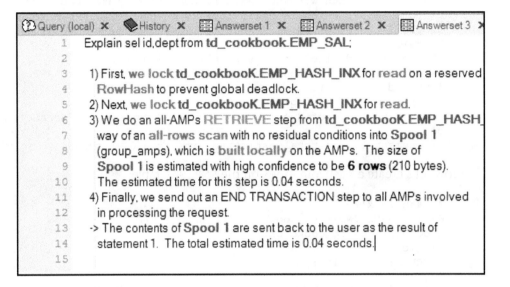

How it works...

Points to consider about the hash index definition are:

- Each hash index row contains the department id and the department name.
- Specifying the department id is unnecessary, since it is the primary index of the base table and will therefore be automatically included.
- The BY clause indicates that the rows of this index will be distributed by the department id hash value.
- The ORDER BY clause indicates that the index rows will be ordered on each AMP in sequence by the department id hash value. The column specified in the BY clause should be part of the columns which make up the hash index. The BY clause comes with the ORDER BY clause.

Unlike join indexes, hash indexes can only be on a single table.

A hash index is not allowed with a NOPI table.

A hash index requires permanent space in the user or database. A table defined with a hash index can't be dropped without the hash index first getting dropped.

Use the following code to show or drop the hash index defined on the table:

```
/*Command to show/drop hash index*/
      SHOW HASH INDEX
      DROP HASH INDEX
```

There's more...

You can use the following SQL when you want to check the indexes in the Teradata database system:

```
SELECT databasename, tablename, columnname, indextype, indexnumber,
indexname FROM
dbc.indices
ORDER BY
indextype
```

The following are the types of indexes available:

IndexType	Description
P	Non-partitioned primary
Q	Partitioned primary
S	Secondary
J	Join
N	Hash
K	Primary key
U	Unique constraint
V	Value ordered secondary

H	Hash ordered ALL covering secondary
O	Valued ordered ALL covering secondary
I	Ordering column of a composite secondary index
M	Multi-column statistics
D	Derived column partitioned statistics
1	field1 column of a join or hash index
2	field2 column of a join or hash index

Hash indexes for primary partitioned indexes improve the performance of PPI tables. Hash indexes defined on PPI tables should be ORDER BY HASH or ORDER BY VALUES:

```
/*ORDER BY HASH IDX*/
CREATE HASH INDEX EMP_hash
(employee_id, dpt_id) ON EMP_hash
BY (employee_id)
ORDER BY VALUES(employee_id);
```

5
Mixing Strategies – Joining of Tables

In this chapter, we will cover:

- Identifying skewness in joins
- Identifying right columns for joins
- Eliminating product joins
- Improving left joins
- Improving Teradata joins

Introduction

A **data warehouse** is comprised of many tables, and we rarely get an answer with one table alone. To get business answers, we need to join two or more tables. In upcoming recipes, we will see how to improve this joining and troubleshoot some of the issues that occur while joining tables.

We will answer the following questions in our recipes:

- What join types are supported in Teradata
- The difference between outer and inner joins
- Resolving product joins
- How to improve join performance

The following illustration gives a better understanding of the relationship:

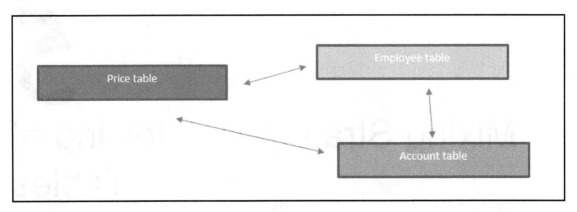

There are two methods of writing joins; one is with *Oracle* syntax, and the other ANSI, which is the recommended one. The following is a query with Oracle syntax:

```
/*Query with Oracle Syntax*/
SELECT  A.QTR_YEAR, A.WEEK_YEAR ,  B.INVOICE_NME
FROM  Table_A.CUR  A, Table_B.INVOICE_CNTY b ,
WHERE  B.store_Id=A.CNTY_id
and A.type_name='MOD'
GROUP BY 1,  2;
/*Query With ANSI Syntax*/
SELECT  A.QTR_YEAR, A.WEEK_YEAR ,  B.INVOICE_NME
FROM  Table_A.CUR  A,
INNER JOIN Table_B.INVOICE_CNTY b
ON B.store_Id=A.CNTY_id
Where
A.type_name='MOD'
GROUP BY 1,  2;
```

Before we start on the recipe, let's brush up on types of joins in Teradata:

- **INNER JOIN:** Also know as **EQUI-JOIN**, when used, it will display all the matching rows. The row must exist in each table, thus the term **INNER JOIN**. The following is the syntax for inner join:

```
/* Teradata SQL syntax INNER JOIN */
SELECT  A.item_id
,A.end_dt
,B.rev_curncy
FROM  item_tbl  A
,rev_tbl  B
```

```
WHERE   A.item_id = B.item_id
AND   A.end_dt = B.end_dt;
```

This query only retrieves rows based on the following join conditions: `item_id` matches and `end_dt` matches.

- **LEFT/RIGHT OUTER JOIN or LEFT/RIGHT JOIN:** Returns all rows from the *left* table or *right* (when right join used), and only those rows that match from the *right* table. This is handy when there may be missing values in the *left* table, but you want to get a description or other information from the *right* table. The following code shows an OUTER JOIN query:

```
/* Teradata SQL syntax OUTER JOIN */
SELECT   A.item_id
,A.end_dt
FROM   item   A
LEFT OUTER JOIN currencies   B
ON   A.curncy_id = B.curncy_id
and b.curncy_id=4
WHERE   A.end_dt = '2017-10-04';
```

Any conditions that apply to the outer table must be part of the `JOIN`.

- **FULL OUTER JOIN:** Used when you want to retrieve every row, whether there is a match or not, based on the join criteria. Full outer join has to be joined with caution. Think of joining two big tables with billions of rows in them. Each row has been matched with each row of the other table. So when do you use full outer join? In the case of data integrity checks, to see if tables have a 1-1 relationship between them. Following code shows full outer join at work.

```
/*Full OUTER join query*/
SELECT   item.END_DT
,CASE WHEN   item.ITEM_ID IS NOT NULL   AND other.ITEM_ID   IS NOT
NULL   THEN 'Exists in Both'
WHEN   item.ITEM_ID IS NOT NULL   AND other.ITEM_ID   IS NULL   THEN
'Cold Missing'   WHEN   item.ITEM_ID IS NULL   AND other.ITEM_ID   IS
NOT NULL   THEN 'Item Missing'   END   AS DataIntegrityCheck /* CASE
statement to check if row present in table */
, COUNT(*) AS Cnt
FROM   ITEM item
FULL OUTER JOIN Other_ITEM Other
ON   ( other.ITEM_ID = item.ITEM_ID
```

```
        AND other.END_DT = item.END_DT)
WHERE  item.END_DT = '2017-10-05'
        AND  item.END_DT = '2017-10-05'
GROUP  BY 1,2;
```

- **CROSS JOIN**: In the CROSS JOIN or Cartesian product, every column in the *left* table is joined to every column in the *right* table! So, if you have a one billion row table and CROSS JOIN it to a 100 row table, your answer set will have 100 billion rows! There are uses for deliberate cross joins in SQL that will be discussed later. In a Cartesian product, a WHERE clause can restrict the amount of rows considered. The following shows a CROSS JOIN query:

```
/*QUERY with CROSS JOIN*/
SELECT    C.CAL_DATE
, A.CRYN_CODE
FROM  SYS_CALENDAR C
CROSS JOIN CODES A
WHERE  C.CAL_DATE BETWEEN CURRENT_DATE - 10 AND CURRENT_DATE
ORDER BY 1,2;
```

As you can see, there are many joins you can use to marry your table, but which one gets your business answer depends on the requirements:

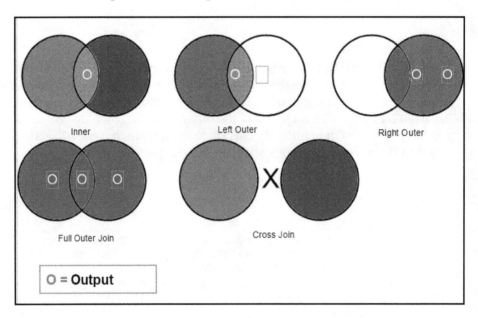

Identifying skewness in joins

Skewness is the system killer. The magic of Teradata is in its parallelism, which distributes the work/data across many processing elements; this magic can turn into mush if the work/data is distributed in an uneven or disproportionate manner. Skew is when one or more of the **Access Module Processors (AMPs)** get a larger than average share of the work.

We need to understand that an absolute even distribution is rarely achievable on a single query event. It is recommended not to consider the operation skewed until the portion consumed by the hot AMP exceeds four to five times the average.

Whatever kind of skewness there is on a system, it reduces and degrades system parallelism. When skewness occurs in a query, it slows down the join processing, and for that reason joining does not occur with full efficiency, which in turn consumes more CPU and runtime for the query.

The distribution of rows directly affects the benefits of parallelism. The more uniform the distribution of rows, the more the parallelism, as shown in the image that follows:

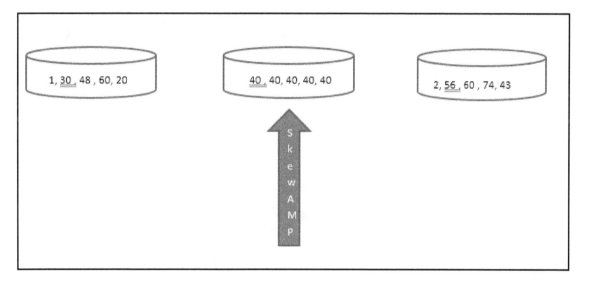

In this recipe, we will find out a way to help you reduce the naturally occurring skewness in join.

Getting ready

You need to connect to the Teradata system. Identify the queries that are having performance issues due to skew joins.

Let's create two tables, A and B, with the following structure, and insert values into them. We will induce natural skewness in table A.

We have only two AMP quiescent system, skewness, CPU and query run time will be much less than the actual Teradata production box. Create tables with the following code for DDL and data, as shown:

```
/**Table A with Skewness**/
CREATE volatile SET TABLE td_cookbook.A_with_skew ,NO FALLBACK ,
     NO BEFORE JOURNAL,
     NO AFTER JOURNAL,
     CHECKSUM = DEFAULT,
     DEFAULT MERGEBLOCKRATIO
     (
     cust_id integer,
Cust_name varchar(32),
City varchar(18)
     )
     PRIMARY INDEX ( cust_id );

/*Insert Values in Table A*/
insert into td_cookbook.A_with_skew values (,'Rakesh Jha','AJM');
insert into td_cookbook.A_with_skew values (,'Tom A','CA');
insert into td_cookbook.A_with_skew values (,'Namcie R','IN');
insert into td_cookbook.A_with_skew values (,'Ab Kh','VIC');
insert into td_cookbook.A_with_skew values (,'Man Jav','PUN');
insert into td_cookbook.A_with_skew values (,'Rajesj Jav','MUM');
insert into td_cookbook.A_with_skew values (,'Donald T','NY');
insert into td_cookbook.A_with_skew values (,'Erica Sven','MS');
insert into td_cookbook.A_with_skew values (,'Holly W','TS');
insert into td_cookbook.A_with_skew values (2,'Mnai W','BHK');
insert into td_cookbook.A_with_skew values (3,'Raji W','HAD');
insert into td_cookbook.A_with_skew values (4,'Raji W','HAD');
```

In `Table A`, we have kept some values as `NULL`; rows of these values will be skewed and hold onto only one AMP, as shown in the following block of code:

```
/*Table B without skew*/
CREATE SET TABLE td_cookbook.B_with_nonskew ,NO FALLBACK ,
     NO BEFORE JOURNAL,
     NO AFTER JOURNAL,
     CHECKSUM = DEFAULT,
     DEFAULT MERGEBLOCKRATIO
     (
     cust_id integer,
Sal integer
     )
     PRIMARY INDEX ( cust_id );

/*Insert Value in table B*/
insert into td_cookbook.B_with_nonskew values (1,2000);
insert into td_cookbook.B_with_nonskew values (2,2100);
insert into td_cookbook.B_with_nonskew values (3,2200);
insert into td_cookbook.B_with_nonskew values (4,2400);
insert into td_cookbook.B_with_nonskew values (5,2600);
insert into td_cookbook.B_with_nonskew values (6,2600);
```

In `Table B`, we will insert values without any skew. `CUST_ID` in `Table A` (`A_with_skew`) will be skewed on `NULL`, whereas in `Table B` (`B_with_nonskew`), it won't be. The following will be the data in both the tables:

td_cookbook.A_with_skew			td_cookbook.B_with_nonskew	
Column1	**Column2**	**Column3**	**cust_id**	**Sal**
cust_id	Cust_name	City	1	2,000
?	Rakesh Jha	AJM	2	2,100
?	Tom A	CA	3	2,200
?	Namcie R	IN	4	2,400
?	Ab Kh	VIC	5	2,600
?	Man Jav	PUN	6	2,600
?	Rajesj Jav	MUM		
?	Donald T	NY		
?	Erica Sven	MS		
?	Holly W	TS		
2	Mnai W	BHK		
3	Raji W	HAD		
4	Raji W	HAD		

A good proportion of customer records will have null values for the `CUST_ID` column. During the join step, the AMP holding these records will be skewed, which will cause skewness in the overall query.

How to do it...

1. Connect to Teradata SQLA or Studio.
2. The following query is joined on skew columns, which is `CUST_ID`:

```
/*Skew join query*/
sel A.* ,b.sal
from td_cookbook.A_with_skew A
inner join
td_cookbook.B_with_nonskew B
on a.cust_id=b.cust_id;
```

3. To resolve skew on joining columns, we fill first check what values are skewed. The following query will show values that are skewed on one AMP:

```
/* To check SKEW value*/
LOCKING ROW FOR ACCESS
SELECT cust_id,count(*)
FROM td_cookbook.A_with_skew
group by 1 order by 2 desc;
```

4. The following output shows `CUST_ID` ? has 9 values from table A. Next, we will check the row distribution of table B:

CUST_ID	Count(*)
?	9
2	1
4	1
3	1

The values of table A

5. The following will be the query to show the data skewness in table B:

CUST_ID	Count(*)
1	1
4	1
2	1
6	1
3	1
5	1

6. There are many ways to reduce or improve the query performance. Let's check method 1.

7. **Method 1**: Multiply the primary key of the table with -1 (where value is '?'). This has to be done in the ETL layer. Casting in the view wouldn't help with the redistribution. The following is the table view:

td_cookbook.A_with_skew		
Column1	**Column2**	**Column3**
cust_id	Cust_name	City
-2	Rakesh Jha	AJM
-3	Tom A	CA
-4	Namcie R	IN

8. We will use `UNION ALL`. The upper part of the query will have values with skew and other parts without skew values, as shown in the following block:

```
/* UNION ALL To reduce skew*/
SELECT cust_id, name
(
sel cust_id,name
from skew_tableA A,
nonskew_tableB B
on A.cust_id=B.cust_id
where a.cust_id=<skew_value>

UNION ALL

sel cust_id,name
```

```
from skew_tableA A,
nonskew_tableB B
on A.cust_id=B.cust_id
where a.cust_id not in (<skew_value>)
)a
  GROUP BY 1,2
```

9. Breaking the query into multiple parts, with and without skew, improves join performance, and redistribution of tables occurs without much impact.

10. You can compare the CPU, I/O, and Active time of the original query and recommended query.

How it works...

As shown in the recipe steps, the issue was due to the result of carrying an unknown dimension.

Randomly distributing the unknown dimension on a range of negative key values is an effective means to address this problem.

80% of the business is done by a small number of customers. Primary indexes might be fine, but you still have data skew on dynamic joins. Reducing skewness on joins is a major challenge for developers when designing the process, be it ETL or business reports. Skewed joins may over kill the system and can help in arising *hot* AMP situations on the Teradata box.

Sub-optimal or skewed queries can be identified at runtime by looking at viewpoint, which will have a skew percentage displayed on the session information screen. This value is calculated on the CPU consumed during the last updated interval (usually 60 seconds). This is not likely to be representative of what has been occurring over the course of the query operation. The following is the snippet of a viewpoint showing various performance parameters:

METRIC	VALUE	THRESHOLDS	LAST 15 MINUTES
CPU Utilization	57.3%		
User	49.19%		
System	8.114%		
Wait I/O	10.17%		
Node CPU Skew	0.39%		
Node I/O Skew	0.902%		
AMP CPU Skew	2.246%		
AMP I/O Skew	4.303%		
AMP Worker Tasks	4		
Total Disk Space	54.48%		
Max Disk By AMP	55.98%		
Component Down	0		
Memory Used	40.3K		
Max Spool By AMP	0.071%		
Memory Failures	0		

Viewpoint showing various performance parameters

The Teradata hashing algorithm assigns hash bucket zero to all keys having values of NULL, 0, or space. The specific AMP which has hash bucket zero assigned to it will be different on each system. Execute the following SQL to see where it is assigned on your system:

```
/*To identify the AMP*/
SELECT        HASHAMP(HASHBUCKET(HASHROW(NULL))) AS TheNullAmp;
```

If the operation you are working on is running hot or skewed on this amp, there is a good indication that nulls, 0s, or spaces are generating the skew in that particular step.

There's more...

Statistics also play a key role in data distribution when joins are skewed. You need to make sure the optimizer always has correct information regarding tables involved in the query.

A skewed distribution will likely be a result of the optimizer having insufficient information on which to recognize the skewed condition. Skewed queries run longer, and a less parallel efficiency query will run longer. A longer running query means it blocks any new work on a system which has throttle implemented on workloads.

Identify the right columns for joins

A **data warehouse** is a collection of objects such as databases, tables, users, and many others. Tables hold data which is used to drive business insights and analytics. To get answers to many business requirements, it becomes necessity to join multiple tables.

Not only is this type of join important, but it is also important which columns need to be joined. In this recipe, we will explore which types of columns are good candidates for joins. But sometimes, joining columns can't be changed because of business requirements.

The following are some data types that can be used in Teradata:

Data Type	Length (Bytes)	Description
ByteINT	1	Ranges from -127 to +127
CHAR	Fixed format	These data types represent character data: Type Varchar, CLOB
DATE	4	Format YYYYYMMDD
TIME	6/8	Format Time or Timestamp value HHMMSS.nnnnnn or HHMMSS.nnnnnn+HHMM
ARRAY/VARRAY	Fixed format	User-defined type
BIGINT	8	Numeric data type
DECIMAL	1-16	Range from 1-38

Like other programming languages, Teradata SQL also has some reserved keywords that can't be used as identifiers to name objects. Some examples are DATE and YEAR words.

Getting ready

You need to be connected to the Teradata database using SQLA or Studio.

How to do it...

1. For any given query, we will derive the DDL of the objects in the query.
2. Write SHOW in front of the query and execute it to get the list of all objects in the query with their definitions, as shown in the following block:

   ```
   /*DDL of object*/
   SHOW sel A.* ,b.sal
   from td_cookbook.A_with_join A
   inner join
   td_cookbook.B_with_nonjoin B
   on a.cust_id=b.cust_id
   where a.cust_id is not null
   ```

3. Once you have the DDL of all the objects, check the columns involved in the joins. Are they PI columns or PPI columns? Is there any join index on these joining columns?
4. Execute EXPLAIN for the query by pressing *F6* in SQLA or writing EXPLAIN in front of the query and pressing *F5*:

   ```
   /*EXPLAIN of qery*/
   EXPLAIN sel A.* ,b.sal
   from td_cookbook.A_with_join A
   inner join
   td_cookbook.B_with_nonjoin B
   on a.cust_id=b.cust_id
   where a.cust_id is not null
   ```

5. Then, check for the data type of these queries. Make sure that only similar data type columns are joined: a varchar is joined to a varchar or a decimal is joined to a decimal. Any non-data type join which is varchar to decimal will result in poor join performance.
6. Also, if possible, make sure long-length varchar columns are avoided in joins.
7. Check if any function is used in a join condition, like COALESCE, CASE, or any other. Conditions in join columns need to be avoided. They make join CPU intensive.

8. Statistics also need to be checked on joining columns. HELP STATS TABLENAME will reveal stats on columns in the table. If stats are out of date, you need to refresh them on the table:

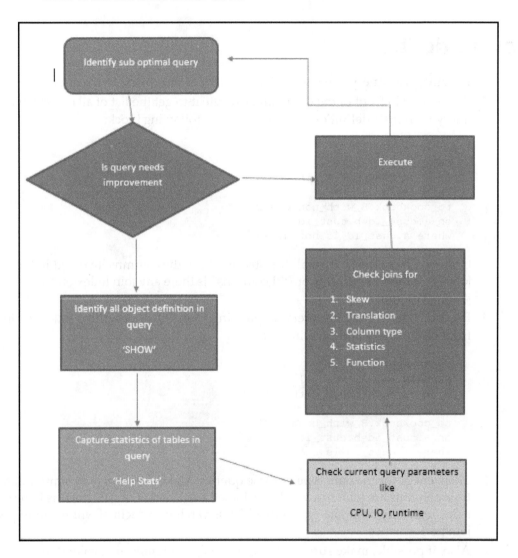

How it works...

Now we understand how important joins are in queries. The performance of a query mainly depends on the joins in the query. Sometimes, due to business requirements, we come across situations were skewed joins or unnecessary joins become necessary. Those scenarios are rare in occurrence.

Let's see how joins work:

Nature of Join	How Join Occurs
PI to PI	No redistribution. Local AMP join.
PI to Non PI	NON PI table will be redistributed. Smaller table should be duplicated on AMPs.
Non PI to Non PI	Tables will be redistributed based on joining columns. Statistics play important role.
PPI to PPI	Row key based merge join. Only partitions are joined.
PPI to NPPI	Sliding window merge join. It is like a product join for partitioned based tables.
Unmatched datatype	Conversion of data type; translation will occur.
Use of Function	Statistics could be of no use. Each value in a column will be computed, which will increase CPU. Table can go for full table scans.
SKEW values	Redistribution or duplication of table gets impacted. NULL values, if there, need to filtered.
Columns with no or stale stats	Columns of skew values and with millions of rows should have statistics. Can result in product join.

There's more...

The explain plan plays an important role in identifying sub-optimal joins.
Any discrepancies in a join can be checked from the explain plan even before executing the actual query. If you find these keywords in your query, make sure it is tuned before execution:

- Translate
- Product join
- Estimated row 1
- All-rows scan
- Low confidence

Sub-optimal joins not only impact the CPU and runtime, but also SPOOL. Teradata often has to use spool space to hold copies of rows redistributed to do a join. The optimizer minimizes the amount of spool required by:

- Copying only those rows that the query requires
- Doing single-table set selections first (qualifying rows)
- Putting only the smaller tables into spool whenever possible

High spool queries result in spool out error 2646, which needs to be optimized before the next run.

Eliminating product joins

Product joins, cross joins, or Cartesian joins, are mainly created unintentionally. These are the most expensive types of joins when you are joining two tables with millions of rows.

In the cross join, every column in the *left* table is joined to every column in the *right* table! So, if you have a one billion row table and cross join it to a 100 row table, your answer set will have 100 billion rows!

These joins happen when you:

- Mention CROSS join explicitly
- Missed a join condition in a query as shown in following code

- Wrongly used aliases in a query

```
/*Missed join PRODUCT JOIN*/
SELECT
COUNTRY_ID,
REVI_ID,
AUCT_CODE,
FROM
COUNTRIES, -- NO JOIN SPECIFIED
AUCT_TYPES
```

And when you check the EXPLAIN plan for the query, you will get the product join in it:

```
/*EXPLAIN PLAN SHOWING PRODUCT JOIN*/
4) We do an all-AMPs JOIN step from Spool 2 (Last Use) by way of an all-
rows scan, which is joined to Spool 7 (Last Use) by way of an  all-rows
scan.  Spool 2 and Spool 7 are joined using a product  join, with a join
condition of ("(1=1)").  The result goes into  Spool 4 (group_amps), which
is built locally on the AMPs.  The  result spool file will not be cached in
memory.  The size of Spool  4 is estimated with low confidence to be ***
rows (*** bytes).
The estimated time for this step is 291,597,657 hours and 47  minutes.
```

As you can see in the EXPLAIN plan that estimated rows are shown by asterix * which means that estimated rows are extremely high in number, because of which it is not visible in the plan. These types of explain plans need to be investigated without any delay. The following is the image of a **Product Join**:

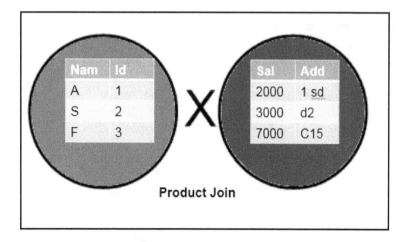

Product Join

In this recipe, we will see how we can remove 'unintentional' product joins. Remember that not all product joins are bad; when relatively small tables are involved, product join works better.

Getting ready

You need to be connected to the Teradata database using SQLA or Studio. Identify the query that you want to investigate for product join.

How to do it...

1. Connect to Teradata using SQLA or Studio.
2. Write SHOW in front of the query and execute it to get the list of all objects in the query, with their definitions.
3. Once you have the DDL of all the objects, check the columns involved in joins.
4. Execute EXPLAIN for the query by pressing *F6* in SQLA or writing EXPLAIN in front of the query and pressing *F5*:

   ```
   /*EXPLAIN of query*/
   EXPLAIN sel A.* ,b.sal
   from td_cookbook.A_with_PJjoin A
   td_cookbook.B_with_nonjoin B -- NO JOIN SPECIFIED
   ```

5. Identify which columns are getting joined using product join.
6. Once identified, check the stats on these columns. No stats or stale stats on columns causes wrong estimations, which causes product joins.

> If, in the redistribution step, you find the number of rows is equivalent to your AMPs in the system, that means the optimizer is estimating only one row. *# of row= estimatednumberrows/numberofAMP*.

7. Collect stats on these columns and check the explain plan again.
8. If you still have PRODUCT JOIN, check for aliases involved. Correct them if required.

9. Next, check for any inequality join conditions, which are conditions involving operations like <, <=, >, and >=. Because of these conditions, the optimizer can go for PRODUCT JOIN.

10. If product join in the query is not due to a human mistake and is because of a business requirement. Mention CROSS JOIN in query.

11. It is advocated that you use the WHERE clause whenever you require doing a CROSS JOIN. The WHERE clause can restrict the amount of rows considered.

12. Linking the two tables on a common field may eliminate an unwanted Cartesian product in some cases; it is equivalent to an INNER JOIN.

 Using the WHERE clause in 'joining' conditions is not ANSI standard, but it is a way to link tables to combine information from different tables.

How it works...

In product join, the smaller row table is usually copied to all the AMPs and prepared to be compared with each row of the other table, which makes the cost of comparison of row high. This is why product join is costly join operation when we compare it to merge/inner join.

Product joins are like any other joins to the optimizer, but they can hamper the system if it is appearing unintentionally.

Primary root causes for resource intensive product joins include:

- Type of join conditions
    - Missing
    - OR-ed join conditions
    - Unequal join conditions
    - Complex CASE
- Missing, stale, or inappropriate statistics (see the following example on stale statistics, which are the most frequent cause)
- Unmatched data types or different data types will typically result in low estimates and costly join logic
- Use of functions in join conditions: TRIM(), UPPER(), and SUBSTRING ()

Let's see an example which is a common occurrence in product joins: missing/stale statistics.

- Table A: Statistics collected when a table had 1,000 rows, but it now has 1,000,000 rows and stats are now stale on it
- Table B: With 50,000 rows and no statistics

If a product join between table A and table B is necessary for a given query, then one of the tables must be duplicated on all AMPs. Table A will be duplicated (remember, the smaller table in this case is table A). Since in reality Table A now has 1,000,000 rows, the optimizer will be making a very bad decision (duplicating 1,000,000 rows instead of 50,000), and the query will run much longer than necessary.

This makes statistics important and needs to be refreshed in timely manner.

Summing up, the following image shows you the steps to perform this recipe:

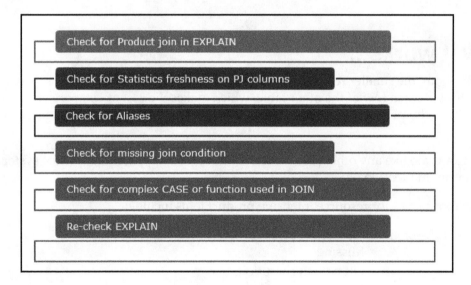

There's more...

We can monitor product join queries in real time from viewpoint. Also, they are available in DBQL/PDCR logs.

As a product join is a calculated ratio of CPU to I/O, this value does not result in an actual product join happening in a query every time. Sometimes, a query doing a full table or high scanning also shows a high value for PJI in viewpoint:

```
/*Calculation of PJI*/
Product Join Indicator, PJI = (AMPCPUTime * 1000) / TotalIOCount
```

So, it becomes important to check the explain plan of the query to see if a product join is actually happening.

See also

- Identifying suspect queries

Improving left join

There can be two kinds of left joins, or outer joins:

- Left outer join
- Right outer join

This type of outer join will return all rows from the *left* or *right* table, and only those rows that match from the *right* or *left* table. This is handy when there may be missing values in the *other* table, but you want to get a description or other information from the *other* table. The following image shows the working of outer joins, represented as a VENN diagram:

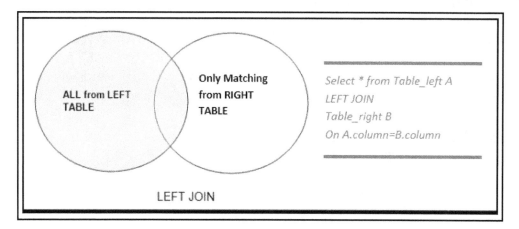

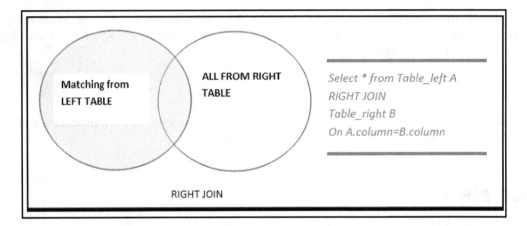

Rows for which matching values are derived will be NULL in each case of join.

Getting ready

You need to connect to the Teradata database using SQLA or Studio. Identify the query in which left join is causing performance issues.

How to do it...

1. Connect to the Teradata database using SQLA or Studio.
2. Write SHOW in front of the query and execute it to get the list of all objects in the query, with their definitions.
3. Once you have DDLs of all the objects, check the columns involved in joins.
4. Execute EXPLAIN for the query by pressing *F6* in SQLA or writing EXPLAIN in front of the query and pressing *F5*. Check for the OUTER keyword, which will indicate that the join is correct:

```
/*EXPLAIN of query*/
EXPLAIN sel A.* ,b.sal
from td_cookbook.A_with_Leftjoin A
left join
td_cookbook.B_with_join B
on a.cust_id=b.cust_id
where B.cust_id is not null
```

5. Check statistics on the columns involved. If required, collect statistics on the column involved in the left join.

6. The `WHERE` clause and `ON` condition should be placed in the right place:
   - Join should be placed on the `ON` clause.
   - The `WHERE` clause for the `INNER` tables are placed on the `ON` clause, while search conditions on the `OUTER` table are placed in the `WHERE` clause. This limits the participant rows from the `OUTER` table and improves performance.
   - Placement of `WHERE` and `ON` changes the result set of the query; take caution when applying them:

```
/*LEFT JOIN*/
SELECT
A.CUST_ID,
B.MONTHLY_SAL
FROM CKBK_DB.CUST A -- OUTER TABLE
LEFT OUTER JOIN
CKBK_DB.HR_block B -- INNER TABLE
ON A.CUST_ID = B.EMP_ID -- CONDITION on the ON Clause
AND
B.DOB_DATE= '1980-02-23' -- FILTER CONDITION ON INNER TABLE
WHERE A.DEPT='COP'-- FILTER CONDITION ON OUTER TABLE
AND A.CRNY_ID= 'IN'
ORDER BY 1,2;
```

7. If the conditions are in the correct place or can't be changed due to business requirements, try to rewrite the query using `NOT EXIST`. The left join can be changed to `NOT EXIST` to improve performance by filtering `NULL` directly when joining columns.

How it works...

Placement of joining and search conditions are important in `LEFT JOIN`. Your result set can change if the conditions are changed. To demonstrate this, let's see an example.

Let's create two tables:

```
CREATE volatile TABLE EMP (
name VARCHAR(25),
ID INT
) on commit preserve rows;
```

```
INSERT into EMP VALUES ('Rosy',2);
INSERT into EMP VALUES ('Emily',2);
INSERT into EMP VALUES ('Tom',1);
INSERT into EMP VALUES ('Ross',3);
INSERT into EMP VALUES ('Mark',null);
INSERT into EMP VALUES ('Dave',null);

CREATE volatile TABLE EMP_SAL
(
id INT,
DEPT varchar(25)
) on commit preserve rows;

INSERT into EMP_SAL VALUES (1,'HR');
INSERT into EMP_SAL VALUES(2,'IT');
INSERT into EMP_SAL VALUES (3,'CMP');
INSERT into EMP_SAL VALUES (4,'MGMT');
```

We get the following tables:

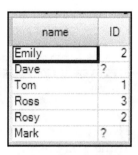

We will first see how simple left join works:

```
/* Simple LEFT JOIN*/
SELECT  *
FROM    EMP F LEFT outer join EMP_SAL FC
ON      F.id = FC.id;
```

From this query, all the columns from the left table will be there, and non-matching rows from the right table will have NULLS.

Next, a left join with the WHERE clause:

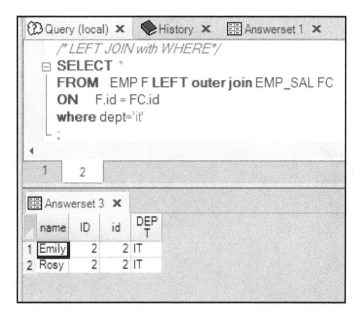

This is equivalent to an INNER JOIN; when you check the explain plan of this query, the optimizer converts it to a merge join. The following is the EXPLAIN plan of the query:

```
/*EXPLAIN PART*/
2) Next, we do an all-AMPs JOIN step from SYSDBA.FC by way of a
   RowHash match scan with a condition of ("SYSDBA.FC.DEPT = 'it'"),
   which is joined to Spool 2 (Last Use) by way of a RowHash match
   scan. SYSDBA.FC and Spool 2 are joined using a merge join, with a
   join condition of ("ID = SYSDBA.FC.id"). The result goes into
   Spool 1 (group_amps), which is built locally on the AMPs. The
   size of Spool 1 is estimated with no confidence to be 6 rows (294
   bytes). The estimated time for this step is 0.05 seconds.
```

A left outer join with the ON clause:

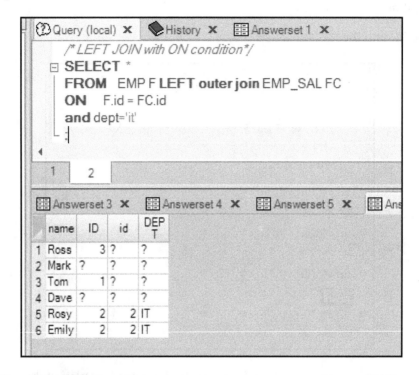

When we move the condition to the ON clause, join becomes `'OUTER LEFT JOIN'`, as seen in the explain plan:

```
/*EXPLAIN PLAN*/
Next, we do an all-AMPs JOIN step from Spool 2 (Last Use) by way
  of a RowHash match scan, which is joined to SYSDBA.FC by way of a
  RowHash match scan with a condition of ("SYSDBA.FC.DEPT = 'it'").
  Spool 2 and SYSDBA.FC are left outer joined using a merge join,
  with condition(s) used for non-matching on left table ("NOT (ID IS
  NULL)"), with a join condition of ("ID = SYSDBA.FC.id"). The
  result goes into Spool 1 (group_amps), which is built locally on
  the AMPs. The size of Spool 1 is estimated with no confidence to
  be 11 rows (539 bytes). The estimated time for this step is 0.05
  seconds.
```

The result set contains all the rows from the left table as the plain left outer join query that we saw in the first query, but in the second table, only those rows are shown which match the condition dept='IT'. Otherwise, it is shown as NULL.

Improving Teradata joins

In this recipe, we will list steps which will guide you to an overall health check of Teradata joins. This will be a high-level view of performance when it comes to JOINS. Steps in this recipe will not be dependent on type of join. You can apply these to any join, based on the problem in the query:

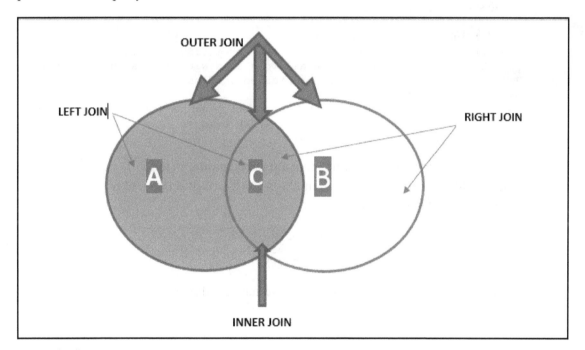

Getting ready

You need to connect to the Teradata database using SQLA or Studio.

How to do it...

1. Connect to the Teradata database using SQLA or Studio.
2. Write SHOW in front of the query and execute it to get the list of all objects in the query, with their definitions.
3. Once you have the DDLs of all the objects, check the columns involved in joins.
4. Execute EXPLAIN for the query by pressing *F6* in SQLA or writing EXPLAIN in front of the query and pressing *F5*.
5. In EXPLAIN, check for extremely high estimated rows or extremely low estimated rows and time; if these estimations are not in relation to table statistics, refresh the stats on the columns:

   ```
   /*High Estimated Explain*/
   1) We do an all-AMPs RETRIEVE step from SYSDBA.FC in view
   SYSDBA.SITES by way of an all-rows scan with no residual conditions
   into Spool 7 (all_amps) (compressed columns allowed), which is
   duplicated on all AMPs.
   The size of Spool 7 is estimated with high confidence to be
   123,121,232,255,840rows (***,721,920 bytes). The estimated time
   for this step is 234.01 hours.
   ```

6. Check for skewness in columns that are participating in joins.
7. Check for data type conversion in EXPLAIN. If you find one that needs it, change the data type in the join:

   ```
   Then we do a SORT to order Spool 3 by
   the hash code of (SYSDBA.Table_A.EMP_Id (FLOAT, FORMAT
   -9.99999999999999E-999') (FLOAT)).
   ```

8. Check for the join type and focus to eliminate product join if found in EXPLAIN:

   ```
   ) We do an all-AMPs JOIN step from Spool 1 (Last Use) by way of an
   all-rows scan, which is joined to Spool 6 (Last Use) by way of an
   all-rows scan. Spool 1 and Spool 6 are joined using a product
   join, with a join condition of ("SITE_ID =SITE_ID"). The result
   goes into Spool 8 (all_amps) (compressed columns allowed),  which
   is built locally on the AMPs.
   ```

9. Try to transform the sliding window merge join to a row-key based merge join.
10. If LEFT OUTER JOIN exists and there is also a condition on the WHERE clause on the right table, logically, this makes the outer join an INNER JOIN. Place a condition in the right order or change LEFT JOIN to INNER JOIN.

11. Reconsider the `PI` of tables to improve the join performance on larger tables.

12. Make sure the duplicated table is the smaller one in the join. Statistics can let to improper table joins.

13. Recheck the `EXPLAIN` after making changes, if all the keywords and joins are as per requirement.

14. Avoid join on large `VARCHAR` columns, as each record can be of variable length and
    that makes it more costly to join fields in a record.

15. Make sure no function is used on joining columns. Avoid a `TRIM()`, `AVG()` kind of function from join. Make use of derive columns in join to improve performance.

16. Try to convert sub queries in query into joins for better performance:

```
/*Sub query*/
SELECT first_name
, last_name
, deprt_number
FROM employee
WHERE deprt_number IN
(SELECT department_number
FROM department
WHERE department_name LIKE 'IT');

/*Subquery to JOIN*/
SELECT e.first_name
, e.last_name
, e.department_number
FROM employee e INNER JOIN
department d
ON e.department_number =
d.department_number
WHERE d.department_name LIKE
'IT';
```

17. Query performance needs to be checked from time to time. An increase in data volume and stats can change the optimizer plan of execution.

How it works...

Determining the cost of the query is the main job of the optimizer. The costs of columns used in joins come from statistics. The explain plan is not stored for a given query because the data may have changed between executions.

Row Estimates:

- May be estimated using random samples, statistics, or indexes
- Are assigned a confidence level - high, low, or none
- Affect timing estimates - more rows, more time needed

Timings:

- Used to determine the 'lowest cost' plan
- Total cost generated if all processing steps have assigned costs
- Not intended to predict wall-clock time, useful for comparisons

Miscellaneous Notes:

- Estimates too large to display show three asterisks (***)
- The accuracy of the time estimate depends upon the accuracy of the row estimate

JOIN Type:

- Depends on the costs and conditions placed on columns
- Can be manipulated because of stale or no statistics

6
Building Loading Utility – Replication and Loading

In this chapter, we will cover:

- Loading data from Flat to Teradata
- Resolving FastLoad error 2652
- Using Multiload to delete
- Resolving MLOAD error 2571
- Resolving Failure 7547
- Upserting data using MLOAD
- Loading data from one Teradata Database to another

Introduction

The Teradata Database provides several utilities to load, delete, or update large volumes of data. Utilities are the most efficient way to load data into a database. Utilities are designed to utilize the parallel architecture of Teradata while inserting, deleting, or updating data. This also means that if they are not designed properly, these utilities can have performance impacts on the system.

The following are the utilities in Teradata:

- **Fastload**: Bulk load utility
- **Mload**: Bulk load utility
- **Fastexport**: Bulk export utility
- **BTEQ**: Use of transient journal
- **TPUMP**: Use of transient journal

Let's see how these utilities compare with each other:

Utility Name	Type	Advantages	Disadvantages
Fastload	Single table bulk load	• Fastest • Table with NoPI supported • Supports error limits and checkpoint/ restart • Both support multi-value compression and PPI	• Inserts only • Empty target table required • Fallback, permanent journal are applied after the FastLoad is complete • Secondary indexes, triggers, join indexes, and referential integrity must be applied after the FastLoad is complete • No updates/deletes • No duplicate rows inserted
Multiload	Multi-table bulk load and delete	• Up to five tables can be loaded • Updates/deletes can be performed in block mode • Use table-level lock	• Unique secondary indexes, triggers, join indexes, and referential integrity must be dropped before and recreated after the multiload • NoPI tables not supported

Fastexport	Bulk extract	• Multiple tables can be joined to extract data • 64K block • NOSPOOL option available to improve performance • Has an advantage over BTEQ • Automated restart • Applies read lock	• Cannot use SELECT with equality condition for a primary index, PI, or unique secondary index
BTEQ	Traditional load unload utility	• Simple INSERT/SELECT sql, no special script required • Best to use with smaller dataset • Offers rollback functionality • Works with all types of indexes	• Slowest of all • Insert one row at a time • One session per BTEQ query • No restart capability

Whatever utility we choose to load/unload data, it all requires better design. A utility is used to its full capacity if it is designed in an efficient manner. A good choice of PI, the right number of sessions, and well-designed workload management affects the speed of a utility.

 NoPI tables allow you to create tables with no primary indexes to improve the performance of Fastload and Teradata Parallel Transporter.

The following image shows the traditional **Extract, Transformation, Load ETL method;** load utilities perform all these tasks from end to end:

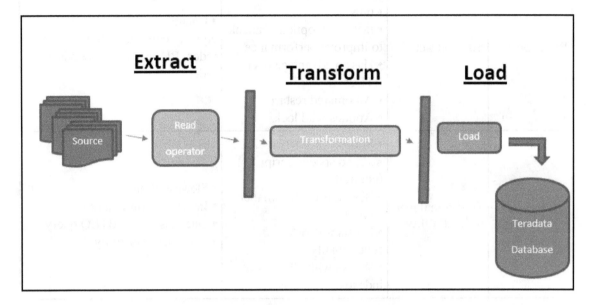

Loading data from flat to Teradata

In the following recipe, we will use FastLoad to load data from a flat file to Teradata. The following are some known issues which degrade the performance of the load utility:

- Unclean data decreases the efficiency of the apply phase
- Unclean data, like duplicate unique indexes, duplicate rows, and constraint violations put loads on error tables
- Uneven distribution of rows

The loading of data is done in staging tables when following the traditional ETL process. We can club FastLoad with SQLs to increase the performance of ETL, as shown in the following figure:

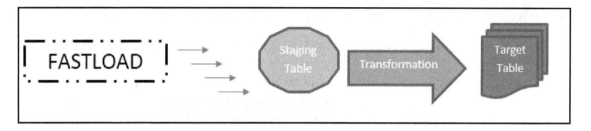

Fastload can be invoked on a channel attached system to load data via a disk or using a flat file on a network attached system. You can load data from:

- Special input module (INMOD) routines
- Any other device providing properly formatted source data

Getting ready

The following are some prerequisites before loading data using FastLoad:

- Target table in Teradata should be empty
- Log table to capture all processing
- Flat file CSV format or delimited

We will use the FastLoad utility installed on your machine. It is part of the standard TTU installation.

Create a text file with the following records, and name the file accounts_data.txt:

```
**Save it to local drive folder**
10|Raj|S|1980-01-05|1200|1
11|Dhruv|Kumar|1983-03-05|2010|1
12|Pete|Lee|1983-04-01|2009|2
13|James|Stuart|1984-11-06|2014|2
14|Robert|Paul|1984-12-01|2015|3
```

A user requires the following privileges/rights in order to execute the FastLoad:

- SELECT and INSERT (CREATE and DROP or DELETE) access to target or loading table.
- CREATE and DROP TABLE on error tables.
- SELECT, INSERT, UPDATE, and DELETE are required privileges for the user PUBLIC on the restart log table (SYSADMIN.FASTLOG). There will be a row in the FASTLOG table for each FastLoad job that has not completed in the system.

How to do it...

1. Log on to FastLoad utility. Click on the Start menu and search for FastLoad. Click on **Teradata Fastload** from the search results:

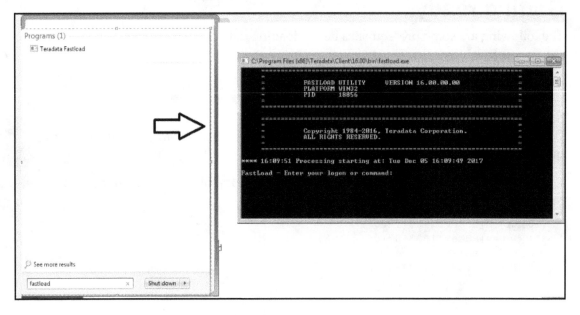

Screenshot of Teradata Fastload

2. Capture the flat file name which we are going to load into the Teradata Database. For this case, we will use a | separated file.

3. Use the following code to load the data specified in the file to the Teradata Database `cookbook_fl`:

```
.LOGON 127.0.0.1/dbc,dbc /* servername/userid,password */
/* if you are using LDAP mechanism then use .logmech ldap before
.logon statement for authentication*/
.SESSIONS 4;
.CHECKPOINT 10;  /* When to take checkpoint */
.DATABASE COOKBOOK_FL /* Set default database */
DROP TABLE TEST_FL; /*To drop existing staging table*/
DROP TABLE ERR_FL1; /*To Drop error table*/
DROP TABLE ERR_FL2; /*To Drop error table*/
CREATE MULTISET TABLE TEST_FL ,NO FALLBACK ,NO BEFORE JOURNAL,
NO AFTER JOURNAL,
CHECKSUM = DEFAULT,
DEFAULT MERGEBLOCKRATIO
(
Name VARCHAR(30),
Sr_NAME VARCHAR(30) CHARACTER SET LATIN NOT CASESPECIFIC),
dob date,
Sal Decimal(18,0),
Id INT(2)
)
PRIMARY INDEX ( Name,id );
/*SET RECORD is used to define the delimiter used in file, here |
is the delimiter for current flat file*/
SET RECORD VARTEXT "|";
/*to define the structure of the file use DEFINE and mention
the file path from which, table will be loaded*/
DEFINE Name (VARCHAR(6))
,Sr_NAME (VARCHAR(20))
,dob (VARCHAR(10))
,Sal (VARCHAR(30))
,ID (VARCHAR(2))
FILE = C:/tmp/accounts_data.txt; /*flat file path*/
/*BEGIN will start the load process */
BEGIN LOADING TEST_FL
ERRORFILES ERR_FL1,DEV.ERR_FL2;
INSERT INTO TEST_FL
VALUES(:Name,:Sr_NAME,:dob,:Sal,:id);
END LOADING;
LOGOFF; /*last statement in the FastLoad script*/
```

4. Once the input file `accounts_data.txt` is created and the FastLoad script is saved as `cookbook_fl`, execute the script using this command:

```
/*Fastload execution command*/
FastLoad < EmployeeLoad.fl > log_fl.log /* Specify the output in
log file */
```

How it works...

Fast job is divided into two phases:

1. **Phase 1 – Acquisition Phase**: The **parsing engine** (**PE**) receives data from the input file and sends it directly to **Access Module Processors, AMPs**. One session is used for an SQL session to define AMP steps, and the others for the SQL session for the log table. Data is sent in 64K blocks of records to each AMP. AMPs hash each record to the correct receiving AMP. At the end of phase 1, AMPs have rows in non-hash sequences.

2. **Phase 1 – Application Phase:** When the `END LOADING` statement is received, the application phase of the FastLoad script starts. In this phase, the parcel received in step 1 will be sorted and sent to its destinations. AMP sorts the records on row hash and writes them to disk. Locks on target tables are released and error tables are dropped.

 To enable FastLoad on channel enabled systems (mainframe), use `EXEC TDSFAST FDLOPT= [PARAMETERS]`.

`PARAMETERS` can be:

- `BUFSIZE=kb`
- `CHARSET=charsetname`
- `INMODETYPE=SAS_C`

There's more...

The following is the list of common terms used in the FastLoad script:

- LOGON: Logs in to Teradata and initiates one or more sessions.
- DATABASE: Sets the default database.
- BEGIN LOADING: Identifies the table to be loaded.
- SESSIONS: Number of sessions logged on with a LOGON command. Teradata Active System Management, TASM, enabled systems govern/supersede the number of sessions defined in this option.
- SLEEP: Minutes before the FastLoad retries a log on operation.
- TENACITY: Number of hours that FastLoad continues trying to log on when the maximum number of load jobs is already running on the Teradata Database.
- ERRLIMIT: Maximum number of errors detected during the loading phase of a FastLoad job. Processing stops when the limit is reached.
- ERRORFILES: Identifies the two error tables that need to be created/updated.
- CHECKPOINT: Defines when to take checkpoint. Set a checkpoint at 10% of your total row-count in the file. It's an overhead and doesn't need to be used after every row.
- SET RECORD: Specifies if the input file format is formatted, binary, text, or unformatted.
- DEFINE: Defines the input file layout.
- FILE: Specifies the input filename and path.
- INSERT: Inserts the records from the input file into the target table.
- END LOADING: Initiates phase 2 of the FastLoad. Distributes the records into the target table.
- LOGOFF: Ends all sessions and terminates FastLoad.

Resolving FastLoad error 2652

When data is being loaded via FastLoad, a table lock is placed on the target table. This means that the table is unavailable for any other operations. A lock on a table is only released when FastLoad encounters the END LOADING command, which terminates phase 2, the so-called application phase. FastLoad may get terminated in phase 1 due to any of the following reasons:

- Load script results in failure (error code 8 or 12)
- Load script is aborted by admin or some other session
- FastLoad fails due to bad record or file
- Forgetting to add end loading statement in script

If so, it keeps a lock on the table, which needs to be released manually. In this recipe, we will see the steps to release FastLoad locks.

Getting ready

Identify the table on which FastLoad is been ended pre-maturely and tables are in locked state. You need to have valid credentials for the Teradata Database.

Execute the dummy FastLoad script from the same user or the user which has write access to the lock table.

A user requires the following privileges/rights in order to execute the FastLoad:

- SELECT and INSERT (CREATE and DROP or DELETE) access to the target or loading table.
- CREATE and DROP TABLE on error tables.
- SELECT, INSERT, UPDATE, and DELETE are required privileges for the user PUBLIC on the restart log table (SYSADMIN.FASTLOG). There will be a row in the FASTLOG table for each FastLoad job that has not completed in the system.

How to do it...

1. Open a notepad and create the following script:

   ```
   .LOGON 127.0.0.1/dbc, dbc; /* Vaild system name and credentials to
   your system */
   .DATABASE Database_Name; /* database under which locked table is */
   erorfiles errortable_name, uv_tablename /* same error table name as
   in script */
   begin loading locked_table; /* table which is getting 2652 error */
   .END LOADING; /* to end pahse 2 and release the lock */
   .LOGOFF;
   ```

2. Save it as dummy_fl.txt.
3. Open the windows Command Prompt and execute this using the FastLoad command, as shown in the following screenshot:

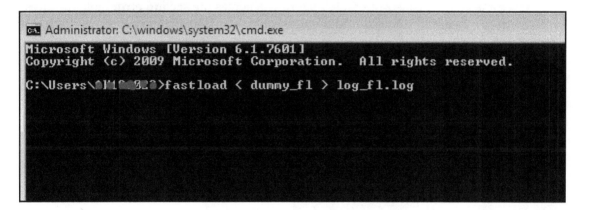

4. This dummy script with no insert statement should release the lock on the target table.
5. Execute Select on the locked table to see if the lock is released on the table.

How it works...

As FastLoad is designed to work only on empty tables, it becomes necessary that the loading of the table finishes in one go. If the load script is errored out prematurely in phase 2, without encountering the END loading command, it leaves a lock on loading the table.

Fastload locks can't be released via the HUT utility, as there are *no* technical lock on the table.

To execute FastLoad, the following are some requirements:

- **Log table**: FastLoad puts its progress information in the fastlog table.
- **EMPTY TABLE**: FastLoad needs the table to be empty before inserting rows into that table.
- **TWO ERROR TABLES**: FastLoad requires two error tables to be created; you just need to name them, and no ddl is required. The **first error** table records any translation or constraint violation error, whereas the **second error** table captures errors related to the duplication of values for **Unique Primary Indexes (UPI)**.

After the completion of FastLoad, you can analyze these error tables as to why the records got rejected.

There's more...

If this does not fix the issue, you need to drop the target table and error tables associated with it. Before proceeding with dropping tables, check with the administrator to abort any FastLoad sessions associated with this table.

Using MultiLoad to delete

MultiLoad, unlike FastLoad, has the capability to not only insert, but can also be used for update, delete, and upserts. MultiLoad can be executed on channels and network connected systems. You can insert up to five non-empty tables using MultiLoad.

Traditional MLOAD is not capable of loading data into tables that have USI-unique secondary indexes, RI-referential integrity, JI-join indexes, NoPI, or tables with triggers. But MLOADX overcomes this limitation and loads data into any table with the earlier restrictions.

In this recipe, we will use MLOAD to delete the rows, based on the equality conditions mentioned.

MLOAD delete should be chosen over SQL delete when a large number of rows need to be deleted and the table size is big.

Getting ready

A user requires the following privileges/rights in order to execute the MultiLoad:

- SELECT and INSERT (CREATE and DROP or DELETE) access to the target or loading table
- SELECT, INSERT, UPDATE, and DELETE are required privileges for the user PUBLIC on the log table

Identify the table on which you need to execute the delete statement. In this recipe, we will delete rows from <table name> and <pic>.

How to do it...

1. Open a notepad and write the following script, with the table from which you want to delete the rows. Save the file as delete_ml.txt:

```
.LOGTABLE    Logtable_del;
.SET ERROROUT STDOUT /* Output to file */
.LOGON 127.0.0.1/sysdba,password;
.BEGIN DELETE MLOAD TABLES Accounts_ml_del;
DELETE FROM Employee WHERE Sal = 0;
.END MLOAD;
.LOGOFF;
```

2. Execute the following to execute the created mload script:

```
/*MLOAD execution*/
mload < delete_ml.txt > ml_del.log
```

How it works...

Delete tasks work similarly to IMPORT tasks, with some differences:

- Deleting based on an equality UPI value is not permitted
- No acquisition phase, because there are no variable input records to apply
- The application phase reads each target block and deletes qualifying rows

MultiLoad DELETE versus SQL DELETE:

- MultiLoad DELETE is faster and uses less disk space and I/O (no transient journal).
- MultiLoad DELETE is restartable. If SQL DELETE is aborted, transient journal applies, and rows are rolled back to the original state. SQL DELETE can be resubmitted, but starts from the beginning.
- Good for tables with a large number of rows and which are not partitioned.

There's more...

As there is no transient journaling available in MLOAD DELETE when the database restarts or the host utility restarts, MLOAD determines its stop point and restarts from there.

Use .IMPORT INLINE filename_del to pass a single row containing the file to delete the rows based on values in the file.

Resolving MLOAD error 2571

MLOAD works in five phases, unlike FastLoad, which only works in two phases. MLOAD can fail in either phase three or four. Figure shows 5 stages of MLOAD.

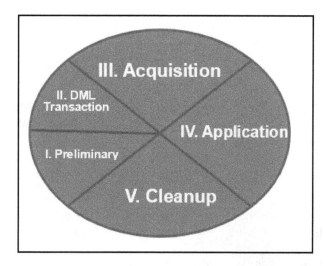

1. **Preliminary**: Basic setup. Syntax checking, establishing session with the Teradata Database, creation of error tables (two error tables per target table), and the creation of work tables and log tables are done in this phase.

2. **DML Transaction phase**: Request is parse through PE and a step plan is generated. Steps and DML are then sent to AMP and stored in appropriate work tables for each target table. Input data sent will be stored in these work tables, which will be applied to the target table later on.

3. **Acquisition phase**: Unsorted data is sent to AMP in blocks of 64K. Rows are hashed by PI and sent to appropriate AMPs. Utility places locks on target tables in preparation for the application phase to apply rows in target tables.

4. **Application phase**: Changes are applied to target tables and NUSI subtables. Lock on table is held in this phase.

5. **Cleanup phase**: If the error code of all the steps is 0, MLOAD successfully completes and releases all the locks on the specified table. This being the case, all empty error tables, worktables, and the log table are dropped.

Getting ready

Identify the table which is getting affected by error 2571. Make sure no host utility is running on this table and the load job is in a failed state for this table.

How to do it...

1. Check on viewpoint for any active utility job for this table.
2. If you find any active job, let it complete.
3. If there is a reason that you need to release the lock, first abort all the sessions of the host utility from viewpoint. Ask your administrator to do it.
4. Execute the following command:

```
RELEASE MLOAD <databasename.tablename>;
>
```

5. If you get a `Not able to release MLOAD Lock` error, execute the following command:

```
/* Release lock in application phase */
RELEASE MLOAD <databasename.tablename> in apply;
```

6. Once the locks are released you need to drop all the associated error tables, the log table, and work tables with it.
7. Re-execute `MLOAD` after correcting the error.

How it works...

The `Mload` utility places a lock in table headers to alert other utilities that a MultiLoad is in session for this table. They include:

- **Acquisition lock:**
  - DML allows all
  - DDL allows `DROP` only
- **Application lock:**
  - DML allows `SELECT` with `ACCESS` only
  - DDL allows `DROP` only

There's more...

If the release lock statement still gives an error and does not release the lock on the table, you need to use `SELECT` with the `ACCESS` lock to copy the content of the locked table to a new one and drop the locked tables.

If you start receiving the error `7446 Mload table %ID cannot be released because NUSI exists`, you need to drop all the NUSI on the table and use `ALTER Table` to non-fallback to accomplish the task.

Resolving failure 7547

This error is associated with the `UPDATE` statement, which could be SQL based or could be in `MLOAD`.

Various times, while updating the set of rows in a table, the update fails on `Failure 7547 Target row updated by multiple source rows`.

This error will happen when you update the target with multiple rows from the source. This means there are duplicated values present in the source tables.

Getting ready

Let's create sample volatile tables and insert values into them. After that, we will execute the `UPDATE` command, which will fail to result in 7547:

1. Create a `TARGET TABLE` with the following DDL and insert values into it:

```
** TARGET TABLE**
create volatile table accounts
(
CUST_ID,
CUST_NAME,
Sal
)with data
primary index(cust_id)
insert values (1,'will',2000);
insert values (2,'bekky',2800);
insert values (3,'himesh',4000);
```

2. Create a `SOURCE TABLE` with the following DDL and insert values into it:

```
** SOURCE TABLE**
create volatile table Hr_payhike
(
CUST_ID,
CUST_NAME,
Sal_hike
```

```
) with data
primary index(cust_id)
insert values (1,'will',2030);
insert values (1,'bekky',3800);
insert values (3,'himesh',7000);
```

3. Execute the MLOAD script. Following the snippet from the MLOAD script, only update part (which will fail):

```
/* Snippet from MLOAD update */
UPDATE ACC
FROM ACCOUNTS ACC , Hr_payhike SUPD
SET Sal= TUPD.Sal_hike
WHERE
Acc.CUST_ID = SUPD.CUST_ID;
```

Failure: Target row updated by multiple source rows

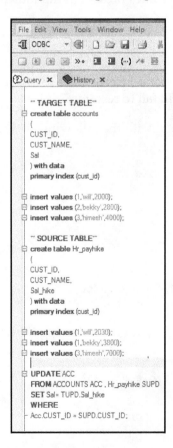

How to do it...

1. Check for duplicate values in the source table using the following:

    ```
    /*Check for duplicate values in source table*/
    SELECT cust_id,count(*)
    from Hr_payhike
    group by 1 order by 2 desc
    ```

2. The output will be generated with CUST_ID =1 and has two values which are causing errors. The reason for this is that while updating the TARGET table, the optimizer won't be able to understand from which row it should update the TARGET row. Who's salary will be updated Will or Bekky?

3. To resolve the error, execute the following update query:

    ```
    /* Update part of MLOAD */
    UPDATE ACC
    FROM ACCOUNTS ACC ,
    ( SELECT
    CUST_ID,
    CUST_NAME,
    SAL_HIKE
    FROM
    Hr_payhike
    QUALIFY ROW_NUMBER() OVER (PARTITION BY CUST_ID ORDER BY
    CUST_NAME,SAL_HIKE DESC)=1) SUPD
    SET Sal= SUPD.Sal_hike
    WHERE
    Acc.CUST_ID = SUPD.CUST_ID;
    ```

4. Now, the update will run without error.

How it works...

Failure will happen when you update the target with multiple rows from the source. If you defined a primary index column for your target, and if those columns are in an update query condition, this error will occur.

There's more...

To further resolve this, you can delete the duplicate from the source table itself and execute the original update without any modification. But if the source data can't be changed, then you need to change the update statement.

Upserting data using MLOAD

Assume a scenario where you need to update the existing records based on certain criteria conditions and non-updating records are inserted into the table. This update and insert combined in one SQL are called as UPSERT.

UPSERT is not an SQL command, but a loading technique where missing rows are inserted and existing records are updated.

TMPUP and MLOAD can both be used for this purpose.

In this recipe, we will create a sample table in the Teradata Database, and then we will update the existing records in the sample table and add new records if any. The MLOAD script will be used for this.

Getting ready

Connect to Teradata Database using SQLA or Studio. We will create the following table in one of the databases:

```
                    MultiLoad Acquisition Phase
====================================================================
**** 10:15:04 UTY0817 MultiLoad submitting the following request:
BEGIN TRANSACTION;
**** 10:15:04 UTY0817 MultiLoad submitting the following request:
CHECKPOINT LOADING INTERVAL 0;
**** 10:15:04 UTY0817 MultiLoad submitting the following request:
CHECKPOINT LOADING INTERVAL 0;
**** 10:15:05 UTY0817 MultiLoad submitting the following request:
CHECKPOINT LOADING INTERVAL 0;
**** 10:15:06 UTY0817 MultiLoad submitting the following request:
USING Ckpt(VARBYTE(1024)) INSERT SYSDBA.Restartlog723_mld       (Logty
Seq, MLoadSeq, MLoadImpSeq, MLoadSrcSeq,
MiscInt1,MiscInt2,MiscInt3,MiscInt4,
MiscInt5,MiscInt6,MiscInt7,MiscInt8,CkptInterval,byteflag,MLoadCkpt)
  VALUES (110, 1, 0, 1, 0, 0, 0, 0, 0, 0, 0, 0, 0, 1, :Ckpt);
**** 10:15:06 UTY0817 MultiLoad submitting the following request:
CHECKPOINT LOADING INTERVAL 0;
**** 10:15:07 UTY0817 MultiLoad submitting the following request:
USING Ckpt(VARBYTE(1024)) INSERT SYSDBA.Restartlog723_mld       (Logty
Seq, MLoadSeq, MLoadImpSeq, MLoadSrcSeq,
MiscInt1,MiscInt2,MiscInt3,MiscInt4,
MiscInt5,MiscInt6,MiscInt7,MiscInt8,CkptInterval,byteflag,MLoadCkpt)
  VALUES (110, 1, 1, 1, 0, 4, 4, 4, 4, 0, 0, 0, 0, 0, 1, :Ckpt);
**** 10:15:07 UTY0826 A checkpoint has been taken, recording that end of file
has been reached for IMPORT 1 of this MultiLoad Import task.
**** 10:15:07 UTY0817 MultiLoad submitting the following request:
CHECKPOINT LOADING INTERVAL 1;
**** 10:15:08 UTY0817 MultiLoad submitting the following request:
USING Ckpt(VARBYTE(1024)) INSERT SYSDBA.Restartlog723_mld
(Logtype, Seq, MLoadSeq, MLoadImpSeq, MLoadSrcSeq,
MiscInt1,MiscInt2,MiscInt3,MiscInt4,
MiscInt5,MiscInt6,MiscInt7,MiscInt8,CkptInterval,byteflag,MLoadCkpt)
  VALUES (110, 1, 2, 1, 0, 4, 4, 4, 4, 0, 0, 0, 0, 1, 1, :Ckpt);
**** 10:15:08 UTY1803 Import processing statistics
.                                     IMPORT  1      Total thus far
.                                     ========       ==============
Candidate records considered:........      4.......             4
Apply conditions satisfied:.........      4.......             4
Candidate records not applied:.......      0.......             0
Candidate records rejected:.........      0.......             0
**** 10:15:08 UTY1821 Acquisition Phase statistics
Elapsed time:   00:00:04
CPU time:       0.0156001 Seconds
MB/sec:         2.5e-005
MB/cpusec:      0.00641022
**** 10:15:08 UTY0817 MultiLoad submitting the following request:
CHECKPOINT LOADING INTERVAL 1;
**** 10:15:09 UTY0817 MultiLoad submitting the following request:
CHECKPOINT LOADING INTERVAL 1 END;
**** 10:15:11 UTY0817 MultiLoad submitting the following request:
INS SYSDBA.Restartlog723_mld (LogType, Seq, MLoadSeq)VALUES(130, 1, 30);
```

```
Query (local) ✕   History ✕   Answerset 1 ✕   Answerse

CREATE SET TABLE td_cookbook_nyse.mktprice ,NO FALLBACK ,
    NO BEFORE JOURNAL,
    NO AFTER JOURNAL,
    CHECKSUM = DEFAULT,
    DEFAULT MERGEBLOCKRATIO
    (
    symbol CHAR(10) CHARACTER SET LATIN NOT CASESPECIFIC,
    id varchar(10),
    open_share DECIMAL(18,0)
    )
    PRIMARY INDEX ( id );
```

```
/*UPSERT create table*/
CREATE SET TABLE td_cookbook_nyse.mktprice ,NO FALLBACK ,
     NO BEFORE JOURNAL,
     NO AFTER JOURNAL,
     CHECKSUM = DEFAULT,
     DEFAULT MERGEBLOCKRATIO
     (
     symbol CHAR(10) CHARACTER SET LATIN NOT CASESPECIFIC,
      id varchar(10),
      open_share DECIMAL(18,0)
      )
     PRIMARY INDEX ( id );
```

Let's populate this table with some data. UPSERT will be done based on these values:

```
/*Insert values*/
insert into td_cookbook_nyse.mktprice values ('tdc','1',200);
insert into td_cookbook_nyse.mktprice values  ('Goog','2',520);
insert into td_cookbook_nyse.mktprice values ('YAHOO','3',70);
insert into td_cookbook_nyse.mktprice values ('UB','4',20);
```

Let's create a raw file, which will be ', ' separated. We will add four values to this file. Rows which will be based on this raw file will be updated, and new values will be inserted into the table. Save this file into any folder on the local desktop with the name price_match.txt

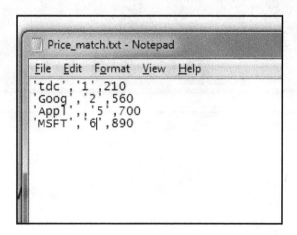

```
/*Raw data for UPSERT*/
tdc,1,210
Goog,2,560
Appl,,5,700 /* Missing id column value */
MSFT,6,890
```

How to do it...

1. Connect to the Teradata Database via SQLA or Studio.

2. Create the following MLOAD script and save it on the local desktop:

```
/*UPSERT script*/
.LOGTABLE Restart_log_ml;
.LOGON 192.168.0.12/sysdba,password;
.BEGIN IMPORT MLOAD TABLES td_cookbook_nyse.mktprice;
.LAYOUT Inputfile_layout; /* Definition of input layout */
.FIELD in_symbol * VARCHAR(25);
.FIELD in_id * varchar(10);
.FIELD in_open_share * VARCHAR(30);
.DML LABEL Fix_Price DO INSERT FOR MISSING UPDATE
ROWS;/*Definitionofan UPSERT*/

 UPDATE td_cookbook_nyse.mktprice SET open_share = :in_open_share
 WHERE symbol = :in_symbol
and id=:in_id
;

 INSERT INTO td_cookbook_nyse.mktprice VALUES
(:in_symbol,in_id,:in_open_share);
.IMPORT INFILE C:\Users\AK\Desktop\CookBook\Price_match.txt /*File
name to import from*/
FORMAT VARTEXT ','
LAYOUT Inputfile_layout APPLY Fix_Price;
.END MLOAD;
.LOGOFF;
```

3. Open Windows command prompt and execute the following command:

```
/*MLOAD execution command*/
mload < path_name\filename > ml_upsert.log
```

4. Once the command is complete, you can execute `more` to check the log file:

```
                      MultiLoad Acquisition Phase
==============================================================================
**** 10:15:04 UTY0817 MultiLoad submitting the following request:
BEGIN TRANSACTION;
**** 10:15:04 UTY0817 MultiLoad submitting the following request:
CHECKPOINT LOADING INTERVAL 0;
**** 10:15:04 UTY0817 MultiLoad submitting the following request:
CHECKPOINT LOADING INTERVAL 0;
**** 10:15:05 UTY0817 MultiLoad submitting the following request:
CHECKPOINT LOADING INTERVAL 0;
**** 10:15:06 UTY0817 MultiLoad submitting the following request:
USING Ckpt(VARBYTE(1024)) INSERT SYSDBA.Restartlog723_mld       (Logty
Seq, MLoadSeq, MLoadImpSeq, MLoadSrcSeq,
MiscInt1,MiscInt2,MiscInt3,MiscInt4,
MiscInt5,MiscInt6,MiscInt7,MiscInt8,CkptInterval,byteflag,MLoadCkpt)
   VALUES (110, 1, 0, 1, 0, 0, 0, 0, 0, 0, 0, 0, 0, 1, :Ckpt);
**** 10:15:06 UTY0817 MultiLoad submitting the following request:
CHECKPOINT LOADING INTERVAL 0;
**** 10:15:07 UTY0817 MultiLoad submitting the following request:
USING Ckpt(VARBYTE(1024)) INSERT SYSDBA.Restartlog723_mld       (Logty
Seq, MLoadSeq, MLoadImpSeq, MLoadSrcSeq,
MiscInt1,MiscInt2,MiscInt3,MiscInt4,
MiscInt5,MiscInt6,MiscInt7,MiscInt8,CkptInterval,byteflag,MLoadCkpt)
   VALUES (110, 1, 1, 0, 4, 4, 4, 4, 0, 0, 0, 0, 0, 1, :Ckpt);
**** 10:15:07 UTY0826 A checkpoint has been taken, recording that end of file
has been reached for IMPORT 1 of this MultiLoad Import task.
**** 10:15:07 UTY0817 MultiLoad submitting the following request:
CHECKPOINT LOADING INTERVAL 1;
**** 10:15:08 UTY0817 MultiLoad submitting the following request:
USING Ckpt(VARBYTE(1024)) INSERT SYSDBA.Restartlog723_mld
(Logtype, Seq, MLoadImpSeq, MLoadSrcSeq,
MiscInt1,MiscInt2,MiscInt3,MiscInt4,
MiscInt5,MiscInt6,MiscInt7,MiscInt8,CkptInterval,byteflag,MLoadCkpt)
   VALUES (110, 1, 2, 1, 0, 4, 4, 4, 4, 0, 0, 0, 0, 1, 1, :Ckpt);
**** 10:15:08 UTY1803 Import processing statistics
 .                                          IMPORT  1      Total thus far
 .                                          ========       ==============
Candidate records considered:........         4......            4
Apply conditions satisfied:.......            4......            4
Candidate records not applied:......          0......            0
Candidate records rejected:..........         0......            0
**** 10:15:08 UTY1821 Aquisition Phase statistics
Elapsed time:    00:00:04
CPU time:        0.0156001 Seconds
MB/sec:          2.5e-005
MB/cpusec:       0.00641022
**** 10:15:08 UTY0817 MultiLoad submitting the following request:
CHECKPOINT LOADING INTERVAL 1;
**** 10:15:09 UTY0817 MultiLoad submitting the following request:
CHECKPOINT LOADING INTERVAL 1 END;
**** 10:15:11 UTY0817 MultiLoad submitting the following request:
INS SYSDBA.Restartlog723_mld (LogType, Seq, MLoadSeq)VALUES(130, 1, 30);
```

5. We can see that all four records have been applied without any record being error out.

6. Execute the `Select` command on the table to verify the results:

symbol ▽	id	open_share
1 YAHOO	3	70
2 UB	4	20
3 tdc	1	210
4 MSFT	6	890
5 Goog	2	560
6 Appl	?	5

How it works...

In our script, we have the following update condition:

```
UPDATE td_cookbook_nyse.mktprice SET open_share = :in_open_share
 WHERE symbol = :in_symbol
and id=:in_id
;
```

Records in the file will be checked against the table in Teradata. We have only two matching records, which are `tdc` and `Goog`; their values will be updated in the table and the new values `Appl` and `MSFT` will be written to the table as new records as shown in figure:

sym bol ▽	id	open_s hare
1 YAHOO	3	70
2 UB	4	20
3 tdc	1	210
4 MSFT	6	890
5 Goog	2	560
6 Appl	?	5

Have you noticed the ? against `Appl`? This is because, in our raw file, we have kept this value as missing.

There's more...

There are many operators in MLOAD, some are descried as follows:

- `.LAYOUT`: Reads input variables from a host input data file.
- `.BEGIN`: Specifies the tables, and optionally, the work and the error tables used in this MultiLoad job. Also used to specify miscellaneous options, such as checkpoint, sessions, and so on.

```
.BEGIN   [IMPORT] [DELETE] MLOAD
TABLES     tname1, tname2, ...
WORKTABLES   wt_table1, wt_table2 /* could be database.tablename */
ERRORTABLES   et_table1 uv_table1, et_table2 uv_table2 /* Default
ET_Tablename */
ERRLIMIT    errcount  [errpercent] /*Approximate # of data errors
```

```
permitted during Acquisition */
CHECKPOINT    rate   (Default - 15 min.)
SESSIONS      limit  (Default - 1 per AMP + 2) /* Workload dependent
*/
TENACITY      hours  (Default - 4 hours)
SLEEP    minutes  (Default - 6 minutes)
```

- `.FIELD`: Inputs fields supporting redefinition and concatenation.
- `.DML`: Defines labels, along with error treatment conditions, for one or more `INSERT`s, `UPDATE`s or `DELETE`s.

Loading data from a one Teradata Database to another

In this recipe, we will lay the steps for how to transfer data from one Teradata Database to another.

This scenario is very common when you have a production database and you need to transfer pieces of rows to your development or testing box. We will use two separate Teradata boxes and copy tables from one to another using the Teradara parallel transporter, the TPT utility.

The **Teradara parallel transporter** (**TPT**) utility has the following features:

- Extracts data
- Loads data
- Updates data

TPT can be invoked via SQL like scripting, by using an API, or with a GUI interface known as TPT wizard. In this recipe, we will use TPT wizard. It is part of the standard Teradata Tools and Utility package, TTU.

The following is the comparison between TPT operators and Teradata utilities:

TPT operator	Teradata equivalent utility	Purpose
DDL operator	BTEQ	DDL, DML, and DCL statements
EXPORT operator	FastExport	Exports data from Teradata Database
LOAD	FastLoad	Loads data into empty table in Teradata
Stream operator	Tpump	Real-time data load using SQL protocol
Update operator	MultiLoad	Update, insert, and delete rows to existing tables

TPT is made of the following components:

- Load operator
- Update operator
- Export operator
- Stream

Getting ready

As we are going to transfer data from one Teradata box to another, you need to run two instances of VMs.

> Copy the Teradata VM image into two different locations to start two instances of Teradata on VMs.

Once you have your two VMs up and running, grab the IP addresses on both the machines. These IPs will be used to connect via TPT wizard.

To find IPs on Linux boxes, we use `ip addr`. Can we seen in following figure.

```
Terminal                                                    _ □ ✕

File  Edit  View  Terminal  Help
Your use is subject to the terms and conditions of
        the click through agreement that brought you to this
        screen ("TERADATA EXPRESS") EVALUATION AND DEVELOPMENT
        LICENSE AGREEMENT), including the restriction that this
        evaluation copy is not for production use.
TD-EXPRESS:~ # ip addr
1: lo: <LOOPBACK,UP,LOWER_UP> mtu 16436 qdisc noqueue state UNKNOWN
    link/loopback 00:00:00:00:00:00 brd 00:00:00:00:00:00
    inet 127.0.0.1/8 brd 127.255.255.255 scope host lo
    inet 127.0.0.2/8 brd 127.255.255.255 scope host secondary lo
    inet6 ::1/128 scope host
       valid_lft forever preferred_lft forever
2: eth0: <BROADCAST,MULTICAST,UP,LOWER_UP> mtu 1500 qdisc pfifo_fast state UP ql
en 1000
    link/ether 00:0c:29:2a:91:f3 brd ff:ff:ff:ff:ff:ff
    inet6 fe80::20c:29ff:fe2a:91f3/64 scope link tentative flags 08
       valid_lft forever preferred_lft forever
TD-EXPRESS:~ #
```

In the source VM, we will create the following table:

```
/*TPT source table*/
CREATE SET TABLE td_cookbook_nyse.tpt_source,NO FALLBACK ,
    NO BEFORE JOURNAL,
    NO AFTER JOURNAL,
    CHECKSUM = DEFAULT,
    DEFAULT MERGEBLOCKRATIO
    (
                symbol CHAR(10) CHARACTER SET LATIN NOT CASESPECIFIC,
                id char(2),
      open_share DECIMAL(18,0)
                )
    PRIMARY INDEX ( id );
```

We will insert the following rows:

```
/*TPT table insert values*/
insert into td_cookbook_nyse.mktprice values ('TDC',4,220);
insert into td_cookbook_nyse.mktprice values ('GOOG',9,250);
insert into td_cookbook_nyse.mktprice values ('APPL',14,260);
insert into td_cookbook_nyse.mktprice values ('MSFT',17,210);
insert into td_cookbook_nyse.mktprice values ('UBR',3,720);
insert into td_cookbook_nyse.mktprice values ('ITUN',2,320);
```

Second VMware would be running our target Teradata box, we will be copying data into this target Teradata instance. A target table is created with same DDL as source.

How to do it...

1. Open the **Teradata Parallel Transporter** wizard.
2. Click on **Edit,** then the **New** option:

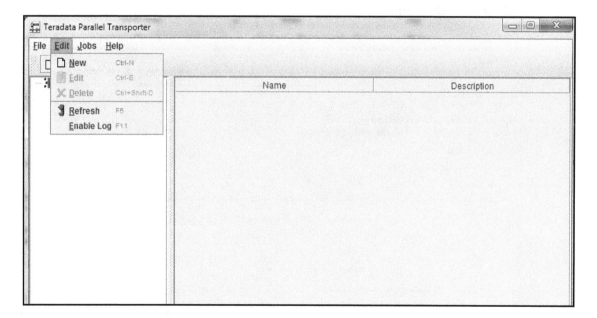

3. Give your **Job Name** as you like. In this, we will connect to the source system, the system from which data will be copied:

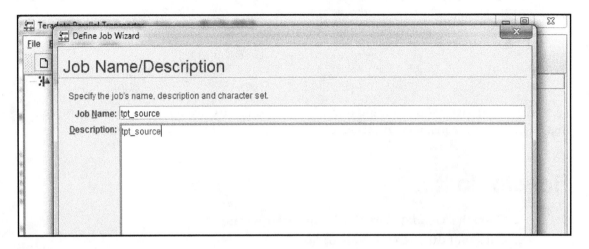

4. Connect to the source system:

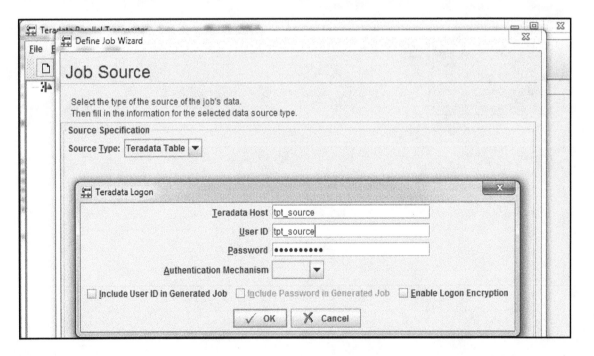

5. Select the source/destination table and column that you want to copy from. From the drop-down menu, select the **Teradata Table** option from the **Job Source** dialog box to log on to your Teradata system. Then select a specific table as a data source for a job, as shown in figure.

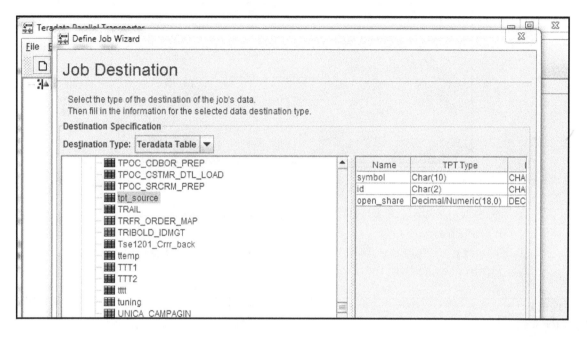

6. Click **Next**, and the **Job Destination** box will appear. In this, we will select where the data will be stored in the destination or target Teradata box, check following figure.

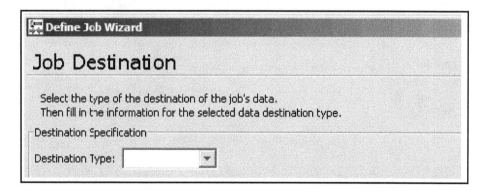

7. We will select the option **Teradata table** from the drop-down menu.
8. On the next screen, you need to log on to the target Teradata box, as seen in the following screenshot:

Teradata Logon screen

9. The next screen will be **Job destination**, and the database object will be displayed in a tree format.
10. Select **Load Operator** from the next screen option. Read the other options if required, as shown in the following screenshot:

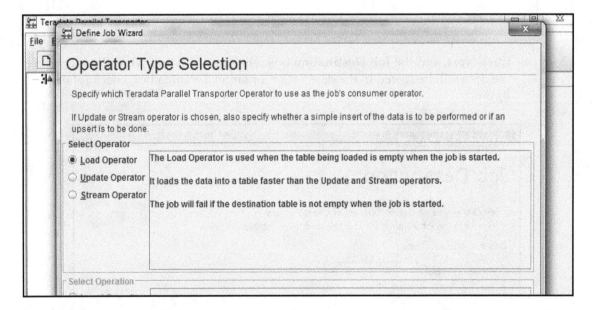

11. In the next screen, map the columns from the source to target. If the number of columns is mismatched between the source and destination, manual mapping will be required. The following is a snapshot of how the screen looks:

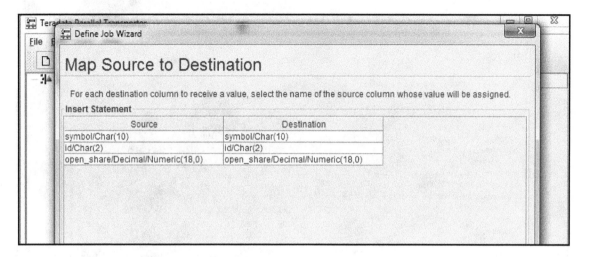

12. Click **Next** to open the **Finish Job** dialog box, as shown in the following screenshot:

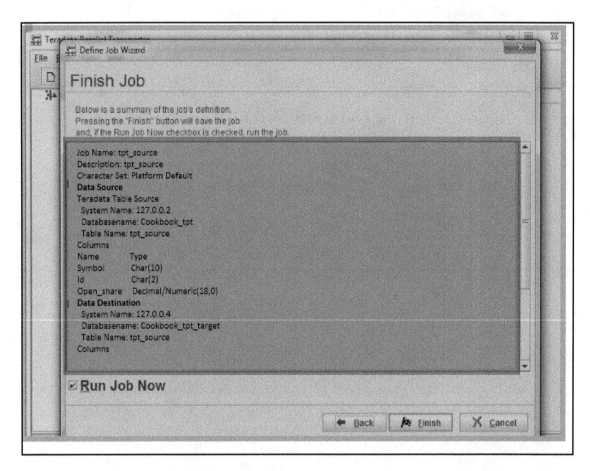

The Finish Job dialog box

13. After clicking on **Finish Job**, the **Run** window will appear:

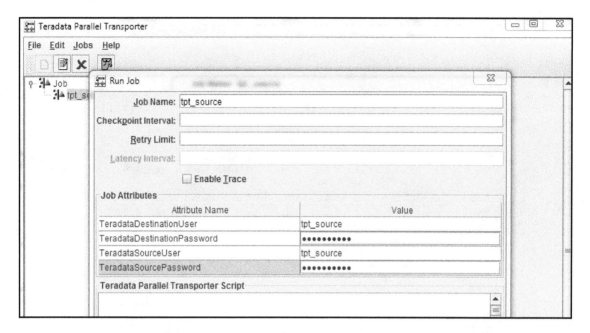

14. Enter the **Checkpoint Interval,** the time in seconds between checkpoint intervals. The value chosen should be of minutes and not in seconds.

15. If **Job Attributes** is available, type the name and password for the source table and the target table.

16. Check the output of the job in the following window:

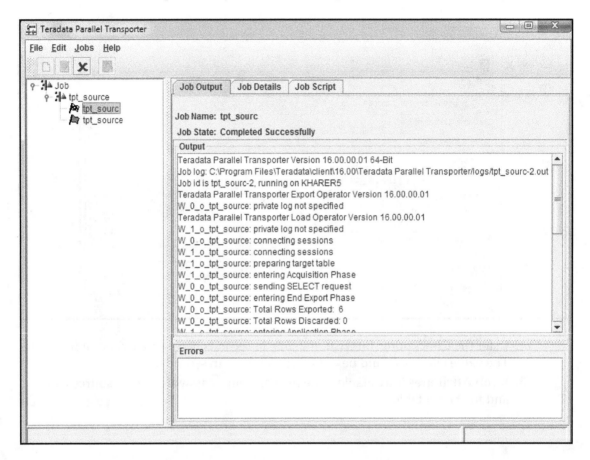

17. Do a SELECT on the target table to verify the data in the table.

18. The following is the script generated at the backend that can be used to execute by changing the parameters:

```
/*TPT script*/

/* 1 */
/* 2 */
/* 3 */ DEFINE JOB tpt_source
/* 4 */ DESCRIPTION 'tpt_source'
/* 5 */ (
/* 6 */ DEFINE OPERATOR W_1_o_tpt_source
/* 7 */ TYPE LOAD
/* 8 */ SCHEMA *
```

```
/* 9 */ ATTRIBUTES
/* 10 */ (
/* 11 */ VARCHAR UserName,
/* 12 */ VARCHAR UserPassword,
/* 13 */ VARCHAR LogonMech,
/* 14 */ VARCHAR LogonMechData,
/* 15 */ VARCHAR LogTable,
/* 16 */ VARCHAR TargetTable,
/* 17 */ INTEGER BufferSize,
/* 18 */ INTEGER ErrorLimit,
/* 19 */ INTEGER MaxSessions,
/* 20 */ INTEGER MinSessions,
/* 21 */ INTEGER TenacityHours,
/* 22 */ INTEGER TenacitySleep,
/* 23 */ VARCHAR AccountID,
/* 24 */ VARCHAR DateForm,
/* 25 */ VARCHAR ErrorTable1,
/* 26 */ VARCHAR ErrorTable2,
/* 27 */ VARCHAR NotifyExit,
/* 28 */ VARCHAR NotifyExitIsDLL,
/* 29 */ VARCHAR NotifyLevel,
/* 30 */ VARCHAR NotifyMethod,
/* 31 */ VARCHAR NotifyString,
/* 32 */ VARCHAR PauseAcq,
/* 33 */ VARCHAR PrivateLogName,
/* 34 */ VARCHAR TdpId,
/* 35 */ VARCHAR TraceLevel,
/* 36 */ VARCHAR WorkingDatabase
/* 37 */ );
/* 38 */
/* 39 */ DEFINE SCHEMA W_0_s_tpt_source
/* 40 */ (
/* 41 */ symbol CHARACTER(10),
/* 42 */ id_1 CHARACTER(2),
/* 43 */ open_share DECIMAL(18)
/* 44 */ );
/* 45 */
/* 46 */ DEFINE OPERATOR W_0_o_tpt_source
/* 47 */ TYPE EXPORT
/* 48 */ SCHEMA W_0_s_tpt_source
/* 49 */ ATTRIBUTES
/* 50 */ (
/* 51 */ VARCHAR UserName,
/* 52 */ VARCHAR UserPassword,
/* 53 */ VARCHAR LogonMech,
/* 54 */ VARCHAR LogonMechData,
/* 55 */ VARCHAR SelectStmt,
/* 56 */ INTEGER BlockSize,
```

```
/* 57 */ INTEGER MaxSessions,
/* 58 */ INTEGER MinSessions,
/* 59 */ INTEGER TenacityHours,
/* 60 */ INTEGER TenacitySleep,
/* 61 */ INTEGER MaxDecimalDigits,
/* 62 */ VARCHAR AccountID,
/* 63 */ VARCHAR DateForm,
/* 64 */ VARCHAR NotifyExit,
/* 65 */ VARCHAR NotifyExitIsDLL,
/* 66 */ VARCHAR NotifyLevel,
/* 67 */ VARCHAR NotifyMethod,
/* 68 */ VARCHAR NotifyString,
/* 69 */ VARCHAR PrivateLogName,
/* 70 */ VARCHAR TdpId,
/* 71 */ VARCHAR TraceLevel,
/* 72 */ VARCHAR WorkingDatabase
/* 73 */ );
/* 74 */
/* 75 */ APPLY
/* 76 */ (
/* 77 */ 'INSERT INTO COOKBOOK_TPT_TARGET.tpt_source
(symbol,id,open_share)
VALUES (:symbol,:id_1,:open_share);'
/* 78 */
/* 79 */ TO OPERATOR
/* 80 */ (/* 81 */ W_1_o_tpt_source[1]/* 82 */ /* 83 */
        ATTRIBUTES
/* 84 */ (
/* 85 */ UserName = @TeradataDestinationUser,/* 86 */
                        UserPassword =
@TeradataDestinationPassword,
/* 87 */ LogonMech = '',
/* 88 */ LogTable = 'COOKBOOK_WORK_IN.tpt_source_log',
/* 89 */ TargetTable = 'COOKBOOK_tpt.tpt_source',
/* 90 */ TdpId = '127.0.0.2'
/* 91 */ )
/* 92 */ )/* 93 */ SELECT * FROM OPERATOR
/* 94 */ (
/* 95 */ W_0_o_tpt_source[1]
/* 96 */
/* 97 */ ATTRIBUTES
/* 98 */ (
/* 99 */ UserName = @TeradataSourceUser,
/* 100 */ UserPassword = @TeradataSourcePassword,
/* 101 */ SelectStmt = 'SELECT symbol,id,open_share FROM
COOKBOOK_TPT.tpt_source;',
/* 102 */ TdpId = '127.0.0.4'
/* 103 */ )
```

```
/* 104 */ );
/* 105 */ );
```

How it works...

TPT uses a data stream which acts as a pipeline between operators, instead of serial like its counterpart utilities like fastload and Mload. The pipe established between operators helps in high-speed data transfer without been written to disk.

Data is written from one operator into the data stream, which acts as a **source** for another operator. Same is been illustrated in following figure.

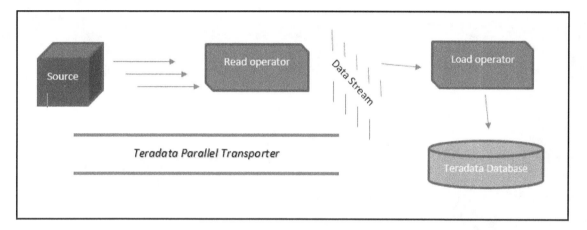

This can be seen the figure that how the data flows through the TPT.

How it works...

7
Monitoring the better way

In this chapter, let's learn about the general approach for monitoring your work on the Teradata system. The following recipes will be covered in this chapter:

- Configuring the viewpoint portlet
- Identifying killer queries in viewpoint
- Setting up viewpoint alerts
- Changing and managing filters
- Changing and managing throttle
- Defining a ruleset
- Creating a TASM exception

Introduction

There are many ways to monitor the performance of your work. Teradata has tools like viewpoint, where individual users can log on and check how their queries are executing on the system and how it is affecting the other workloads on the system. It empowers individual users to track their work, based on which they can take informed decisions about their queries. Inefficient requests can be killed or performance can be improve.

There are some terms that a user must understand when monitoring queries and workloads.

A query should be the perfect mix of CPU, I/O, and runtime. Finding that perfect mix is a critical task and takes a lot of effort sometimes. With today's growing query complexity and various different analysis needs, optimizing SQLs can be a daunting task.

Monitoring not only involves optimization techniques on the query level, but also on the system level. Like queries, there are some other system parameters that we need to keep track of:

- Nodes utilization
- AMP utilization
- PE utilization
- Logical disk utilization
- Network traffic on nodes
- Memory allocation, paging, and swapping activities on the nodes

To cook a good pizza, you not only need fresh ingredients, but you need a good oven to bake the pizza in, too.

Before we start monitoring and analyzing these parameters, let's understand what they stand for:

- **Average node CPU busy**: Average CPU busy, of all nodes.
- **Average AMP CPU busy**: Average CPU busy, of all AMP Vprocs.
- **Maximum node CPU busy**: Maximum CPU busy, of all nodes.
- **Maximum AMP CPU busy**: Maximum CPU busy, of all AMP Vprocs.
- **Node CPU skewing**: The ratio indicates how much longer work is taking than if the work was perfectly distributed over all nodes. *Skew = MAX(CPU) / AVG (CPU)*.
- **CPUUServ**: This column is derived from the `ResUsage` table, indicating the time, in centiseconds, the CPU is busy executing operating service code (that is, operating system services).
- **CPUUExec**: This column is derived from the `ResUsage` table, indicating the time, in centiseconds, the CPU is busy executing user service code.
- **MaxIOAmpNumber**: The number of the AMP with the highest I/O usage for this step:

```
/*BUSY CPU QUERY PER NODE*/
SELECT
NodeId as NodeID
,AVG(((CPUUserv + CPUUExec)/Nullifzero(NCPUs))/secs)as NodeCPUBsy
FROM
DBC.RESUSAGESPMA
where thedate=date
group by 1
```

There are many parameters that can be derived, as discussed, from the so-called performance tables. You just need to know what you are looking for.

We have various ways to monitor system resources. We can either build reports on tables, or we can use visual tools, like viewpoint, that show live system activity. But for historical data imprints and to check raw data, tables are your best bet. You need to know what to look for, and where to look for it, when it comes to data. There are several tables in Teradata that record the system activity over a period and can be useful to track the activity:

Table Name	What it Tracks
ResUsageIpma	System-wide node information
ResUsageIvpr	System-wide virtual processor information
ResUsageScpu	Information specific to the CPUs with the nodes
ResUSageShst	Information specific to the host channels and LANs that communicate with the Teradata RDBMS
ResUsageSldv	To measure max I/O response times
ResUsageSpma	System-wide node-level information
ResUsageSvpr	Data specific to each virtual processor (AMPs and PEs) and its file system; cache hit percentage

Let's talk about some of the tables in detail:

- **DBC.AccountInfo**: Provides a valid account name for a user. Columns like username or account name can be joined, with other tables, to the resources usage on the account level for active users on the system.
- **DBC.AMPUsage:** Provides details regarding the resources used in an AMP Vproc by user and account.

Data in this table is written in history tables after one day:

```
/* HOT AMP Execute this query in 10 mins interval to check which
AMP causes high CPU repeaditly*/
SELECT Vproc, sum(diskio),sum(cputime) from dbc.ampusage group by
1,2
```

Data in this table can be used for a plot trending graph and can be used for planning the capacity of the system. As data in this table is computed on AMP/Vproc, it can be used to identify slow AMPs when the system is running a skew work:

```
/*Number of AMP's on system*/
Select count(distinct Vproc) from dbc.ampusage
```

- **DBQL**: Used to log query activity for analysis. Query counts and response times can be charted and SQL text and processing steps can be analyzed. There are different sets of tables in DBQL that provide historical records, duration, performance, and activity on the system:
    - **DBQLogTbl**: Under DBQL, provides individual user query logging data, like CPU, I/O, parse time, SQL text. You can derive other performance related columns from this table.
    - **DBQLStepTbl**: This table consists of the step-level activity recorded, like CPU, I/O, and rows, for each query which has logging enabled. Check the following code.

```
/*STEP table*/
SELECT stepname,StepLev1Num,StepLev2Num,CPUTime,SpoolUsage
from dbc.dbqlsteptbl where queryid=163435711352446508
```

In this chapter, we will learn about how to monitor and manage the Teradata database.

Configuring the viewpoint portlet

Teradata viewpoint is an integrated, drop-in appliance with a rich, powerful, and robust web-based (and now mobile-based) interface that can monitor multiple Teradata database systems and provide actionable monitoring and management information to end users, DBAs, and managers.

Teradata viewpoint has many portlets, categorized under different subjects or contents, that need to be monitored or have actions taken upon them. Portlets are added to pages, and you can either have one portlet per page or many portlets on one page.

Teradata viewpoint 16.10 is the latest viewpoint available on the market.

Getting ready

You need to log on to the Teradata viewpoint page using a web browser.

How to do it...

1. Once logged on, you will be presented with a blank page (if the default portlet was not added by the admin before):

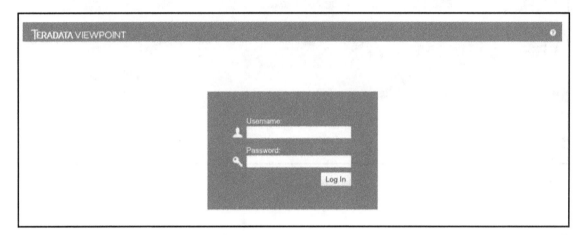

Viewpoint login page

2. Click on **add content**. This portlet will allow you to add several portlets to the page in a single go; you can add the same portlet multiple times, if required, by clicking on it.
3. Click **add**.
4. Select which portlets will be added to the page.

5. If you require adding multiple pages, click on **Add** to add more pages, and then add portlets to it. The following screenshot illustrates searching for a particular portlet:

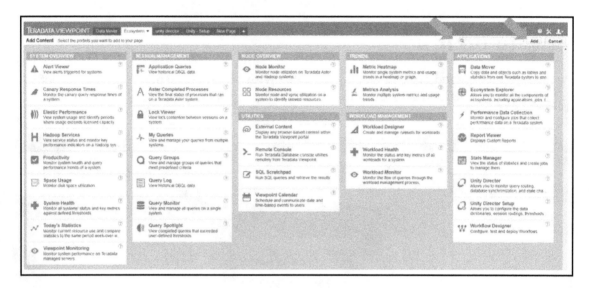

Viewpoint portlet page

How it works...

Teradata viewpoint is the one-stop shop for monitoring all the activities that are associated with the Teradata system. With the evolution of big data, viewpoint also gives you the capability to monitor the Hadoop jobs interacting with your Teradata system.

A user has multiple portlet at his disposal. Choosing the right portlet for its work is important. Or you might end up with multiple pages and portlets. One must also understand the reporting done by viewpoint; the interpretation of the data displayed by viewpoint lies with its users.

Some portlets, and their uses, are as follows:

Portlet	Function
Query monitor	Live view of queries executing on Teradata and Aster systems. Most used portlet.
System health	Live system performance indicator for Teradata, Hadoop, and Aster systems.
SQL scratchpad	Allows connecting to Teradata system to execute queries.
Alert viewer	Display and manage alerts for Teradata, Hadoop, and Aster systems.
Node resources	Monitor node and AMP/Vproc usage.
Query spotlight	Set of queries in a selected period of time.
Space usage	Monitoring and managing Teradata, Hadoop, and Aster database disk space.
Productivity	Graphical trend reporting, displaying current versus historical trends of key system metrics.
Hadoop services	Monitors status of Hadoop services.
Remote Console	Teradata database console utilities via your web browser.
Aster process	View of Aster process on the system.
Lock Viewer	Displays lock information of Teradata system.
External content	Allows integration of external content into viewpoint portlet.
Metric heatmap	Resources (CPU, IO, AWT) visualization in hotspot map.

Identifying killer queries in viewpoint

With thousands and millions of queries coming in and out of the Teradata system, it is important to find high-impact queries. Teradata provides various tools for query and workload management so that the system works at optimal performance.

We can use system tables like `resusage` and `pdcrinfo` to get the poorly performing user queries, which could be high CPU, I/O, and skewness. These could also be monitored in real time by using a GUI interface called **viewpoint**. You can also go back in time and check for the queries that have caused an adverse impact on the system.

In this recipe, we will use viewpoint to identify high impact or killer queries on your Teradata platform.

Getting ready

You need to log in to Teradata viewpoint and enable query monitoring and the query spotlight portlet.

How to do it...

1. Log in to Teradata viewpoint using your credentials.
2. Go to the query monitor portlet. All the live queries on the system can be seen here.
3. To identify currently impacting queries directly use TOP session by, you can sort current executing sessions by, as this highlighted in the screenshot:

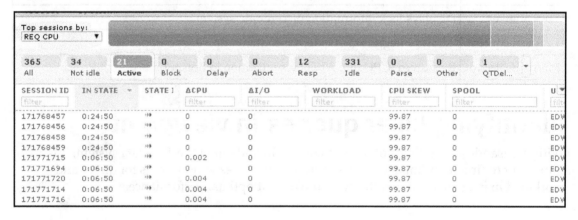

Query Monitor Portlet

4. In the query monitor, you can sort queries based on runtime, CPU, I/O, CPU usage, and many other parameters. This can be seen in the following figure:

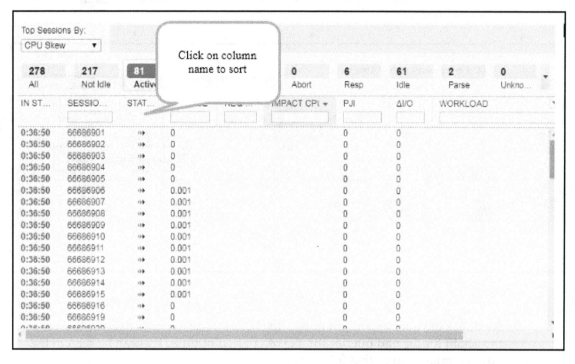

Query Monitor Portlet

5. To rewind and check previous executing sessions, click on the rewind window. Select the time to which you want to go back and check the system state. The rewind time on viewpoint depends on how much data has been retrieved in the viewpoint database. For better monitoring, it is recommended to save data for at least six months in the viewpoint database:

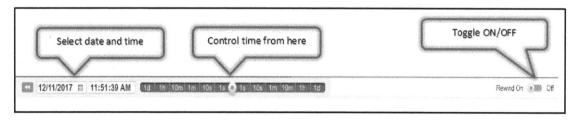

Viewpoint Rewind Option

6. If you require any session to be highlighted in the query monitor when it crosses a certain threshold, like duration, click on **properties** to open a configuration tab, and then put in the threshold values desired for the columns. Check the following figure:

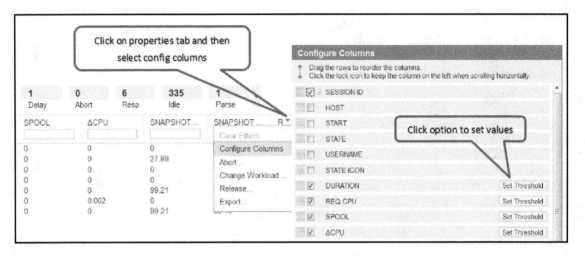

Viewpoint Configuration Option

7. Next, use the query spotlight portlet to check all sessions which cross the threshold for the bad queries for a given period of time. This can be seen in the query monitor figure that follows:

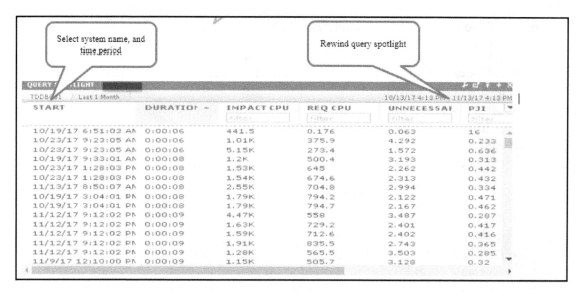

Query Spotlight Portlet

How it works...

The Teradata database provides fantastic live monitoring, which enables you to see the progress of submitted queries and target longer running and high resource consuming queries. It helps you to optimize them. After you have identified a problem query, you can take corrective measures by:

- Aborting the executing query right away
- Changing the workload
- Capturing the data and tuning the query before the next execution

The detail session view provides a table listing the sessions, account strings, users, or utilities running on the database.

You can also export the data, from either the query monitor as a whole or from a session window (for a particular query), into a .csv file. More importantly, wherever you see the **EXPORT** option, you can capture the data into a .csv file for analysis.

When you click on any session for analysis, you might see many parameters, and to make sense of some of them, check the following definitions:

- **CPU busy time**: `CPUUServ` + `CPUUExec`. This will be the total CPU, including the user and the system.
- **CPUIoWait**: This column is derived from the `ResUsage` table, indicating the total centiseconds that the CPU was idle while waiting for the disk or BYNET I/O to complete.
- **OS as % of CPU**: This is used to understand a balance between the operating system and database software CPU usage, calculated as *SUM(CPUUServ) * 100 / NULLIFZERO(SUM(CPUBusy))*.
- **Request CPU**: Number of CPU seconds that have been used by the current step in the query.
- **Delta CPU**: Number of CPU seconds consumed during the latest session sampling period. This can be used to identify sessions that took more CPU at the last sampling time. If the value under this column is not changing for longer duration, it can indicate hung system issues.
- **Request I/O**: Total number of I/Os for the current request.
- **I/O Skew**: In percentage, represent skewness of a query when compared to the hottest AMP. I/O taken during the last sample period to the average AMP I/O count during the last sample period.
- **Disk I/Os**: Number of I/Os and volume in KB, which can be used to calculate MB/sec per node.

There's more...

The key metrics to look for include:

- Response time
- Resource utilization
- Data growth, such as number of rows or changes in data demographics (unique values)
- Changes in data access (insert, delete, update)
- Increases in the number of active sessions (concurrent queries)
- Keeping a record of environmental changes, such as new applications or changes in data loading strategies (node, AMP, cache)

As the saying goes, prevention is better than cure. A monitoring system has its benefits:

- Manage available resources optimally
- Maximize the value of a data warehouse investment
- Extend the life of the current Teradata investment
- Ensure that actions are being taken to meet the service levels that the business needs
- Align client business priorities with job/query-level system resource priorities
- Maximize query performance and data load performance

The following table shows some key measures and tools that are at the disposal of admins to monitor the performance of the system:

Measure	Tool	Tracking/Recording	What to Check
Response time	Canary Queries	Response time samples, avg response time in workload	Avg run time over the day. Samples can be compared to get optimal response time.
Resource utilization	DBQL, resusage, ampusage	High CPU, high I/O, node usage	High CPU, product join, and I/O intensive queries. Peaks, avg, day-wise data.
Growth	DBC, PDCR	Table size, skew	Data growth, driving factors, a sudden increase in space.
Data access	DBC, query logging	Data access by users and batch	Change in access pattern, hot and old tables. High usage tables.
Run time	Query logging, PDCR	Workload-wise, day-wise break up	Specific increase in run time. Kind of query, access specific database.
Active users	Logoff, ACCTG	Workload-wise, AVG, active session, concurrent sessions	Unique active users, state-wise, access usage.
Utility jobs	PDCR	Kind of load jobs active, separate workload wise	Rows loading using utility, kind of users using it. Most favorite utility in user community.

Although the standard monitoring and other best practices can be in place, you always need to set up an alarm system in case runaway queries or unaccounted activity occurs on the system. We will discuss these alerts at length in upcoming recipes.

Setting up viewpoint alerts

Teradata provides many tools to monitor and manage your database. Viewpoint is one of the tools that provides you an inner view of your database. Viewpoint not only helps you to govern your jobs on the system, but reports any unwanted activity on the system. With Teradata viewpoint 16.0, you can use viewpoint on your mobile devices, too.

Viewpoint is a best friend tool for any admin to monitor the system in real time. Teradata makes it possible to live view your whole system in a 360-view. You can do the following with Teradata viewpoint:

- Create and manage a workload
- View and report Hadoop and Aster systems
- Manage and report query activity
- Use the remote console utility
- Monitor and manage PDCR jobs
- Monitor and manage backup jobs
- Monitor viewpoint on mobile
- Manage and report space
- Manage and report CPU, I/O, and other performance parameters

Viewpoint alerts can be set up for all activities that you monitor on viewpoint. Some cases include high PJI sessions, high spool consuming sessions, and long running sessions. Through viewpoint, you can set thresholds for such cases, which trigger events in the forms of email, SQL executions, and so on, when such an event occurs; for example, if you want to receive an email alert for the sessions you are monitoring on viewpoint which exceed a certain spool limit. Alerts monitor the performance of a system and automatically take action when events occur. You can add, copy, and configure alerts, as well as migrate Teradata Manager Alerts. You can activate alert actions that send a notification, or take some other type of action, when a metric exceeds a threshold.

In this recipe, we will create and set up the thresholds of an alert.

Getting ready

You need to connect to Teradata viewpoint and log in using an administrator account, with access to creating alerts.

How to do it...

1. Log in to Teradata viewpoint using an admin account.
2. Click on the tools icon in the upper right-hand corner, as shown in the screenshot:

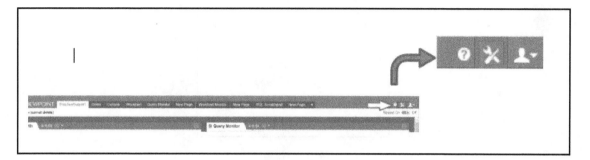

Viewpoint Configuration Option

3. An administrative window will open; click on **Alert Setup,** as shown in the following screenshot:

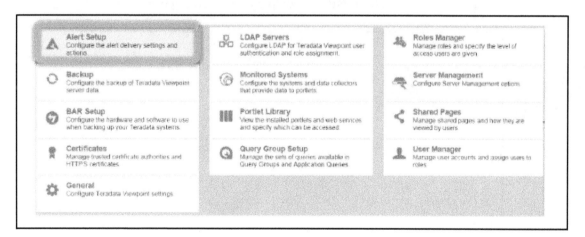

Viewpoint Setting Page

4. Next, we will click on **Delivery Settings**, which will help you to deliver alerts via email or store them in Teradata tables. In this recipe, we will set up email delivery. As highlighted in the figure, click on **Delivery Settings | Email**:

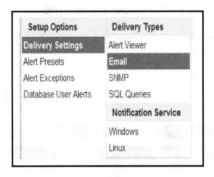

Alert Settings

5. In the next window, we will be entering information regarding your email server, like smtp host, port number, and login details. On this page, under **Login,** it is recommended to use an anonymous login. Provide the email address (probably a group distribution list, dl) with the display name you want:

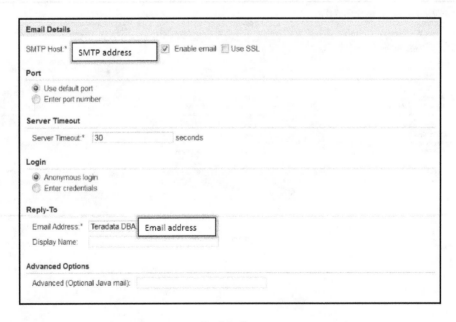

Alert Option Page

6. There are also other options in alert setup that you can configure if required, like scheduling the time from which an alert will start.

7. Once you have configured the alert settings in the alert setup window, you can now open the **Monitored Systems** window to start adding alerts on various activities:

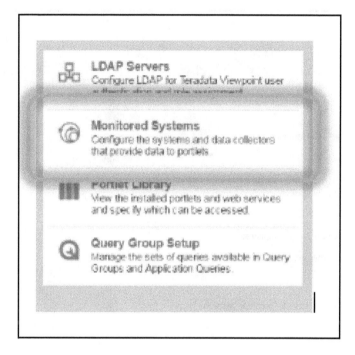

Viewpoint Setting Page

8. Select your system under the **Systems** tab and then select **Alerts** under the **Setup** tab. Under the **Alert Types** tab, select the activity on which you want to set the alert. Since we are interested in setting alerts on sessions, we will select **Session** under the **Alert Types** tab. In the following screenshot, we have set up a table space alert on a transient journal table under DBC:

Table Space Alert Setting

9. Under **Alert Action**, you can select the following action, if you want to take an action other than email:

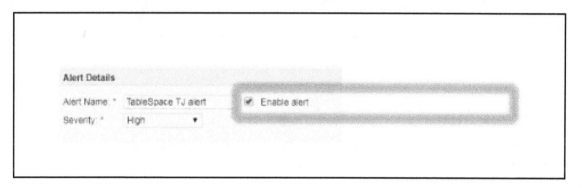

Alert Action

10. Click **Apply** to activate the alert. If you want to disable the alert, uncheck the following option:

Alert Action

How it works...

Once you have set up the alert on the viewpoint, the defined action on alert will take place. You can also define the time over which this alert won't run twice. If you reduce this value to the minimum, you will get flooded with email alerts. This value should be based on the importance or urgency of the alert.

As we know, we can also schedule alerts based on the time of the day. These alerts are useful when we have separate windows defined, for example, if you want to have backup related alerts only on weekends and not on weekdays. As shown in the following screenshot, you can select appropriate timings as per requirement:

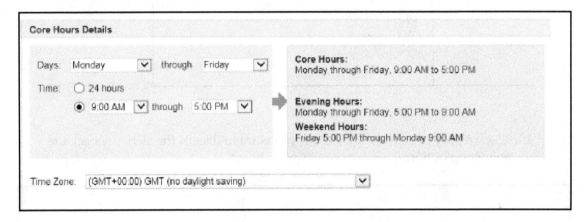

Alert setting

There's more...

There are many different types of alerts that you can configure on viewpoint. The following is a list of alert types:

- Canary queries
- HDFS, MapReduce (HDP 1.1 and 1.3)
- Node
- Process
- System
- Vproc
- Data collectors
- Database space
- Events
- Session
- System dealt
- Table space

Teradata viewpoint is also available on a cloud platform. You can install viewpoint from the AWS cloud market platform. Viewpoint can be used to view one standalone system or multiple systems in a cluster.

There are three viewpoint options available in this offer:

- Single Teradata system viewpoint
- Multiple Teradata systems viewpoint
- Single Teradata system with Teradata data lab

Changing and managing filters

Teradata workload designer portlet on viewpoint helps you to manage and create workloads. As we know, a workload on a system has many parameters attached to it. Any query, before hitting the system, needs to be classified under a particular workload. Once classified, this query goes through a filter check. Imagine this filter as a security guard for a building; he keeps a note of everyone going into a building. And if he has a list of people who are not allowed to enter a building, he will disallow them and stop them from entering the building.

Workload throttle works in the same fashion. Filters stop or give warnings, based on bad queries hitting the system. You can define rules like:

- Block high estimated runtime queries
- Block queries on selected objects
- Block queries with certain join times
- Block queries with high row estimations
- Block queries from specific users or IPs

It is recommended to create a filter in warning mode first before aborting queries, so that you can make sure throttles are working as expected. The figure shows the **Filter** option from viewpoint:

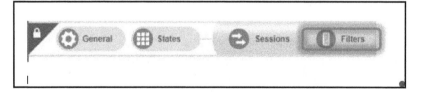

Workload Filter Option

Getting ready

You need to connect to Teradata viewpoint and open the viewpoint workload designer portlet.

How to do it...

1. You need to connect to Teradata viewpoint using an admin account.
2. Open any previously defined ruleset. Click on Rule set and select the option **Unlock,** and then **Show**. The following is the block diagram representing the workload designer view:

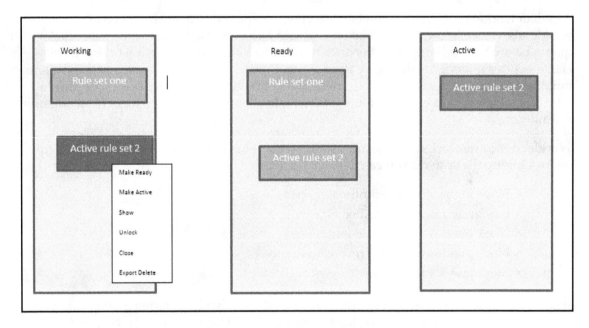

Workload Designer

3. Next, click on **Show** to open the ruleset.

4. In the next window, click on the filter window:

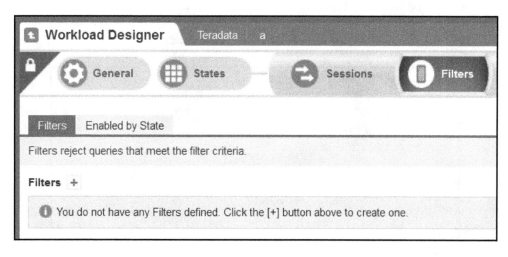

Workload Designer Window

5. Provide the name and description of the filter, so that its role can be identified:

Workload Designer Setting

6. Next, click on the **Classification** tab; here we will define filter rules based on selection criteria to stop queries from entering the system. You can select from various options from the drop-down menu; we will select the Request source option in this recipe, as shown in the screenshot:

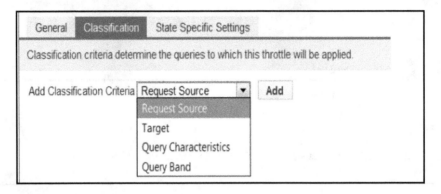

Workload Designer Classification Setting

7. In this recipe, we will select a Profile, and restrict users under selected profile. Check the following figure from viewpoint.

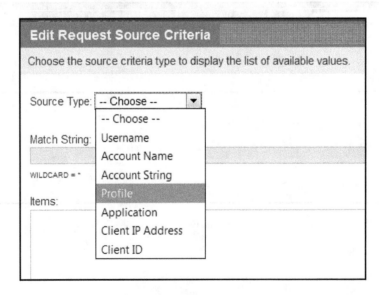

Workload Designer Classification Setting

8. Next, from the list of profile displayed, select one or multiple profiles on which you want to restrict access. We will select all profiles by using * as show in figure.

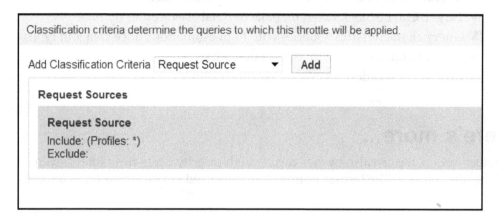

Classification criteria determine the queries to which this throttle will be applied.

Add Classification Criteria Request Source ▼ **Add**

Request Sources

Request Source
Include: (Profiles: *)
Exclude:

Workload Designer Classification Setting

9. Next, click on the **State** option and select under which you want this filter to be enabled.
10. Once done, click on **Save**.
11. To take this filter into effect, you need to go to the main option in step 1 and click on **Ready** for the ruleset. And once your ruleset is in a ready state, click on **Active**. And once your workload is in an active state, a new filter will be activated.

How it works...

Filters are a great way to stop any bad query or limit the certain object or user access to the system. It's a preventative measure that can help admins to avoid any unwanted activity on the system.

By limiting object or user access, it also helps to maintain security access to the system. Tables with critical data or information can be blocked and reported from time to time.

As we have seen, the following criteria can be used to filter queries or users:

- **Request source**: Can block one or a set of IPs or users
- **Target**: Can be block based on table or database or other options
- **Query characteristics**: Queries with high estimations or certain join types
- **Query band**: Queries with certain query bands
- **Utility**: Application specific or loading utilities

There's more...

In another option, we can also bypass certain high priority users from filters, even if they meet the filter criteria. The bypass option should be used very cautiously, as bypass is not applied at the rule level.

 DBC user is always bypassed.

Another way to use the filter option in a cautioned way is to use it under the **warning mode**. This will check the queries for filter rules and, based on the rule met, instead of aborting, it will only give a warning. These queries will be recorded in the DBQL table. Admins can plot the data against the incoming request and the warning it is creating. If you find that the number of warnings is high, it means high impact work is coming into the system. But it is also recommended to check that only the right queries are creating warnings, and if you find some rightful query being classified as a warning, you might want to change the filter.

Changing and managing throttle

Teradata workload management provides another great way to optimize and monitor your system.

Throttles help in limiting the work coming into the system. They are a way to reduce and maintain concurrent queries or requests on the system. Imagine a highway without a red light in place. There would be no traffic management, and all the roads would become jammed. Even if your roads are capable of handling high amounts of traffic, unmanaged traffic will create chaos.

Similar is true for the Teradata database; to keep the system throughput effective all the time, it is important to limit the number of work requests coming into the system.

The following flowchart shows the lifetime of a query on a system:

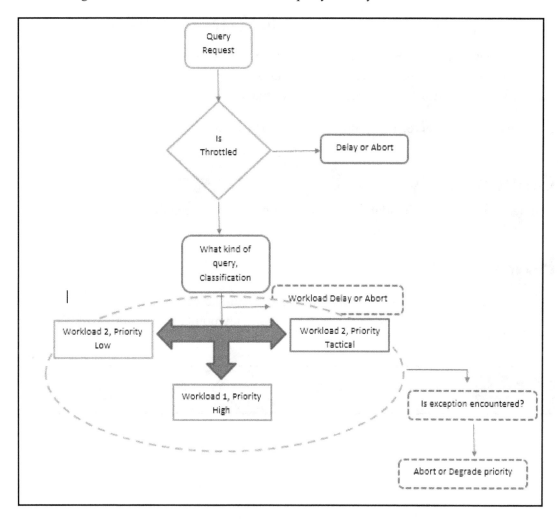

Query Request Workflow

Teradata 16 has a feature known as **flex throttle**, which is self intelligent throttle that auto-adjusts itself based on the system workload.

The following are some different kinds of throttles available:

- **Session throttles** limit active sessions and reject new sessions
- **Query throttles** limit concurrent queries and reject/delay new queries
- **Utility throttles** limit concurrent utility jobs and reject/delay new jobs

In this recipe, we will create a throttle definition for a workload.

Getting ready

You need to connect to Teradata viewpoint using an admin account.

How to do it...

1. Log in to Teradata viewpoint using an admin account.
2. Open the **Workload Designer** portlet on viewpoint. Click on the **Throttle** option, as highlighted in the following figure:

Workload Throttle Option

3. Next, under the system throttle, click on the + sign to create a new throttle, as shown in the following screenshot; enter a name and description as required:

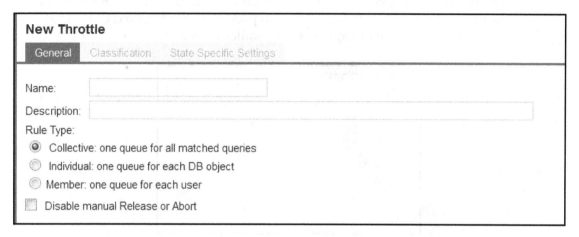

New Throttle

| General | Classification | State Specific Settings |

Name:

Description:

Rule Type:

⦿ Collective: one queue for all matched queries

◯ Individual: one queue for each DB object

◯ Member: one queue for each user

☐ Disable manual Release or Abort

Workload Throttle Setting

4. Next, click on the **Classification** tab, and select **Request Source** from the drop-down menu under **Add Classification Criteria**. This can be seen in the following screenshot:

5. Once you have clicked on **Request Source**, the next window will pop up with an edit option for the selected source. From the drop-down menu choose the **profile** option. This will populate all the profiles in your system. Select the required profile and click on **OK**.

> To select all profiles, write * in the profile name column.

6. You can also exclude some users or utilities in that profile from this throttle, as required.

7. Next, click on the state **Specific** tab. In this tab, we will specify the limit or throttle value. The number mentioned here will allow only that count of requests for the throttle created. Also, you have a option to delay or reject the query that meets the threshold limit. In our case, all profile users are limited to 10. That means the total count of requests from profiles is limited to 10:

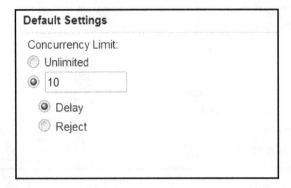

Workload Throttle Setting

8. Once done, click on **Save**.
9. To make this throttle active, you need to go to the main option in step 1 and click on **Ready for the ruleset**. And once your ruleset is in a ready state, click on **Active**. And once your ruleset is in an active state, the new throttle will be activated.

How it works...

Throttles works on four levels in Teradata (from Teradata database version 16.0). A request, once classified into a particular workload, needs to go through all the throttles, if defined on the system. These throttles can be:

- The entire system
- Workload specific or groups of throttles
- Virtual partitions
- Utility jobs

You also need to take a note that the throttle does not affect jobs already running on the system; once a job/request is in an active state, it can't be put into delay. To take care of these active jobs, the Teradata workload has exceptions defined.

One other way to check if your throttles are working fine is to check the delay queue. If your request is delayed for more time and in a high number from a particular throttle rule, you might need to increase the throttling value.

Throttle values should be reviewed every month; you need to carefully decide on the number you choose to throttle. A high number can allow more users on the system, and too low can make the system under perform.

Every workload needs to be associated with a throttle. If not, unlimited work can hit the system, making it busy and degrading the performance.

There's more...

Each resource in any system is supposed to be working at 100% efficiency, unless they are bound to some lower limit due to restrictions. CPUs are supposed to run at a maximum of 100% at nodes.

CPU usage is reported out of 100% for each core, so the total amount of CPU power to be used in a dual core system would be 200%, and a quad core, 400%, depending on cores in the CPU. So, when we have multiple CPUs in a system, how should we calculate CPU busy percentage across all the nodes?

To calculate how busy the CPUs are within a node, we need to normalize the CPU over the node level; for this, we add together all the CPUs in a node, and then divided by the number of CPUs in the node, to arrive at a number with a maximum value of 100%. Normalized values are the standard for reporting CPU busy in the ResUsage macro reports and in Teradata viewpoint screens. Un-normalized values represent the actual values of the CPUs in a node and are used for analysis at the individual Vproc level, AMPs, and PEs.

A high number of requests hitting the system requires CPU and other resources from the system. Throttling is a way to limit the resources for requests. Admins need to record high concurrency time periods on the system and compare them to the resource utilization in that time period. If concurrency is the driving factor for resource consumption, then an admin might require to limit the requests.

Defining a ruleset

A **ruleset** makes the definition of workload load designer on to system. It is a collection of settings that together makes up the workload management environment. A ruleset includes all the workloads expected to be used when the ruleset is active, as well as all throttles, filters, and exceptions.

A ruleset contains:

- The state definition
- Filters
- Throttles
- Exceptions
- Workload definitions
- Virtual partitions

It also includes virtual partition settings for the workloads that make up the ruleset, and the ruleset captures any automated changes to settings that have been defined, as well as the events that trigger such changes.

If you need to make changes on any settings of throttles or filters, you need to open a ruleset, make the changes, and activate the ruleset.

A ruleset has three stages, which can be seen in the following figure:

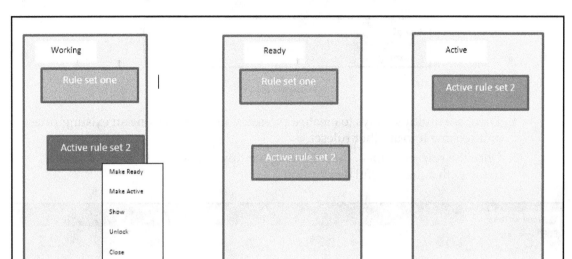

Workload Designer

- **Working**: Collection of all rulesets. From here you can delete, unlock, show, and make a ruleset ready.
- **Ready**: Stage before activating a ruleset.
- **Active**: In this stage, you will find only one ruleset, which is currently active on the system. Ruleset once in ready state, auto transitioned into ready state.

Getting ready

You need to connect to Teradata viewpoint using an admin account.

How to do it...

1. Log in to Teradata viewpoint using an admin account.
2. Open the Teradata workload designer portlet.

3. Click on the + sign over the Working block, as shown here:

Workload Designer

4. There are multiple ways to create a ruleset; you can also clone an existing ruleset and rename it to another ruleset.

5. Once the ruleset is open, the following window will open. Give the ruleset a name with a meaningful description:

Workload Designer Ruleset

6. Now, start defining other parameters in the ruleset to make it complete. The following are the parts that make up a ruleset:

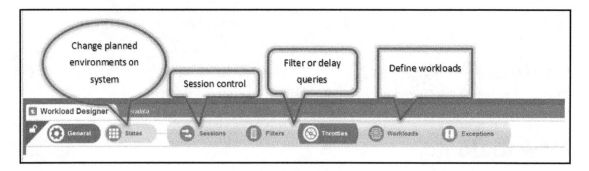

Workload Designer

7. Once you are done defining all the parameters, save the ruleset.

8. To activate, make the ruleset ready, and it will be auto-transit into an active state.

How it works...

A ruleset, once activated, governs the system based on all the settings and parameters defined in it. Only one ruleset can be active at a particular time. You can make another ruleset active as many times as you want, but it is not recommended to make multiple changes to a ruleset and activate it over and over again.

You can also export a ruleset into an XML format. This exported ruleset can be used on another system.

To export a ruleset under the working block, click on any ruleset that you want to export, and then save it in an XML format, as shown in the following screenshot:

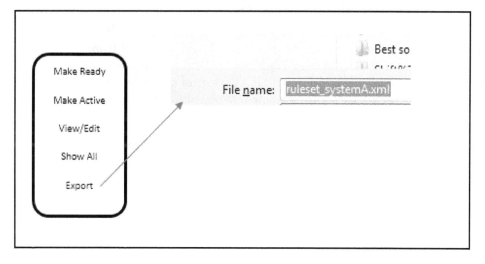

Workload Designer Export Option

Now, to import the saved ruleset onto another system, click on the icon over the working block and choose a ruleset from its saved location, as shown in the following screenshot:

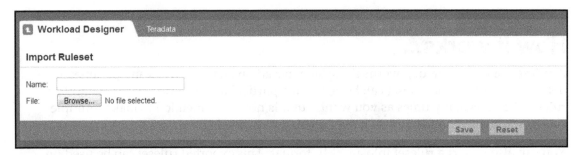

Workload Designer Export Option

Creating a TASM exception

To maintain system availability at an optimal level all the time, TASM provides various tools to accomplish it. We have filters defined to block any request from coming onto the system, throttles to limit the number of requests coming onto the system, and then we have exceptions on the system. Exceptions are used to control any active work on the system. Once a query is active, there should be some way to control it; this is where exceptions come into play.

Exceptions make sure that any request/query that is active on the system is controlled, and if at any step it crosses the threshold, it needs to be controlled, as a query has many steps and sometimes till run time we don't know actual resource consumption of the request. But once it starts consuming resources, it needs to be monitored.

Using exception processing, TASM can detect when an individual query crosses a defined threshold so that a targeted action can be taken with regards to the request.

In this recipe, we will define an I/O exception for a workload.

Getting ready

You need to connect to Teradata viewpoint using an admin account.

How to do it...

1. Connect to Teradata viewpoint using an admin account.
2. Open a workload designer portlet.
3. Unlock any ruleset and click on **show**.
4. Once in a ruleset, click on the **Workloads** tab on the ruleset window. You can also click on the **Exception** tab, under which you will see a list of exceptions on the system. But in this recipe, we will create a workload specific exception:

Workload Option

5. Once clicked, you can see the list of workloads on the system.
6. Click on any of the workloads under which you want to create an exception.
7. Click on the **Exceptions** tab, as marked in the figure:

Workload Exception Option

8. Once the **Exception** window is open, fill in the following fields:

Workload Exception Setting

9. Next, in the **Criteria** window, choose the following fields, and fill in the threshold values:

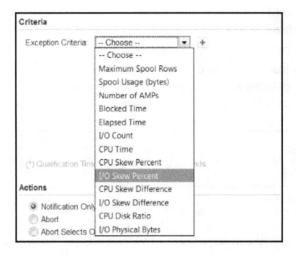

Workload Exception Criteria Option

10. Next is the action you would like to take when the exception is met. In this, we will use a notification only, and send the email when the exception has occurred. Check the following screenshot:

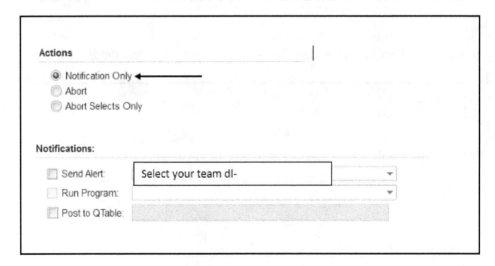

Workload Exception Notification Option

11. When you select the **Notification Only** action, in the next window, provide the email address to which the notification will be sent, as shown in previous figure.

12. Click on **Save** and the **Exception** window will be closed.

How it works...

Once an exception criteria is met by a query, the corresponding action will be performed. A query can be either aborted, notified, degraded to a lower workload, or any other program can be executed.

The following are some types of exception criteria that can be defined:

- Maximum spool rows
- I/O count
- Spool size
- Blocked time
- Elapsed time
- Number of AMPs
- CPU time (sum over all nodes)
- Tactical CPU usage threshold (per node)
- Tactical I/O physical bytes (per node)
- I/O physical bytes
- CPU disk ratio
- Skew - Can be CPU or I/O

It can also be checked in the following screenshot:

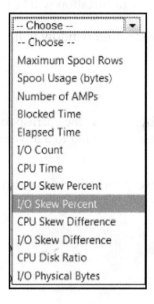

Workload Exception Option

When multiple exceptions are used, they are clubbed using the AND condition, meaning all the rules should be true to trigger the defined exception.

8

Collect Statistics the Better Way

In this chapter, we will cover:

- How to collect statistics
- Identifying stats for a table
- Identifying multi-column stats
- How to collect expression stats
- How to copy statistics
- Using `help` and `show` to resolve stats issues

Introduction

Statistics, by definition, are the collection, organization, analysis, interpretation, and presentation of data.

-Source Wikipedia

The mathematical study of the theoretical nature of such distributions and tests.

-Source Dictionary

In Teradata, the STATISTICS command will gather and store demographic data for one or more columns or indices of a table or join index.

Statistics help in analyzing things based on aggregation of data. They turn data into useful information so that actions can be taken or predictions can be made.

The same goes for Teradata. The Teradata optimizer uses statistics to develop plans for query executions:

The optimizer generates several plans before choosing the most optimized one, based on cost. The estimations that we see in explain plans are derived from data demographics of the table which the optimizer collects while doing a statistics collection.

Stats collection can be a resource-intensive operation if large tables are involved; hence, it needs to be scheduled in non-peak hours for large production tables.

 With Teradata 13.10, you can now grant or revoke stats on a user to control stats collection. STATISTICS privileges must be granted to run and collect stats: GRANT STATISTICS ON Databasename.Tablename TO username;

Caution must be taken while collecting statistics. This chapter emphasizes some important aspects of statistics:

- Identifying stats for a table
- Copy / help / show
- System table for stats
- 14.++ recommendations (only the best)

Cost-based optimizer

Here, "cost" is the CPU, the I/Os, the joins, the number of estimated rows, AMPs, and so on. The optimizer evaluates the costs of all reasonable execution plans, and the best choice is used.

The following is a list of what should be optimized:

- Kinds of joins
- Access paths
- Row relocations
- Ordering of joins

As in a maze, you only have one perfect path from entry to exit; the optimizer generates an execution plan for a query. The numbers of rows and other demographics of a table, and the column parts of the join conditions, help the optimizer decide which table in the join will be distributed or duplicated, what kind of join will be used, and, in the case of multi-table joins, the order of joins.

Evolution of statistics

Statistics have come a long way since V2R1, where only 100 intervals were supported to collect stats on statements themselves. Following figure shows the evolution of statistics since its release.

Statistics Version	Teradata Database Release Introduced	Description
1	V2R1	Initial version. Supports up to 100 intervals.
2	V2R5	Added sampling fields to interval 0. Supports up to 100 intervals.
3	12.0	Added new fields NumAllNulls and AvgAMPRPV to interval 0. Raised the default max detailed intervals to 200.
4	12.0.3	Added new fields AllAMPSampleEst and OneAMPSampleEst to interval 0 for better data growth detection.
5	14.0	New histogram layout, larger value length, modifiable number of intervals, history records and SUMMARY statistics.
6	14.10 (with NoDot0BackDown set to TRUE)	New fields added to interval 0 to support UDI counts.

Teradata Database 14.10 Statistics Enhancements

Statistics in Teradata keep on evolving, and collecting statistics continues to become more dynamic and less resource-intensive.

Now, let's check out some recommendations to be followed. Statistics collection depends upon many things, as we have seen: data demographics, type of stats, system configuration, and many more things.

There are a few questions that we need to answer before diving into recipes.

Make sure your statistics collection process answers the following questions:

- What stats need to be collected? Identify tables, databases, and queries
- Where in the transformation and loading processes do stats need to be collected, and how often?
- What is the stat collection schedule?
- Are statistics on single or multi-column?
- Are statistics full, summary, or sample?

These are some basic tips for use Teradata 14.10 and onwards:

- Enable `NoDot0Backdown` to `true` to make use of the new version 6 for collecting statistics.
- Enable `DBQL OBJECT USE COUNT, OUC` to get information about all DML statements, as shown in following code.

```
/*usecount logging enable*/
BEGIN QUERY LOGGING WITH USECOUNT ON "DatabaseNAME";
```

- Use the system default threshold option to reduce the resources by statistics recollection.
- Collect full stats on small and skewed tables.
- Stats on NUSI to avoid full table scan.
- Stale stats are far more dangerous than no stats.
- DBS control to set a number of AMPs for random AMP samples.
- Sample stats for big tables.
- Extrapolations are not carried for temporary tables.
- To do a recollection of existing stats on the table, use `COLLECT STATS ON TABLENAME;`.
- Extrapolations are done on `DATE` columns.
- `DBC.ObjectUsage` to the collected statistics repository `DBC.StatsTbl` to find the statistics that are not used.
- Drop the existing statistics if changing to full from the sample.
- Statistics should be executed in separate workloads and should be throttle via CPU and I/O bound.
- Use new syntax for statistics collection to reduce resource consumption.

- Collecting stats on expressions should be done carefully. Collection statistics on changing expressions should be avoided.
- Do not copy or transfer the SUMMARY statistics; always recollect them.

Statistics collection is a useful and powerful tool that boosts system performance. A lot of efforts have been put into making statistics collection more optimized. The fine line between what to collect and what not to should be understood and looked into.

Happy collecting stats!

How to collect statistics

In most cases, tuning a poorly performing query starts with taking a look at the collected stats on the tables involved. One wrong/stale stat, or no stats on tables, can turn a regular query into a shark query that eats up all resources on the system. Let's explore more about how and when to collect these statistics.

The following is the EXPLAIN plan of some query:

```
2) Next, we execute the following steps in parallel.
    1) We do an all-AMPs RETRIEVE step from SYSDBA.SITE_ID in view
SYSDBA_VIEWS.SITES_IDV by way of an all-rows scan with no residual
conditions into Spool 2 (all_amps) (compressed columns allowed), which is
duplicated on all AMPs. The size of Spool 2 is estimated with high
confidence to be 55,220rows (5,521,220 bytes).  The estimated time for this
step is 0.05 seconds.
```

If you need to retrieve statistics data on a system, there are a few tables in DBC where metadata for stats are stored, they are:

- DBC.ColumnStatsV: Gives stats information of 'single' column stats of StatsType in ('T', 'I', 'N', 'B'). There is one more view, which gives the same information: DBC.ExpSt.

- DBC.IndexStatsV: Gives stats information of index stats.
- DBC.TempTableStatsV: Gives stats information of materialized temporary tables (GTT)(Statstype = M)
- DBC.ObjectUsage: Used when USECOUNT is enabled, to help stats extrapolation. It captures table row count, which helps in building the history records.

You can use these system tables to identify stale and unwanted statistics and improve your stats strategy or process.

Getting ready

You need to connect to the Teradata database using the Teradata studio or SQLA. Identity the table on which stats need to be collected. You also need to have collect stats permission on the database for executing the collect stats statement.

Let's create a table with the following DDL and insert data into it:

```
/*Sample table for Statistics*/
CREATE volatile TABLE EMP_SAL_STATS
(
id INT,
DEPT varchar(25)
) on commit preserve rows;

INSERT into EMP_SAL_STATS VALUES (1,'HR');
INSERT into EMP_SAL_STATS VALUES (2,'IT');
INSERT into EMP_SAL_STATS VALUES (3,'CMP');
INSERT into EMP_SAL_STATS VALUES (4,'MGMT');
```

Now, let's run the following command and see the output:

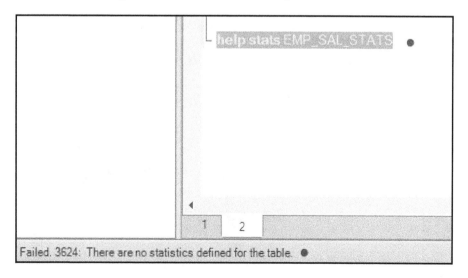

How to do it...

1. There are two ways to collect stats; first, the old way:

```
COLLECT STATISTICS COLUMN
(p_pricetime,p_priceID)
ON prices;
COLLECT STATISTICS COLUMN
(p_pricetime)
ON price;
```

The disadvantage of this syntax is the optimizer needs to scan the table twice, hence consuming more resources. Both of the statements here are independent of each other.

2. Secondly, the effective way:

```
COLLECT STATISTICS
 COLUMN (q_area,q_amount) <--Read base table /Index for multicolumn
aggregation
,COLUMN (q_amount) <--Rollup from multicolumn aggregation result
ON quantity;
```

3. Run the following `stats` command on the table defined in the *Getting ready* section:

```
/*Collecting Statistics on table*/
COLLECT STATISTICS
 COLUMN (id,DEPT) --Read base table /Index for multicolumn
aggregation
,COLUMN (id) --Rollup from multicolumn aggregation result
,COLUMN (DEPT) --Rollup from multicolumn aggregation result
ON EMP_SAL_STATS;
```

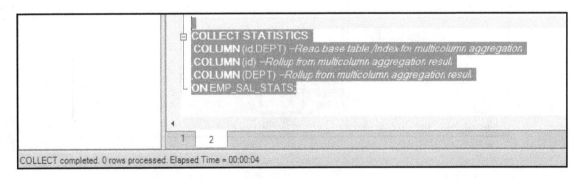

4. As shown in figure we can see that statistics are now collected on the table. We have collected two single-column stats and one multi-column stats.

How it works...

As the same column, q_amount appears in both states, the optimizer will use a multi-column stats spool to derive stats for the single one. This is done on a single scan, hence reducing the spool and resources.

In earlier versions, Teradata collected stats on a table by reading the full table; from version 14.00, it will check for all possible indexes, join indexes, and hash indexes for column access.

Suppose that a table has more than 10 columns and it has a join index present with three columns. Collecting stats on a column which is present in both a table and NON sparse join index, Teradata might choose to access the column through the join index, because the row size in the join index will be smaller than the table, and in turn, it needs to traverse fewer data blocks as compared to a full table.

Old or stale statistics in the warehouse can lead to wrong query plans or estimates, which may take time and unwanted resources for query processing. It is therefore required to refresh the statistics periodically. We can collect the statistics at the column level or at the index level.

 It is recommended to refresh the stats after every 10% of data change.

We can identify this change in the tables which are frequently accessed and modified with inserts, updates, deletes, and so on.

Identifying stats for a table

You can now collect stats on the following objects:

- Columns
- Expression or statement
- Table summary level

With these options in hand, we need to identify when we need to collect stats, on which column, and what type of stats need to be collected.

Statistics are collected on either a table or columns in a table. The following information is collected when we execute the collect statistic command:

- Number of rows in the table
- Average row size
- Information on all indexes in which statistics were collected
- The range of values for the column(s) in which statistics were collected
- The number of rows per value for the column(s) in which statistics were collected
- The number of NULLs for the column(s) in which statistics were collected

In this recipe, we will list steps to identify tables based on size and column types in a table to collect statistics.

Getting ready

You need to connect to the Teradata system using SQLA or Studio.

How to do it...

1. Connect to Teradata using SQLA or Studio.
2. Find the size of tables in the system using the following query. The output will contain databasename, tablename, and the size of the table with skew; it can be seen in the following code:

```
/*Find table size*/
SELECT  B.databasename , B.TableName , SUM ( currentperm ) ( NAMED
CurrentPerm ) ,MAXIMUM ( currentperm ) ( NAMED MaxPerm ) , AVG (
currentperm ) ( NAMED AvgPerm ) ,( ( MAXIMUM ( currentperm ) - AVG
( currentperm )  ) * 100.0  ) / ( MAXIMUM ( currentperm )  ) (
NAMED SkewPercent )
FROM    dbc.tablesize B INNER JOIN DBC.TABLES A
    ON  A.DATABASENAME = B.DATABASENAME
    AND A.TABLENAME = B.TABLENAME
GROUP   BY 1 , 2
ORDER   BY 1 , 2 ;
```

Following is the output of the query.

	DataBaseName	TableName	CurrentPerm	MaxPerm	AvgPerm	SkewPercent
1	AP	athelete_data	2,377,728.00	1,188,864.00	1,188,864.00	0.00
2	AP	countries	6,144.00	3,072.00	3,072.00	0.00
3	DBC	AccessRights	1,191,936.00	595,968.00	595,968.00	0.00
4	DBC	AccessRights_TD14	34,816.00	17,408.00	17,408.00	0.00
5	DBC	AccLogRuleTbl	6,144.00	3,072.00	3,072.00	0.00
6	DBC	AccLogRuleTbl_TD13	6,144.00	3,072.00	3,072.00	0.00
7	DBC	AccLogRuleTbl_TD14	6,144.00	3,072.00	3,072.00	0.00
8	DBC	AccLogTbl	3,072.00	1,536.00	1,536.00	0.00
9	DBC	AccLogTbl_TD14	3,072.00	1,536.00	1,536.00	0.00
10	DBC	Accounts	6,144.00	3,072.00	3,072.00	0.00
11	DBC	Acctg	14,336.00	7,168.00	7,168.00	0.00
12	DBC	ArchiveLoggingObjsTbl	2,048.00	1,024.00	1,024.00	0.00
13	DBC	AsgdSecConstraints	2,048.00	1,024.00	1,024.00	0.00

3. Based on the size of the table, statistics are recommended.
4. The table is categorized based on size, as follows:
    - **Small Tables, Rows <= #AMP**: Tables which have fewer rows than the number of AMPs in your system. Let's say it is an 800 AMP system and a 20 row table. Random AMP sampling won't help in this case, as the optimizer can mess up estimations, as not all the AMPs in the system are carrying the rows for that table. Full table stats can be collected on smaller tables.
    - **Medium Tables, Rows > #AMP**: Tables which have rows greater than the number of AMPs in the system give better estimations, with random AMP sampling if no stats are collected. A point to be noted here is that RAS (random AMP sampling) is not a replacement for full statistics collection. Stats are based on demographics, as it changes estimations and plans of execution get changed, so it is always better to have stats on the table than to not have one. You can always decide on the frequency of stats collection on the table. UPI/USI tables, or tables with nearly unique distribution (~95% rows unique), are good candidates for RAS.

- **Large Tables, Rows >> #AMP**: Collecting stats on large tables can be tricky, as it requires intensive CPU and I/O and execution time. Full collect stats need to be collected on these tables. SUMMARY stats are also good on large tables. It collects summary statistics, such as row count of the table average row size, average block size and so on.
- **Extremely large tables, Rows >>>> #AMP**: We are talking about tables which are 100 TB+ in size. RAS will be best on these, as stats collection on this can take forever. Also, stats collection on one column on this table can jeopardize the execution. With the ever-increasing size of data warehousing tables, you might need to find a way to collect stats on these tables. Summary stats are the way to go for them.

5. Execute SHOW on the table that you have identified to collect stats. This will display the column details and the DDL of the table. Next, we will check statistics collection based on column type:
   - **Unique Primary/Secondary**: Can rely on RAS, but full stats need to be collected if columns are getting used in non-equality predicates and range queries like BETWEEN or LIKE. Frequency of stats collection can, on these columns, be weekly.
   - **PARTITION keyword**: Collecting stats on the PARTITION pseudo column, if the table is partitioned, tells the optimizer how many rows are in each partition. It is very fast, because it reads the cylinder indexes rather than the data tables. SUMMARY stats serve the same purpose and can be used on both PPI and NON PPI tables. PARTITION can be combined with PI columns as multi stats, which is useful for the optimizer to locate PI values in partitions where it exists. Low resource collect stats can be refresh daily or weekly, depending upon the stats collection of partition columns.
   - **Partition column, PPI**: Full or summary collect stats; RAS does not give sound estimations. The DATE partition column should be collected fortnightly on highly changing tables. Delaying stats collection on PPI columns results in bad estimations.
   - **Non-Unique Primary/Secondary**: Full collect stats are recommended because of the nature of the column. More skew on these columns makes them a candidate for full stats. On large tables, to reduce the resources, you can collect stats using the sample. Stats collection frequency can vary from daily to weekly, based on column volatility.

- **DATE/Timestamp columns**: Statistics on date or timestamp columns should be collected daily, as they are the most used and updated columns. It is best to update them at the end of the batch job.
- **Join and Secondary Index**: Stats need to be collected on join indexes or secondary indexes. Single table join indexes can utilize stats on base tables, but with some conditions. For multi-table join index, stats needs to collect on individual join index(s) created table. Even with all the stats collected, usage of a join index from the optimizer is not guaranteed.

6. Based on the table and column type, you can now collect statistics. Use the COLLECT STATISTICS command:

```
/*Collect index table stats*/
COLLECT STATISTICS ON JOIN_INDEX_TBL INDEX (date_start, type_no);
```

How it works...

Let's take an example where we insert rows into a table and the statistics of PI are missing. We will see that the number of rows estimated is equal to the number of AMPs on our system:

```
Number of AMPS: 400

INSERT INTO cookbook_scratch.dw_PI ( main_addnl_type , cre_ts , upd_ts )
SELECT                                  card_main_addnl_type ,
CURRENT_TIMESTAMP ( 0 ) , NULL
FROM     pcookbook_scratch.dw_PI_source ;
```

Now, let's check for the INSERT statement:

```
Before Stats
which is duplicated on the AMPs
The size is estimated with high confidence to be
400 rows.  The estimated time for this step is 0.02 seconds.
```

The estimated number of rows is 400, and as we can see from the explanation, rows are getting duplicated. On a 400 AMP system, if we duplicate one row, estimation will come to 400 rows. Which means the optimizer is estimating one row for the earlier query, which is not right.

Now, let's collect the `stat` on previous query and check explain again:

```
**Collecting statistics**

Collect stat
index (main_addnl_type), --- PI of the table
column (cre_ts)
on
cookbook_scratch.dw_PI_source
```

Let's check explain after collecting statistics:

After Stats
```
The size is estimated with high confidence to be
45,649 rows.  The estimated time for this step is 0.02 seconds.
```

This makes estimation accurate and makes distribution of rows optimized.

There's more...

Statistics are the main input to the optimizer which influence it to create plans or joining strategies. As we saw earlier, it helps the optimizer to make better decisions using actual row counts and data distribution information.

Considerations for collecting statistics:

- Requires a full table scan
- Must be kept current
- May be unnecessary for very large tables

We have techniques with which we can reduce the CPU, I/O, and other resources when collecting statistics:

- **Full stats** are the simplest and are the basic ones. Full data demographics are collected regarding the column(s). You need to understand that these sample/summary stats are different from random AMP sample collect stats, in that these stats are actually collected, unlike RAS. Use the following code for full stats:

```
/*Collect statistics*/
Full collect stats:
 Collect stats <tablename>
```

Sample stats are used only when the percentage of data needs to be collected. Some known advantages of collecting stats via samples are:

- Big tables with full stats can take time and are resource-intensive
- Data is not skewed
- Better to have samples than not have any statistics on a column
- Should be avoided for small and skewed tables
- Not valid for volatile, global volatile, and join indexes

Following table illustrate when to use system based sample and user defined based sample.

Sample type	What's collected
System	System determined percentage of table rows used for statistical information.
Sample n percentage	To scan user-specified percentage of table rows, 2-100, 100 being full stats.

SysSampleOption, defined on your system, defines the sample of stats collection. This option is used when sample stats are based on when system-determined sample stats are collected. Teradata uses the downgrade approach that make sample stats collection smart. It adjusts the sample collection automatically, by understanding data demographics. We can use the following code to collect stats using SAMPLE:

```
/*Statistics using SAMPLE*/
COLLECT STATISTICS
USING <SYSTEM> SAMPLE 5 PERCENT
COLUMN start_dt
ON prod_tables;
```

Summary stats collection: with 14.10, we can now collect stats on the table level. It is represented by a small * in the first line when you do a help or show stats on a table.

These work the same way as the count (*), providing the optimizer a recent row count from the table. Some cons of this are:

- Fast and highly optimized
- Fewer resources
- Gets auto-updated when any stats collection is performed

Following is the resultset of help statistic command on a table.

Date Time	Unique Values	Column Names
17/11/30 16:45:18	12,751,06	*
17/11/30 16:45:19	13,000	start_dt

We have a table, `share_price`, which has 10,000 rows. Now let's try to get the best sample % on which we will be near equal to the actual number of rows before hitting 100%:

Statistic %	Duration (s)	CPU	IO (k)	Confidence	Estimate	Actual
0	N/A	N/A	N/A	No	45,876	10,000
2	1	16.7	38.7	High	2,027	10,000
5	1	40.1	79.7	High	2,681	10,000
10	3.8	78.9	148.4	High	3,308	10,000
20	3.1	158.9	283.8	High	3,970	10,000
40	6.3	317.0	556.3	High	4,768	10,000
80	12.3	626.4	1,101.3	High	8,644	10,000
100	25.9	786.3	1,367.1	High	10,000	10,000

As we increase the percentage of samples, we get close to the actual number. CPU and I/O increase with the sample percentage.

Identifying multi-column stats

With Teradata 14.10, we now have the ability to collect stats not only on columns, but on tables and expressions as well. With better analysis and consideration, you can achieve good performance improvement in queries.

The way you implement collecting statistics plays a vital role in improving performance. We need to discover the optimal way to make use of statistics. Collecting statistics blindly on columns or expressions may help one time, but in the long term it may degrade the performance of the query.

Once we identify the column on which we are ready to collect statistics, we need to identify the type of stats to be collected. Should we collect on them individually, or combine them all into one?

Getting ready

To collect statistics, you need to connect to the Teradata database using Teradata Studio or SQLA.

How to do it...

1. Identify the query on which multi-column stats need to be collected.
2. Identify the columns that are joined using AND conditions. Columns that frequently appear together as selection criteria or join criteria, and for which values are expressed with an equality operator, will benefit from multi-column statistics:

```
/*Multicolumn statistics*/
Collect stat
column (main_addnl_type,cre_ts) --- Multicolumn stats
 on cookbook_scratch.dw_PI_source
```

How it works...

The following example will help you understand and guide you to choose which one you would prefer.

Let's suppose we have four tables, each with a single column primary index, and have five million rows in each of them:

- Table A (PI=x1)
- Table B (PI=y1)
- Table C (PI=y1)
- Table D (PI=x2)

Following the query that we will analyze of multi column statistics.

```
Select A1.*, B2.*, C3.*, D4.*
from A1, B2, C3, D4
where
A1.x1=B2.x1
and
A1.x2=D4.x2
and
A1.x3=007
and
A1.x4='BOND'
and
B2.y1=C3.y1
and
B2.y2 in ('JAI','BOM')
and
C3.z1 = 15
and
C3.z2 = '*'
and
D4.r1 <> 'DELTA'
and
D4.r2 = '7690';
```

Let's suppose we have collected stats on PI columns of all the four tables:

- **STATS ON A (x1,x2)**: Don't collect. Multi-column stats won't be used in this case; each column is used in a different join.
- **STATS ON A (x3,x4)**: Yes, both columns are in equality condition; multi-column stats are good for correlation between the two.
- **STATS ON B (y2)**: Yes, represents a single column constraint for table B. No multi-column advantage.
- **STATS ON C (z1,z2)**: Yes, both columns expressed in equal condition in the query; multi-column stat will be used.
- **STATS ON D (r1,r2)**: Don't collect. Column r1 used in non-equal condition, therefore the multi-column stat will not be used.
- **STATS on D (x2)**: Yes, single join column on table D.

In general, queries with multiple columns that frequently appear together as selection criteria or join criteria, and for which values are expressed with an equality operator, will benefit from multi-column statistics.

Also, it should be noted here that multi-column tends to use more resources and time when compared to single-column stats.

Rollup aggregation, like we saw in the previous chapter, is useful when doing multi-column stats.

There's more...

You can also DROP statistics on the table using the following code:

```
/*DROP Multicolumn statistics*/
DROP STATISTICS ON databasename.tablename COLUMN(column1, column2);
```

For better collection and easy maintenance of multi-column stats, we can name them, and then use it to refresh them if required again:

```
/*Multicolumn Naming*/
COLLECT STATISTICS
COLUMN (Calendar_Date, Product_Number, Outlet_ID)
AS Stats_CalDate_ProdNum_RtlNum -- STATS NAME
ON multi_column_table;
```

Where is the metadata for multi-column, you ask? The MultistatsV table in the DBC database gives stats information of 'multiple' column stats of statstype in ('T', 'I', 'N', 'B'). Another view, which gives the same information, is DBC.MultiExpStatsV.

How to collect expression stats

With 14.10, we can now collect stats on single table expressions. This improves estimations of the query with expressions; stats can be collected as they were with columns:

```
COLLECT [SUMMARY] STATISTICS
[USING options]
COLUMN expr [[AS] statistics_name]
[,COLUMN (expr [..., expr]) [[AS] statistics_name]]
ON [TEMPORARY] <Table>;
```

One of the mandatory requirements of the expression stats is that they need to be named. This name, which follows the same rules as other naming database objects, can be used to recollect, help, show, or drop the statistics.

Getting ready

To collect statistics, you need to connect to the Teradata database using Teradata studio or SQLA.

Identify the expression on which statistics need to be collected.

How to do it...

1. Identify the query on which expression stats need to be collected.
2. Use the following format to collect statistics:

```
COLLECT [SUMMARY] STATISTICS
[USING options]
COLUMN expr [[AS] statistics_name]
[,COLUMN (expr [..., expr]) [[AS] statistics_name]]
ON [TEMPORARY] <Table>;
```

How it works...

Let suppose that for our two tables, `cookbook_t.EXPstats1` has 100 rows and `cookbook_t.EXPstats2` has 100 rows. This means when we join these two tables, rows should be 100*100 = 10,000.

The following query will be used to collect statistics on the expression:

```
/*Query to collect statistics*/
SEL    A.col3 , B.Col1
FROM    cookbook_t.EXPstats1  A
Product  JOIN
cookbook_t.EXPstats2  B
ON  ( CASE WHEN  SUBSTRING( A.col2 FROM 1 FOR 4)   ='this'  THEN  'Y'
ELSE 'N'  END )
=    ( CASE WHEN  SUBSTRING( B.col2 FROM 1 FOR 4)   ='test'  THEN  'Y'
ELSE 'N'  END );
```

Explain plan shown in following block is from a query without having any statistic on expression or any other column:

```
Explanation
---------------------------------------------------------------------We do an all-AMPs JOIN step
from cookbook_t.B by way of an all-rows scan with no residual conditions,
which is joined to Spool 2 (Last Use) by way of an all-rows scan.
cookbook_t.B and Spool 2 are joined using a product join, with a join
condition of ("(( CASE WHEN ((SUBSTR(col2 ,1 ,4 ))= 'test') THEN ('Y') ELSE
('N') END ))=(( CASE WHEN ((SUBSTR(cookbook_t.B.col2 ,1 ,4 ))= 'this') THEN
('Y') ELSE ('N') END ))").  The result goes into Spool 1 (group_amps),
which is built locally on the AMPs.  The size of Spool 1 is estimated with
low confidence to be 3,130 rows (120,450 bytes).  The estimated time for
this step is 0.04 seconds.
```

Let's collect stats using the following code:

```
/*Expression statistics*/

COLLECT STATS COLUMN ( CASE WHEN  SUBSTRING(  col2 FROM 1 FOR 4)   ='this'
THEN  'Y'   ELSE 'N'  END) AS der1_stats  ON  cookbook_t.EXPstats1;

COLLECT STATS COLUMN ( CASE WHEN  SUBSTRING(  col2 FROM 1 FOR 4)   ='test'
THEN  'Y'   ELSE 'N'  END) AS der1_stats ON   cookbook_t.EXPstats2;
```

So, does this help? Let us see the explanation again, as follows:

```
/*EXPLAIN plan after collecting stats on expression*/
Explanation
---------------------------------------------------------------------
We do an all-AMPs JOIN step from Spool 2 (Last Use) by way of a RowHash
match scan, which is joined to Spool 3 (Last Use) by way of a RowHash match
scan.  Spool 2 and Spool 3 are joined using a product join, with a join
condition of ("(( CASE WHEN ((SUBSTR(col2,1 ,4 ))= 'this') THEN ('Y') ELSE
('N') END ))= (( CASE WHEN ((SUBSTR(col2 ,1 ,4 ))= 'test') THEN ('Y') ELSE
('N') END ))").The result goes into Spool 1 (group_amps), which is built
locally on the AMPs.  The size of Spool 1 is estimated with high confidence
to be 100,100 rows (234,900 bytes).  The estimated time for this step is
0.04 seconds.
```

Not only did expression stats get the estimations right, but they also improved query efficiency.

There's more...

Expression stats can be collected on:

- CASE statements
- Aggregation expressions, like SUM, MAX, and so on
- With built-in database functions like date, current_date, and so on
- UDF

> To see expression stats, use the dbc.statsV or show stats command.

How to copy statistics

Collect statistics can be prefixed and used with many commands. It helps to use collect stats efficiently. Some privileges need to be granted when using these commands.

Let us suppose you are tuning a query which involves some terabytes of tables with 100 million rows. You have a requirement to change the PI, or to add a PPI, or to change the joining conditions, to analyze the query. Without changing the definition of the table, you are not able to check the explain plan. The only way you can achieve this is by changing the table structure, which needs a lot of resources and needs to be done during off-peak hours. And you don't even know if changing the DDL will work. So, to achieve this, we can create a copy of the table with the changed PI and copy just stats with no data.

Getting ready

Connect to the Teradata database via Studio or SQLA. Identify tables which stats need to be copied to, and the table from which stats needs to be copied. Both tables from which stats are being copied and to which stats are being copied should have the same ddl structure.

How to do it...

1. Connect Studio or SQLA to the Teradata system.
2. Execute the copy command `Collect stats`:

```
Collect stats on <databasename>.<tablename> from <databasename>.<tablename>
```

How it works...

Here, you can use copy stats to your advantage.

Let's create a table with a changed new structure, as shown here (the source and target table definitions should match):

```
/*DDL for table used*/
CREATE SET TABLE cookbook_sandpit.copy_stats_new ,NO FALLBACK ,
     NO BEFORE JOURNAL,
     NO AFTER JOURNAL,
     CHECKSUM = DEFAULT,
     DEFAULT MERGEBLOCKRATIO
     (
      username varCHAR(30) CHARACTER SET LATIN NOT CASESPECIFIC,
      LogDate DATE FORMAT 'YYYY-MM-DD',
          DatabaseName CHAR(30) CHARACTER SET LATIN NOT CASESPECIFIC,
      TotalCpu FLOAT)
PRIMARY INDEX ( username ,logdate  );
```

This will create an empty table with stats only copied, as follows:

```
/*COPY statistics*/
collect stats on cookbook_sandpit.copy_stats_new from
cookbook_sandpit.copy_stats
```

Now we can replace this new empty table with only stats being copied, to check the explanation and verify if the modified DDL will work or not.

There's more...

Copy statistics are useful when you want to collect stats on tables that are duplicates of existing tables. It helps to avoid recollection of statistics.

Using help and show to resolve query issues

To observe statistics on a table, we use the `help` stats command. This gives an overview of stats collected on the table level:

```
/*Help statistics*/
HELP STATISTICS ON web_clicks;

Date Time              Unique Values    Column Names
--------               --------         -------------------
17/07/07 10:49:55         100                * (represent number of rows in
table)
17/07/07 10:49:55         100                date
```

- `Date Time`: Represents the date and time of stats collected. Helps to identify how old stats are.
- `Unique Values`: Number of unique values for a column, or combination of columns, in case of multi-column stats.
- `Column Name`: Name of the column on which stats are collected. The `HELP STATISTICS` command is enhanced to show the expression statistics. It shows the name given to the expression statistics instead of the actual expressions.

Following is the most popular diagnostic command. It will give you suggestions on stats that need to be collected, based on columns. But due diligence needs to be taken while collecting stats from these recommendations. Not all stats collections work in favor of the query.

```
DIAGNOSTIC HELPSTATS ON FOR SESSION
```

The `SHOW STATISTICS` command is enhanced to show the expression statistics. It shows the name given to the expression statistics, along with the actual expressions. Histograms of tables/columns can be checked by issuing this command.

Getting ready

You need to connect to the Teradata database using SQLA or Studio.

How to do it...

1. Let's create a table using the following DDL:

```
CREATE TABLE cookbook_sandpit.show_me_stats
( employee_is INTEGER ,
Start_date date ,
Year_id INTEGER
) PRIMARY INDEX (employee_is) INDEX (Start_date );
```

2. Now insert some rows into it using data:

```
; INSERT INTO cookbook_sandpit.show_me_stats VALUES
(2,'2017/05/07',102)
; INSERT INTO cookbook_sandpit.show_me_stats VALUES
(3,'2017/05/01',103)
; INSERT INTO cookbook_sandpit.show_me_stats VALUES
(4,'2017/05/07',104)
; INSERT INTO cookbook_sandpit.show_me_stats VALUES
(5,'2017/05/03',105)
; INSERT INTO cookbook_sandpit.show_me_stats VALUES
(6,'2017/05/02',106)
; INSERT INTO cookbook_sandpit.show_me_stats VALUES
(7,'2017/05/08',107)
; INSERT INTO cookbook_sandpit.show_me_stats VALUES
(8,'2017/05/10',108)
; INSERT INTO cookbook_sandpit.show_me_stats VALUES
(9,'2017/05/11',109)
; INSERT INTO cookbook_sandpit.show_me_stats VALUES
(10,'2017/05/14',110)
```

3. Now it's time to `collect` some statistics using the following:

```
collect stats column (employee_is,Start_date) on
cookbook_sandpit.show_me_stats;
collect stats column (employee_is) on
cookbook_sandpit.show_me_stats;
```

4. There is one column stat, one multi-column stat, and table level stats, which get collected automatically.

5. Let's see the summary stats on this on a table level using the following:

```
/*Summary Stats command*/
show summary stats values on cookbook_sandpit.show_me_stats;
/*OUTPUT of Summary statistics*/
COLLECT SUMMARY STATISTICS
ON cookbook_sandpit.show_me_stats
VALUES
(
/** TableLevelSummary **/
/* Version */ 6,
/* NumOfRecords */ 2,
/* Reserved */ 0.000000,
/* Reserved */ 0.000000,
/* CurrSysInsertCnt */ -1,
/* CurrSysDeleteCnt */ -1,
/* CurrSysInsDelResetTS */ TIMESTAMP '9999-12-31 23:59:59-00:00',
/* NumOfCurrSysUpdateCols*/ 0,
/* SummaryRecord[1] */
/* Temperature */ 0,
/* TimeStamp */ TIMESTAMP '2017-08-05 14:29:42-00:00',
/* NumOfAMPs */ 1856,
/* OneAMPSampleEst */ 1856,
/* AllAMPSampleEst */ 10,
/* RowCount */ 9,
/* DelRowCount */ 0,
/* PhyRowCount */ 10,
/* AvgRowsPerBlock */ 0.000000,
/* AvgBlockSize (bytes) */ 0.000000,
/* BLCPctCompressed */ 0.00,
/* BLCBlkUcpuCost */ 0.000000,
/* BLCBlkURatio */ 0.000000,
/* AvgRowSize */ 24.000000,
/* Reserved */ 0.000000,
/* Reserved */ 0.000000,
/* Reserved */ 0.000000,
/* StatsSkipCount */ 0,
/* SysInsertCnt */ 0,
/* SysDeleteCnt */ 0,
/* SysUpdateCnt */ 0,
/* SysInsDelLastResetTS */ TIMESTAMP '9999-12-31 23:59:59-00:00',
/* SummaryRecord[2] */
/* Temperature */ 0,
/* TimeStamp */ TIMESTAMP '2017-08-05 14:29:41-00:00',
/* NumOfAMPs */ 1856,
/* OneAMPSampleEst */ 1856,
/* AllAMPSampleEst */ 10,
```

```
/* RowCount */ 9,
/* DelRowCount */ 0,
/* PhyRowCount */ 10,
/* AvgRowsPerBlock */ 0.000000,
/* AvgBlockSize (bytes) */ 0.000000,
/* BLCPctCompressed */ 0.00,
/* BLCBlkUcpuCost */ 0.000000,
/* BLCBlkURatio */ 0.000000,
/* AvgRowSize */ 24.000000,
/* Reserved */ 0.000000,
/* Reserved */ 0.000000,
/* Reserved */ 0.000000,
/* StatsSkipCount */ 0,
/* SysInsertCnt */ 0,
/* SysDeleteCnt */ 0,
/* SysUpdateCnt */ 0,
/* SysInsDelLastResetTS */ TIMESTAMP '9999-12-31 23:59:59-00:00'
);
```

6. It shows that we have nine rows in the table with a `1856` AMP system.

7. Let's check the values on multi-column stats using the following command:

```
/*show stats value*/
show   stats values
column (employee_is,Start_date)
on
cookbook_sandpit.show_me_stats

 /* MinVal */ 2, DATE '2017-05-07',
 /* MaxVal */ 10, DATE '2017-05-14',
 /* ModeVal */ 2, DATE '2017-05-07',
 /* HighModeFreq */ 1,
 /* NumOfDistinctVals */ 9,
 /* NumOfRows */ 9,
 /** Biased: Value[2], Frequency **/
/* 1 */ 2, DATE '2017-05-07', 1,
 /* 2 */ 3, DATE '2017-05-01', 1,
 /* 3 */ 4, DATE '2017-05-07', 1,
 /* 4 */ 5, DATE '2017-05-03', 1,
 /* 5 */ 6, DATE '2017-05-02', 1,
 /* 6 */ 7, DATE '2017-05-08', 1,
 /* 7 */ 8, DATE '2017-05-10', 1,
 /* 8 */ 9, DATE '2017-05-11', 1,
 /* 9 */ 10, DATE '2017-05-14', 1
```

8. The previous block is a snippet of the output. A biased value shows the frequency of unique values for the combination of columns.

With multi-column show values, you can also identify the values where `maxvalue` length goes greater than `25`. Values in `minval` will be shown as `Truncated`, which means that statistics need to be collected with a new `maxvaluelength`.

9. The following `'Truncated'` command shows that multi-column needs to be recollected:

```
/* MinVal */ 0., 'Truncated', 'Truncated',
/* MaxVal */ 0., 'Truncated', 'Truncated',
/* ModeVal */ 0., 'Truncated', 'Truncated',
```

10. Statistics need to be collected using the max value length to get proper estimations in multi-column. Check the following code for syntax.

```
/*COLLECT STATS  USING MAXVALUELENGTH*/
COLLECT STATS  USING MAXVALUELENGTH 500 COLUMN
employee_is,Start_date ON cookbook_sandpit.show_me_stats
```

How it works...

In earlier version of database, before Teradata 14, the max value for `maxvaluelength` was 16 bytes/ character; from Teradata 14, the default is 25 bytes to max histogram size (64 K). Below table compares two options.

Syntax element	Reason
MAXVALUELENGTH n	The maximum value length for histogram values such as MinValue, ModeValue, MaxValue, BiasedValue, and so on. For single-column statistics with CHAR or VARCHAR type columns, the size is taken as the number of characters. For single-column statistics with non-character type columns and multi-column statistics, the size is taken as the number of bytes. For multi-column statistics, the values are concatenated and truncated to the specified maximum size. The valid range is from 1 to the maximum size of the column for single-column statistics, and from 1 to the combined (sum of all the individual sizes) maximum size of all the columns for multi-column statistics. If a higher size than the maximum size is specified, the system automatically adjusts it to the maximum size. The maximum is subject to adjustment based on the histogram size.
SYSTEM MAXVALUELENGTH	To use the system-determined maximum for histogram building.

Showing stats without values requires *any* privilege on the object/database. Show stats with values require select or dump rights.

We can see that it is easy to get the histogram data, and that it is portable. (Do show stats value and copy/paste/execute results on other systems.)

There's more...

The new table to store stats information is DBC.StatsTbl. Running explain on collect statistics will show you the use of these tables:

```
4) We compute the table-level summary statistics from spool 5 and
save them into Spool 6, which is built locally on a single AMP
derived from the hash of the table id.
5) We lock DBC.StatsTbl for write on a RowHash.
6) We do a Single AMP MERGE Update to DBC.StatsTbl from Spool 5 (Last
Use) by way of a RowHash match scan.
7) We do a Single AMP MERGE Update to DBC.StatsTbl from Spool 6 (Last
Use) by way of a RowHash match scan.
8) We spoil the statistics cache for the table, view or query.
9) We spoil the parser's dictionary cache for the table.
10) Finally, we send out an END TRANSACTION step to all AMPs involved
in processing the request.
-> No rows are returned to the user as the result of statement 1.
```

These tables are used to identify the used and unused tables, and tables on which statistics should be collected.

Object usage count (OUC) is used to track the number of updates, deletes, and insert operations against database objects (except DBC tables). These are stored in a new dictionary table, DBC.ObjectUsage.

The DBQL USECOUNT option also logs the usage of the existing statistics in the DBC.ObjectUsage table with UsageType as 'STA'. This log can also be joined with DBC.StatsTbl to identify the statistics which are never used.

To enable UDI counts usage for the optimizer, use the following code:

```
set the DBS Control field NoDot0Backdown to true
```

Keep USECOUNT logging on for databases whose tables are being analyzed on an ongoing basis. The following code will enable USECOUNT logging:

```
BEGIN QUERY LOGGING WITH USECOUNT ON SandBoxDB;
```

What is the overhead of tracking UDI counts?

The OUC infrastructure uses an in-memory OUC cache to keep track of the access and UDI counts.

Recommendations

- Enabling USECOUNT on all important production databases is recommended
- Do not turn off the object use count logging arbitrarily
- Set the DBS Control internal field NoDot0Backdown to true and enable the DBQL USECOUNT option to enable the optimizer to use UDI counts

Application and OPS DBA Insight

9

In this chapter, we will cover:

- Creating, copying, and dropping tables
- Working with views
- Defining workloads based on application
- Securing passwords using the Teradata Wallet
- Shrinking your data size
- Using Query Band

Introduction

An application in a data warehouse domain represents a business process, a tool, or in some cases a business vertical. Database admins are broadly divided into two classes:

- **System admins**: Who manages the system in a broader perspective
- **Application admins**: Who manages one or more application or tool on the system

System admins are responsible for overall system health; application admins are more focused on application performance and health. Let's look at the various jobs performed by each kind of admin:

System Admin	Application Admin
Responsible for overall health of the system	Only for application
Defines overall system policies	Defines policies based on application as per system policies
Does not maintain service level agreement	Maintains application-based service level agreement
Responsible for system-wide audit and security	Maintains application audit and security defined by system admin
Takes care of overall growth of system	Only for an application they are responsible for

The application DBA are focused on database design and ongoing support, and administration for a specific application or applications. The application DBA is likely to be an expert in writing and debugging application-based issues and resolves data fixes. They should understand the best ways to incorporate database requests into application programs. As we saw in the table, the application DBA must also be capable of performing database change management, performance tuning, and most of the other roles of the DBA for their application. The main difference between the two is the focus of the application DBA; it is on a specific subset of applications rather than the overall DBMS implementation and database environment. But the application DBA must work under the system admin umbrella and create an application-wise policy based on system admin policies.

In this chapter, we will look at recipes that will help application admins to maintain and support applications effectively.

Creating, copying, and dropping tables

Teradata Database uses tables to store data in rows. Tables consist of rows and columns in a database, and can be seen in the following figure:

	Table				

Columns [Fields]

EMP_ID	EMP_NAME	EMP_SAL	EMP_ADD	EMP_City
1	Rose	203	121, Hksi	IN
2	Bose	1343	29, Jhu	MN
3	Philip	332	101, Dt	LR
4	Aks	1323	Gt-192	KL
5	Ross	2324	132, Rd	HF
6	Liberty	26677	9-appt	AD
7	Rajke	4344	Road, 23	AD
8	Snowman	36543	56-Rd	AD
9	Cucus	4676	79-Street	MN

Rows [Records]

Columns Values

In Teradata, you can create the following types of tables:

- **Permanent Table**: Remains in the database until dropped manually:
    - SET
    - MULTISET
- **Temporary Table**: Session based:
    - Derive table
    - Volatile table
    - Global temporary table
    - Queue table
    - Error logging table
    - NOPI table

In this recipe, we will create, drop, and copy data from one table to another.

Getting ready

You need to connect to Teradata Database using SQLA or Studio.

How to do it...

1. Connect to Teradata Database using SQLA or Studio.

2. Create the following permanent table in Database using the following code; it can be seen in the screenshot of SQLA:

```
/*Create set table*/
CREATE volatile TABLE td_cookbook.EMP_TBL
(EMP_ID INTEGER ,
EMP_Name VARCHAR(20),
Sal INTEGER)primary index (EMP_ID)
```

3. Let's insert data into the table by using the following code. Also, check the snippet from SQLA:

```
/*Insert row into table*/
insert into td_cookbook.EMP_TBL values (1,'Andrew',250);
insert into td_cookbook.EMP_TBL values (2,'Rose',232);
```

Following code is show in snippet from SQLA:

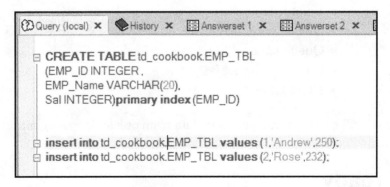

4. We will now copy the data from the table created in step 2 to the new table using the following code:

```
/*Copy table with defination*/
create table td_cookbook.EMP_TBL_CPY as
(sel * from  td_cookbook.EMP_TBL) with data;
```

5. This will create a copy of the first table with the same definition and primary index with data as in source table.

How it works...

As we know, there are two types of tables in Teradata, SET and MULTISET tables, and the main difference between these tables is a SET table doesn't allow duplicate rows whereas a MULTISET table allows it. When we don't specify any option by default, Teradata creates a SET table. You need to specify in DDL if you need a MULTISET table:

```
/*MultiSet table*/
CREATE MULTISET TABLE td_cookbook.EMP_TBL_MULTI
(EMP_ID INTEGER ,
EMP_Name VARCHAR(20),
Sal INTEGER)primary index (EMP_ID)
```

A SET table does not allow duplicate rows, hence for every new row inserted or updated in the table, Teradata checks the violation of uniqueness constraint for each new row (inserted or updated); this is called duplicate row checking, which is overhead on the resources and may cause serious performance issues if the number of records is in large number. It is recommended to use MULTISET when you don't have skewness in the primary index; it improves the performance of INSERT queries.

There's more...

You can also create volatile or other temporary tables using the following codes.

The code for the Volatile table is:

```
/*Create volatile table*/
CREATE Volatile TABLE EMP_TBL_MULTI
(EMP_ID INTEGER ,
EMP_Name VARCHAR(20),
Sal INTEGER)
primary index (EMP_ID)
on commit preserve rows;
```

The code for the GLOBAL TEMPORARY table is:

```
/*Global Temp table*/
CREATE GLOBAL TEMPORARY  TABLE EMP_TBL_GLOBAL
(EMP_ID INTEGER ,
EMP_Name VARCHAR(20),
Sal INTEGER)
primary index (EMP_ID)
on commit preserve rows;
```

on commit preserve rows is used to commit data. Temporary tables make use of user SPOOL space, and both the table definition and data is deleted once the user logs off their session.

Working with views

Views in SQL databases are the virtual tables; any view in a database always sits on top of one or more tables. By definition, VIEW contain rows and columns from a SELECT statement from the real table; it could be a combination of one or more tables:

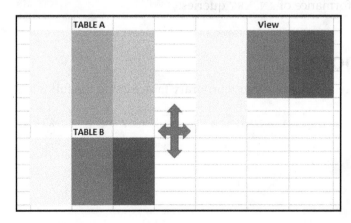

As you can see in the figure, **VIEW** contains 1 column from **TABLE A** and two from **TABLE B**. Tables are joined using a join between two tables.

There are a few benefits when it comes to view creation, and they are as follows:

- Provides a security mechanism
- Can hide the complexity of the table in a view
- Data in the view gets auto-updated whenever the underlying table gets changed
- Statistics defined on the table are available to views also

As a best practice, it is recommended to create a separate database containers for views. As shown in the screenshot, we have two separate containers for tables and views:

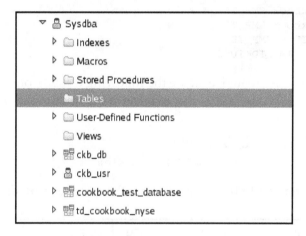

The following is the syntax for creating a view:

```
/*View creating syntax*/
CREATE/REPLACE VIEW <viewname>
AS
<select query>;
```

In this recipe, we will create a view, select data from it, and then drop it.

Getting ready

You need to connect to Teradata Database using SQLA or Studio.

How to do it...

1. Connect to Teradata Database using SQLA or Studio.

2. Create the following view of the tables with a condition of a WHERE clause:

```
/*Create a view*/
CREATE VIEW td_cookbookV.EMP_TBL_View
AS
Select
E.EMP_ID,
D.EMP_DEPT,
D.DEPT_CITY
FROM
td_cookbook.EMP_TBL_A E inner join
td_cookbook.EMP_TBL_B D ON
E.EMP_ID=D.EMP_ID
Where e.EMP_ID=1032
```

3. Once the view is created, execute the following SELECT on td_cookbookV.EMP_TBL_View to retrieve the rows based on the condition defined:

```
/*Select on view*/
SEL * from td_cookbookV.EMP_TBL_View
```

4. The following would be the result set of the query executed:

EMP_ID	EMP_DEPT	DEPT_CITY
1032	2	4

5. Next, we will REPLACE the view using the following code and add an extra column in the current view definition:

```
/*Replace view*/
REPLACE VIEW td_cookbookV.EMP_TBL_View
AS
Select
E.EMP_ID,
D.EMP_DEPT,
D.DEPT_CITY,
E.SAL -- NEW ADDED COLUMN
FROM
```

```
td_cookbook.EMP_TBL_A E inner join
td_cookbook.EMP_TBL_B D ON
E.EMP_ID=D.EMP_ID
Where e.EMP_ID=1032
```

6. Now, let's drop the view we have created. The following code will drop the view:

```
/*Drop view*/
DROP VIEW td_cookbookV.EMP_TBL_View
```

7. View definition will no longer be available.

How it works...

The view created in the recipe will be retrieving rows from the underlying tables. And WHERE in SELECT will be limiting the number of rows.

 The maximum number of columns in a view can be equal to 2,048.

Any view that gets created needs be given select access to base tables, without it your select will error out, giving the error The owner referenced by user does not have insert with GRANT Option.

Following is the statement to give GRANT:

```
/* Grant on view*/
grant select,insert on <tablesdb> to <viewsdb> with grant option;
```

The thing to note here is that the actual view doesn't store any rows in it like a table. The following are some best practices that you must follow when creating views:

- Specify a locking statement like the following; this will help when multiple people try to access the same view, or else blocking will occur:

```
/*locking statement*/
LOCKING ROW FOR ACCESS
CREATE/REPLACE view
<Select statement>
```

- CREATE VIEW in a separate database container. Maintenance of views is easy.
- REPLACE VIEW whenever the underlying table DDL changes.
- Check the validity of the view from time to time. Data/columns in tables changing might require changes to view definition.

There's more...

Like any other object in a database view, the definition is also stored in DBC tables. Use the following statement to get the list of views in your database:

```
/* List all views*/
SELECT databasename,tablename from DBC.TABLES where tablekind='V'
```

The screenshot shows the output from our local database:

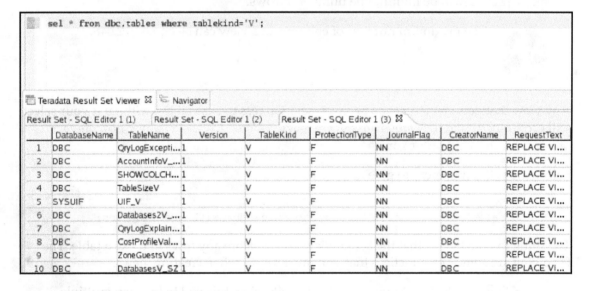

Defining workloads based on application

With millions of queries coming in and out of Teradata Database, it becomes important to manage them better. Low-performance queries need to be demoted or aborted, and critical jobs should be completed as soon as possible.

Your windows also have a workload and process that you can control and give priority to. Kill an application that may have hung your Windows machine. It looks like something like the following image:

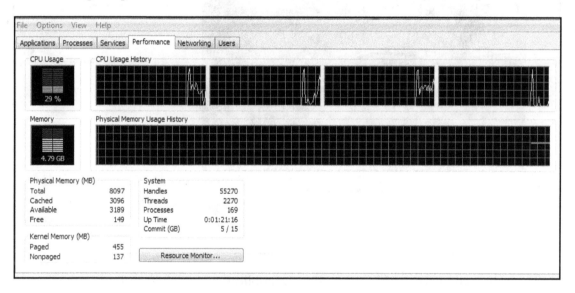

To cater for the need to prioritize the request and to make the system stable, use **Teradata Active System Management** (TASM). The user or batch queries are categorized in the workload. These workloads are then categorized based on their priority. And to further regulate queries in this workload, TASM has filter and throttle created in it.

The following diagram can be used to explain this in a better way:

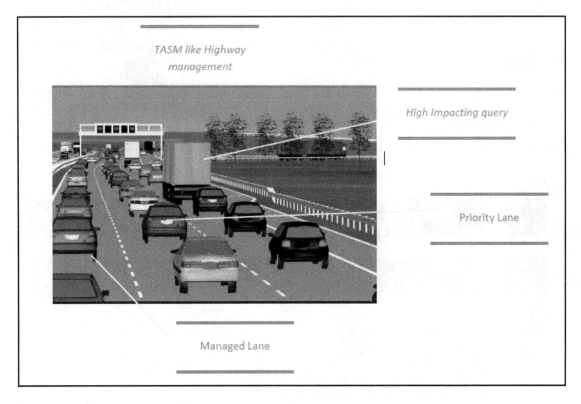

TASM enables admins to set SLGs based on the application, to monitor adherence to them, and to take any necessary steps to reallocate resources to meet business objectives.

Admins can do following with TASM:

- Monitor and regulate queries' concurrent access to Teradata Database
- Manage service-level goals
- Create/manage workload on a system
- Prioritize and optimize workloads
- Block, reject, or abort user queries with defined criteria
- Block access to tables
- Defining alerts on queries or system failures

TASM provides admins with a live view of traffic on the system, which helps admins to identify user queries and tune them if required on the fly. And when you are not monitoring, system alerts can be set up to alert users or admins if something goes wrong on the system or with queries.

From the diagram, let's understand the flow of a query in TASM:

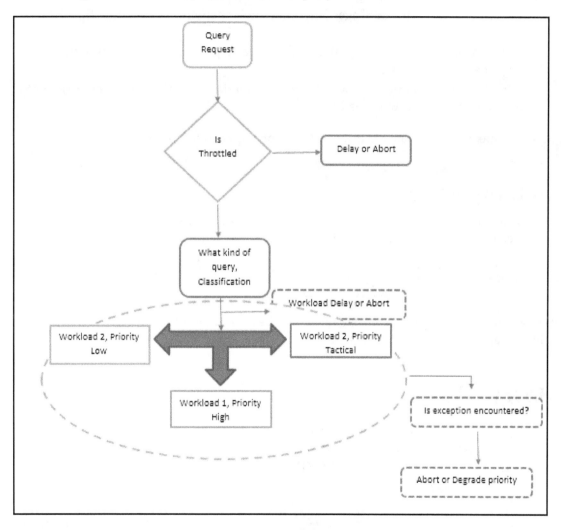

Flowchart of query in TASM

Following are some of the characteristics that defined a workload:

- **Classification criteria**: Characteristics that determine which requests should be assigned to the workload, such as username, profile, and account string.
- **Priority**: This determines how the priority will allocate resources to the requests in the workload during execution. For example, high, medium, or low.
- **Optional throttle settings**: Determines how many requests within this workload can run concurrently.
- **Optional service level goal, SLG**: Either a response time or throughput-based goal sets expectations.
- **Optional exceptions**: A way to manage queries that exhibit characteristics not suitable for this workload.

In this recipe, we will create a workload-based on application profile.

Getting ready

You need to connect to Teradata Viewpoint and have admin access to create a workload. Let's create a profile and then we will relate this profile to a workload:

```
/*Create a profile*/
 CREATE PROFILE finance_workload AS
      DEFAULT DATABASE = td_cookbook;
```

We will map this profile to a workload so that the user in the `finance_workload` profile will be mapped to the new workload.

How to do it...

1. Log in to Teradata Viewpoint using credentials that have access to the workload designer portlet.
2. Open the **WORKLOAD DESIGNER** portlet. It looks something like the following image:

3. Next, click on the **Workload** option in the window. The **General** tab will open up; give the workload a name as highlighted. Enter a **Description** as required:

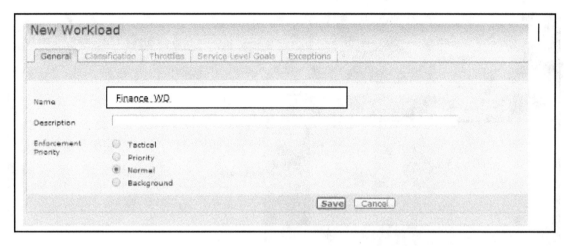

The General tab

4. Next, click on the **Classification** tab. We will map the `finance_workload` profile to this new workload. Click on **Request Source** under add classification criteria:

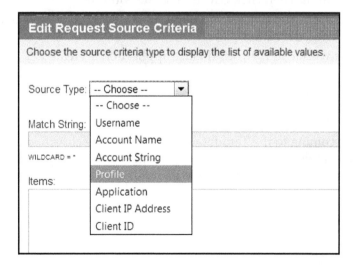

5. Once clicked, an **Edit Request Source Criteria** window will come up. Set **Source Type** as **Profile:**

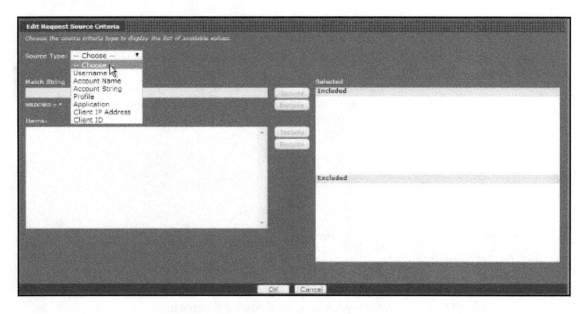

6. Next, a list of profiles will come up. Select the required profile and click on the **Include** button. Then click **OK** to close the window.
7. This will return you to the main window in step 3. Click **Save** to commit to the new workload definition.
8. Your new workload for your finance application is created.

How it works...

Queries or requests coming to the Teradata system need to be classified before they can be allowed to execute on the system. The correct classification of queries helps to give the right priority to queries and helps them to provide their fair share of system resources.

In our recipe, we have used profiles to classify the workload. There are other ways by which we can classify workload, they are:

- **WHO**:
    - **Username**: Admin or high username can be used
    - **Profile**: Best way to classify
    - **Account string**: Second best way to classify
    - **Client IP**: Used to allow or block certain application servers or user machines
- **WHERE**:
    - **Table**: Can abort/delay a query if a certain table is used
    - **View**: Can abort/delay a query if a certain view is referred to
    - **Server object**: Can abort/delay a query if a certain object is referred to
    - **UDF name**: Can abort/delay a query if a certain object is referred to
- **WHAT**:
    - **Join type**: To check a certain type of join, such as product join
    - **Estimated processing time**: If time is high, abort query
    - **Statement type**: Can filter collect stats on certain tables
    - **Single/all-AMP**: Prioritizes requests based on AMP used; used for tactical queries
- **Utility**:
    - **System utility**: Can be mapped to default workload
    - **TPT update operator**: When TPT is used
    - **TPT load operator**: To throttle TPT
    - **JDBC Fastload**: To throttle fast loads
- **QueryBand**:
    - Based on the query band for the specific query

In our recipe, we have classified a request based on profile, but if we want to classify certain users in that profile to another workload we might need to AND the conditions. So, classification in workloads can be clubbed together so that classification can be more granular.

After creation of the workload, it is important to define the throttles option.

There's more...

Application DBAs need to identify the classification of the workload in which the application would be running. This classification mostly remains for a lifetime unless there are major changes that occur on the application side. The nature of the query is still governed by throttles and exceptions, so even if the high priority workload query does something unexpected to the system, TASM has the ability to kill the query and safeguard other applications on the system.

From the Viewpoint workload portlet, you can also witness the health of your workloads. Workloads who have missed their SLGs will be displayed in red. This can be seen in the following figure:

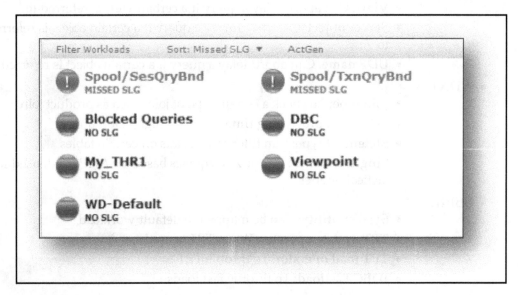

Securing passwords using Teradata Wallet

Teradata Database has many features that make your data and database secure. To continue to make the system more secure, Teradata has introduced Teradata Wallet. Teradata Wallet (TW) is a facility using which you can store sensitive/secret information such as Teradata Database credentials.

What there is in a wallet is known only by the owner of the wallet. The figure shows the visual representation of a vault in which information is secured and can be opened only by the person who is authenticated to do it:

Users save and retrieve credentials by using this utility. This stored information is used while signing in to the Teradata Database using any utility or piece of software that uses Teradata.

The wallet has two parts:

- The **NAME** of the item
- The **VALUE** of the item

Both the NAME and VALUE of the item are sequences of Unicode characters of arbitrary content.

An item name is used to uniquely select an item in the wallet. Value is the content of the item, which could be a password or any other sensitive information. A user is associated only with his own wallet, and the content of any other users is not visible to him.

The Teradata Wallet uses an integrated daemon process which is designed to automatically maintain information to and from the wallet password. This process permits the user to add new password strings to their wallet or to retrieve password-protected strings from the user's wallet, without repeatedly having to provide the wallet password. This mechanism helps (unless the process crashes for some reason) the user not to provide the wallet password even if the user logs back in.

Because the information needed for the password-protected string values in the Teradata Wallet is never saved, the password protection scheme is considered to be more secure than the saved-key protection scheme.

Getting ready

You need to download and install Teradata Wallet from the Teradata Tool and Utility package (TTU).

How to do it...

1. Open Teradata Wallet from program files:

2. A Wallet prompt will open up, as shown in the screenshot:

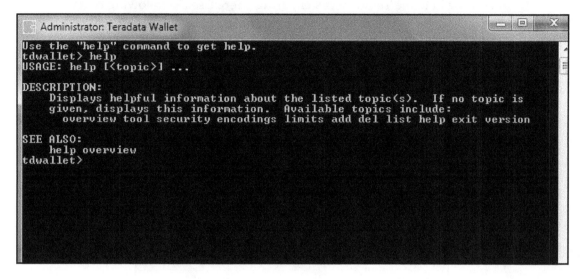

```
Administrator: Teradata Wallet
Use the "help" command to get help.
tdwallet> help
USAGE: help [<topic>] ...

DESCRIPTION:
     Displays helpful information about the listed topic(s).  If no topic is
     given, displays this information.  Available topics include:
       overview tool security encodings limits add del list help exit version

SEE ALSO:
     help overview
tdwallet>
```

3. Issue the following command in the prompt. This will add a Name to wallet, as shown in the screenshot following the code block:

```
/*add string*/
add finance_application
```

```
tdwallet> add finance_application
Enter desired value for the item named "finance_application":
```

4. Next, we will add a password or string to the name. See the following figure:

```
SEE ALSO:
     help overview
tdwallet> add finance_application
Enter desired value for the item named "finance_application":
Item named "finance_application" added.
tdwallet>
```

5. Your wallet, with the `Namefinance_application` is created. Next, we will use this to log in to the Teradata system using `bteq`. Use the following code:

```
/*Use wallet in bteq*/
.logon 192.168.0.12/sysdba,$tdwallet(finance_application)
```

Check the following snippet for details:

```
Teradata BTEQ 16.00.00.02 for WIN32. PID: 11552
Copyright 1984-2016, Teradata Corporation. ALL RIGHTS RESERVED.
Enter your logon or BTEQ command:
.logon 192.168.0.12/sysdba,$tdwallet(finance_application)
```

6. To log in using SQLA, click on the Teradata Wallet string and provide the wallet string as created:

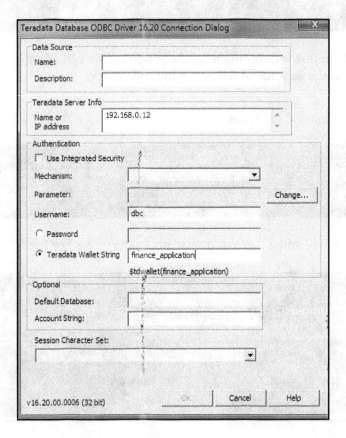

7. You can also add these to shell scripts in Unix machines, as shown in the
    screenshot:

```
My $db = DBI->connect("dbi:ODBC:DSN=$tdserver","$finance_application")
```

How it works...

Teradata Wallet protects each string value using one of the following two protection
schemes:

- **Password**:
    - Not stored anywhere
    - Not written to the hard disk
    - The encryption of string values utilizes a key generated from a
      wallet password
- **Saved-key**:
    - A secret sequence of characters generated from the wallet's
      encryption passphrase

A single Teradata Wallet may contain both password-protected and saved-key protected
string values. Before any password-protected string values can be added to a user's wallet,
the user must establish a wallet password. This wallet password is never saved to any file.

The information stored by Teradata Wallet is segregated by the client user. So, if a given Teradata server or a client machine has two users, **Sam** and **Rose**, then you might visualize the information stored in Teradata Wallet as follows:

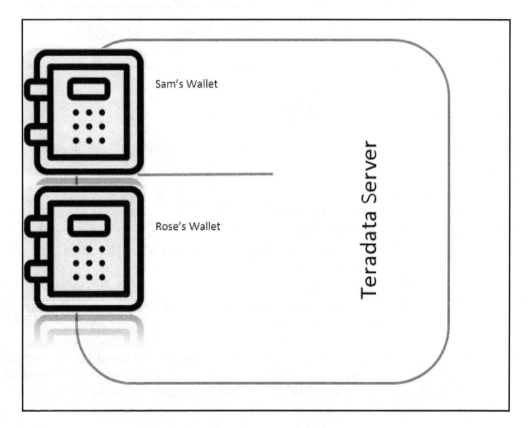

A given user can only access information from his own wallet. The Teradata Wallet software takes extensive measures to protect item values, for example:

- Encrypting item values when passing them to any system call
- Encrypting item values when they are saved on disk

There's more...

Run the following command to access Teradata Wallet online help:

```
tdwallet> help
USAGE: help [<topic>] ...

DESCRIPTION:
    Displays helpful information about the listed topic(s).  If no topic is
    given, displays this information.  Available topics include:
      overview tool security encodings limits add del list help exit version

SEE ALSO:
    help overview
tdwallet>
```

Following are some list of command:

Command	Overview
add <name>	Add an item with the specified name.
addsk <name>	Add an item with the specified name.
del <name>	Delete the item with the specified name.
list	List the names of all items in your wallet.
suppwd	Supply the wallet password after a restart.
forgetpwd	Forget the wallet password. The suppwd command is required to use your wallet again.
exit	Terminate this interactive session if you have entered the tdwallet shell.
chgpwd	Change or establish the wallet password.
chgsavkey	Change or establish the saved-key password.
help [<topic>]...	Output help information for tdwallet.

Shrinking your data size

With increases in data these days, maintaining space on your Teradata system has become important. Businesses now want to capture data of all sorts and want to store it for longer. With data comes insight. Data you might not be using now could become important tomorrow.

This exponential growth in data has presented us with different kinds of problems in data warehouses. With space management and even disks becoming cheap, space is still a concern for businesses when it comes to money.

So, Teradata provides you with many options to manage your space. Compression of data without sacrificing performance; in Teradata you can compress data in the following ways:

- **Multi value compression, MVC**: Software based
- **Algorithmic value compression, ALC**: Software based
- **Block level compression, BLC**: Hardware based

Multi value compression was introduced in TD5; other compression techniques were added with time.

Data you can compress includes:

- Any numeric data type
- Nulls, zeros, blanks
- DATE
- Fixed and Var Character max allowed compress value was 255 till 13.10. But if you are at higher version value is 500.

Data you can't compress includes:

- Primary index column(s)
- Identity columns
- Volatile tables
- Derived tables
- BLOB, CLOB
- Standard RI (can be soft)

In this recipe, we will create a table and compress two columns in that table.

Getting ready

You need to connect to Teradata Database. Let's create the following uncompressed table and insert data into it:

```
/*Create uncompressed table*/
        CREATE TABLE td_cookbook.EMP_SAL
        (
        id INT,
        Sal int,
        dob date,
        o_total int
```

```
    ) primary index( id)
    on commit preserve rows

    INSERT into td_cookbook.EMP_SAL VALUES
(1001,2500,'2017-09-01',890);
    INSERT into td_cookbook.EMP_SAL VALUES
(1002,5500,'2017-09-01',890);
    INSERT into td_cookbook.EMP_SAL VALUES   (1003,500,'2017-09-01',890);
    INSERT into td_cookbook.EMP_SAL VALUES
(1004,54500,'2017-09-05',890);
    INSERT into td_cookbook.EMP_SAL VALUES   (1005,900,'2017-09-05',90);
    INSERT into td_cookbook.EMP_SAL VALUES
(1006,8900,'2017-09-05',800);
    INSERT into td_cookbook.EMP_SAL VALUES
(1007,8200,'2017-08-21',120);
    INSERT into td_cookbook.EMP_SAL VALUES
(1008,6200,'2017-08-06',1230);
    INSERT into td_cookbook.EMP_SAL VALUES
(1009,2300,'2017-08-12',530);
    INSERT into td_cookbook.EMP_SAL VALUES
(1010,9200,'2017-08-15',810);
```

How to do it...

1. You need to connect to Teradata Database using SQLA or Studio.
2. We will now execute the ALTER statement on the DOB column by compressing all values and o_total along with a list of repeating values in these columns.
3. ALTER statement will compresses all values in DOB column:

```
/*Compressing all column values*/
    ALTER TABLE td_cookbook.EMP_SAL
    ADD DOB DATE COMPRESS ; -- ADD COLUMN_NAME DATATYPE
```

4. Next, execute ALTER on the o_total column with a list of repeating values only:

```
/*Compress list of value*/
    ALTER TABLE td_cookbook.EMP_SAL
    ADD o_total INT COMPRESS (890,90);
```

5. Execute SHOW table to check the ddl of the new table and verify that the desired compression has been added to the table definition. Check the following output:

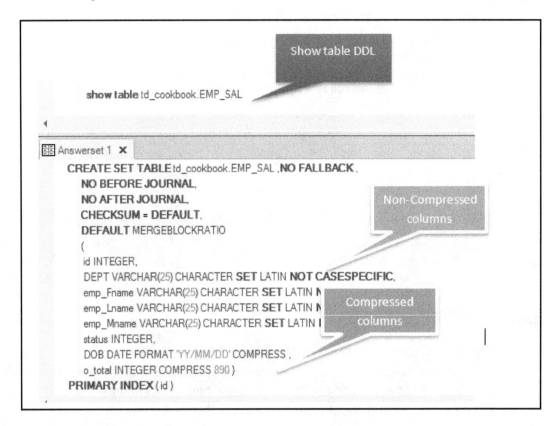

How it works...

Compression is applied on the column level and not on rows. As the name states, it compresses repeated values in a table with NULL, 0, and space. So, what really happens when we issue a compression statement?

In our recipe, the date column takes 4 bytes of space in the table. That means it will occupy 4 bytes of space. Our date column has 6 different values; of them, two are repeating, which are '2017-09-01' and '2017-09-05'. So by applying the MVC technique, Teradata will replace these values with presence bits 01 for '2017-09-01' and 11 for '2017-09-05'; that means only 2 bits instead of 1 byte. These bits are stored in the table header, and when these values are referred to the optimizer replaces these bits with actual values in the table. As the table header resides in memory, there will be no overhead to compress and decompress the data. Here's how the table header and data will look after applying MVC:

Presence Bit O_toal	O_total	DOB	Presence Bit DOB
	Table Header		
	td_cookbook.EMP_SAL		
Compressed Values	90	Uncompressed actual values stored	00000001
	120		00000001
	530		00000001
	800		00000010
	810		00000010
0000 0001			0000001c
000000001			00000011
000000001			00000001
000000001			00000010

All Compressed values

Value 890 in column O_total is compressed so actual values are not stored in the table header like other values shown in the figure. The date column, on the other hand, has all the values compressed, hence no actual date value is stored in the table header. Teradata knows from the table header that o_total has one value compressed and all values for the DOB column. With one presence byte (out of eight), o_total uses 1 bit and DOB column the next 2 bits.

This is how Teradata conserves space without impacting query performance. One might think compressing and un-compressing of data cause CPU resources but that doesn't happen in MVC case.

There's more...

NULL columns are also due for compression in a table. For every nullable column, a presence bit is set to a 1 if that row has a null value in that column for that particular row. Presence bit(s) are also defined for any column with null values. Teradata automatically compresses the NULL values if COMPRESS is defined on that column.

Let's check how MVC improves performance:

- Improves performance of the table where the full scan is happening
- Physical row gets small, which reduces the data blocks, hence less I/O operation

Multivalue compression analysis requires tools, which can execute on the system and generate the DDL of tables which can be compressed. But users can be educated to compress regular values in their tables.

Using query band

Teradata Database provides an intelligent way to tag and track your request when they are in Database. When there are several users executing queries on the system using multiple applications, it becomes important to keep track of the requests in Database. By using Viewpoint, you can view the request status, but to track its resource consumption you require another mechanism. Let's understand query band with an example:

Suppose you have an ETLoad job for an application, and you want to track and analyze the execution of jobs so that if something goes wrong with a job, you know when, what, and where it happened. To make it happen you are required to create a log table where all the activity of the job is recorded. Usually, you would need to log all the steps of your ETL process, and in the logs you would specify unique Load ID, Process ID, Step ID, and so on. You do this because you want to understand which specific request caused performance degradation or failed, and without such logging it would not be possible to distinguish between different runs of your ETL application. A good alternative to this approach would be to associate your queries with Query Band information with Load ID, Process ID, Step ID, and so on. In this way, you would have all the necessary information in DBQL without the necessity to create additional elaborate log tables.

 The Query Band can be set up at the FOR TRANSACTION or FOR SESSION level.

Query band not only helps in identifying your request process—it also helps system admins to allocate resources based on query type. Consider two requests executing in the same workload; now, there is no way to distinguish these two requests from each other. If an admin wants to execute request one in another workload than two, he can't. But if request one has query band, than the admin can create a specific workload for these kinds of query bands. This will help in executing the same profile workload query in two separate workloads.

It helps system administrators to group users and requests based on query bands so that they can allocate proper system resources using TASM.

In this recipe, we will see how to create a query band for a session.

Getting ready

You need to connect to Teradata Database using SQLA or Studio.

How to do it...

1. Connect to Teradata Database using SQLA or Studio.
2. Execute the following statement to enable query band on the session:

   ```
   /*enable query band*/
   SET QUERY_BAND = 'QUERY=Test;ApplicationName=SQLA;' FOR SESSION ;
   ```

3. Now execute any query from SQLA; all the queries associated with the current session will now be executed under this query band:

   ```
   /*sample query*/
   Sel * from dbc.dbase
   ```

4. Now you can retrieve all the queries under this query band from DBQL as follows:

   ```
   /*Get queries under query band*/
   sel query band, querytext,sessionid
   from dbc.dbqlogtbl
   where trim(query band) LIKE '%ApplicationName%';
   ```

How it works...

Query band works in `name:value` pairs and the parameters are then enforced in the current session. A session query band is stored in the session table known as dbc.sessiontbl and recovered after a system reset.

When query band is enabled for a session, all the queries executed in that session will get associated with that. One of the best use cases of query band is when you are optimizing a query. You can set up a query band with post-performance and one-pre-performance. This way, you can track all your work and check the difference to the resource consumption of queries.

You can set up query band using the `VOLATILE` option, in which the `dbc.sessiontbl` will not be updated. This is one way to avoid blocking, caused by query band:

```
/*query band with volatile option*/
SET QUERY_BAND = 'cat=siamese;dog=akita;'FOR SESSION VOLATILE;
```

To turn off query band, use the following code or disconnect the session:

```
SET QUERY_BAND = NONE FOR SESSION;
```

10
DBA Insight

In this chapter, we will cover:

- Creating a Teradata database
- Creating a Teradata user
- Creating profiles and assigning them to users
- Creating a Secure Zone
- Creating user accounts
- Investigating Phantom spool
- Unlocking archive HUT locks

Introduction

While Teradata database has a reputation for lessening the work of a database administrator (DBA), one has to keep in mind that there are some issues which require an administrator's involvement. It could be any of the reason where direct involvement of admin is required. Some of the most frequently occurring issues are:

- Query performance
- System bottleneck
- Space management
- User management

The recipes in this chapter will primarily focus on resolving these issues; we will be using various tools for resolving issues related to user profiles, database space issues, and generating explain plans.

In this chapter, we will use recipes that will help us to create databases and users, and we will use various tools that will help to build a good and streamlined Teradata database system.

Creating a Teradata database

Teradata database is a container of other objects, such as other child databases, tables, stored procedures, indexes, or views. To store these objects, you need to assign space to parent databases you have created; any other objects created in this database will behave as its child and take and release space to its parent database.

To access the database, proper access rights need to be given to a user. It is recommended that only admin team should be allowed to create databases, as databases need to be created in the proper hierarchy while maintaining security compliance.

Getting ready

To step through this recipe, we will connect to the Teradata database instance and use Teradata Studio to execute the `create database` command.

You also need to make sure that you have adequate space in your Teradata database to allocate to your new database.

How to do it...

The following are the steps for creating a Teradata database:

1. Open Teradata Studio and connect to your Teradata system.
2. In the administrator window in Studio, click on **Create a new database**:

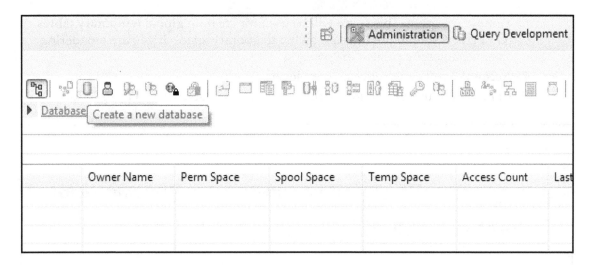

	Owner Name	Perm Space	Spool Space	Temp Space	Access Count	Last

3. It will bring up a box where you need to fill in the details of the new database. In the **General** tab, put in the name of the database, then from the list select the parent under which you want to create this database. The new database will go under **DBC** or the admin database container you might have created on the system, such as **SYSDBA** or **DBA**:

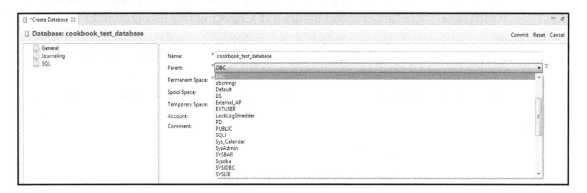

4. **Permanent space**: Space needs to be specified in **KB**, **MB**, **GB**, or **TB**; your selection will be used to store objects in this database. Remember, child databases within this database will be divided among all the other databases.

5. **Spool space**: The next four options are not mandatory. This is usually not required as spool space is drawn from user spool space and the database doesn't require spool.

6. **Temporary space**: This space will be used for creating **global temporary tables** (**GTT**). This should not increase owner temporary space. If you are wondering, Volatile tables are created in spool.

7. **Account**: Imply on user or account level.

8. **Comment**: If useful, put in details as to what this database will be used for:

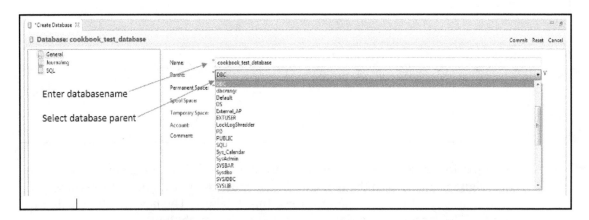

9. Next, click on the **Journaling** option; none of the options under **Journaling** are mandatory. The first option will be **Fallback**. This is not applicable by default but **Fallback** on tables are enabled by default. Checking this box will make all the tables in the database fall back. This is not recommended as normally only main production tables are recommended to fall back. Enabling this will take up double the space on disk:

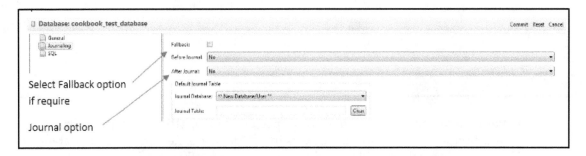

10. **Before Journal**, set to No.

11. **After Journal**, set to No.

12. To check the `sql` of the option we selected, click on the **SQL** option. If required, you can modify the `sql` and copy it to execute it manually from **SQLA** or a **BTEQ**:

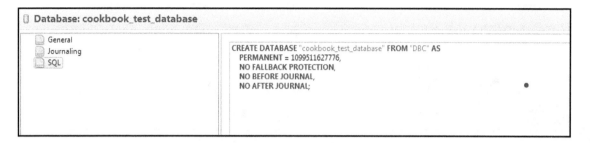

13. Click on **Commit** to create the new database:

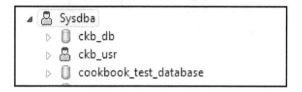

14. The new database will appear under its parent.

How it works...

Database is the main object in Teradata as it holds all the other objects in it. **Option**, specified earlier, will create a database under a parent database which will be used to hold database objects.

There's more...

There are few commands that can be used to display existing databases on the system:

```
Help database
```

This command is used to display the names of all the **Tables (T)**, **Views (V)**, **Macros (M)**, and **Triggers (G)** stored in a database, and table comments. It can be used to quickly find required objects in the database, without writing expensive queries:

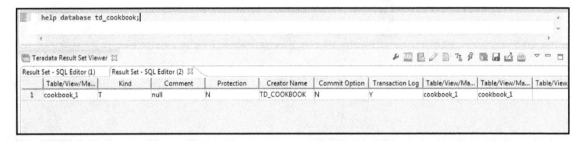

Creating a Teradata database user

In Teradata, a user is an entity that performs actions on the database. It logs onto the system and consumes the resources of the system while performing work. A user can be assigned to individual human users or it could be a batch user that is used to perform ETL or reporting work. Each user has a password, unlike the database. The user can have permanent space and can have spool space allocated to it. It can also own objects, like databases.

Getting ready

To step through this recipe, we will connect to the Teradata database instance and use Teradata Studio to execute the `create user` command.

You need to have admin access to create users on the system.

How to do it...

The following are the steps to create a Teradata database user:

1. Open Teradata Studio and connect to your Teradata system.
2. In the administrator window in Studio, click on **Create a new user**:

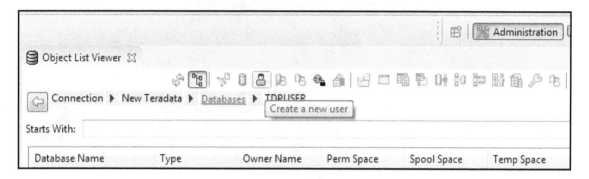

3. It will bring up a box where you need to fill in the details of the new user. In the **General** tab, put in the name of user, then from the list select the parent under which you want to create this user. The option ending with * is mandatory.
4. **Permanent space**: Space needs to be specified in **KB**, **MB**, **GB**, or **TB**; based on your selection, allocated space allows users to store data and other items such as indexes.
5. **Spool space**: Allows users to store intermediate and final rows and volatile tables. With `spool=0`, a user can't execute any queries.
6. **Temporary space**: This space will be used for creating **global temporary tables (GTT)**.
7. **Account**: This needs to be derived from a profile for users.
8. **Default Database**: A database where the user can create volatile tables without specifying the full database name.
9. **Profile name**: Under this, the user will have default roles and other parameters. Parameters defined in the profile supersede the values defined in options, like spool values defined in profiles honored before values defined at the user level.

10. **Role**: Define a default role for each user so it can be used at the time of user logon. The following screenshot gives you an idea of the roles that are to be defined:

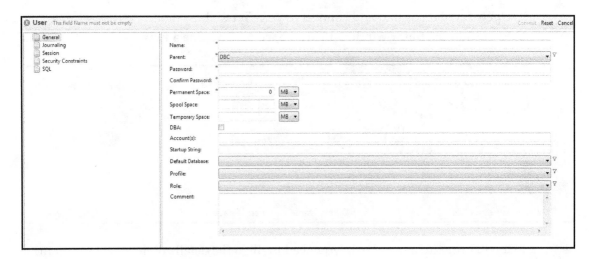

11. Click on the **Journaling** option. **Fallback** creates a duplicate of each table stored in the user space. As best practice, set it to disabled. After clicking on the **Journaling** option, the screen will look as follows:

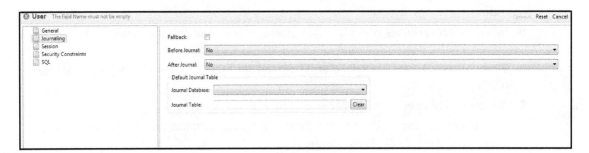

12. **Before Journal**, set to No.

13. **After Journal**, set to No.

14. Select **Session**, objects are setup to default for all users once the database is setup:

15. To check the **SQL** of the option we selected, click on the **SQL** option. If required, you can modify the **SQL** and copy it to execute it manually from SQLA or a BTEQ:

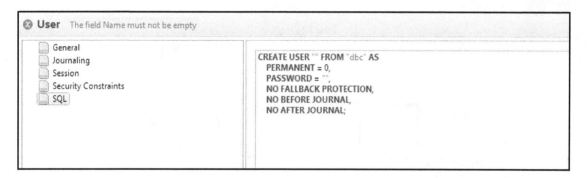

16. A user will be created under the parent, as defined in the options.

How it works...

On the system, users are required to perform certain tasks. When a database is freshly installed, DBC is the only user connected to the database and establishing other objects on the system. We need to identify the types of users on the system and group them according to their functional roles and needs.

There's more...

There are few commands that can be used to display existing databases on the system:

```
Help user <username>
```

This command is used to display the names of all the **Tables (T)**, **Views (V)**, **Macros (M)**, and **Triggers (G)** stored in a user area and table comments.

User creation is somewhat similar to database creation. A user needs to be in a certain hierarchy to fulfill its existence. When the system is installed, DBC, systemfe, and sysadmin are default users that are created on the system. All the space is given to DBC, which sits at top of the hierarchy:

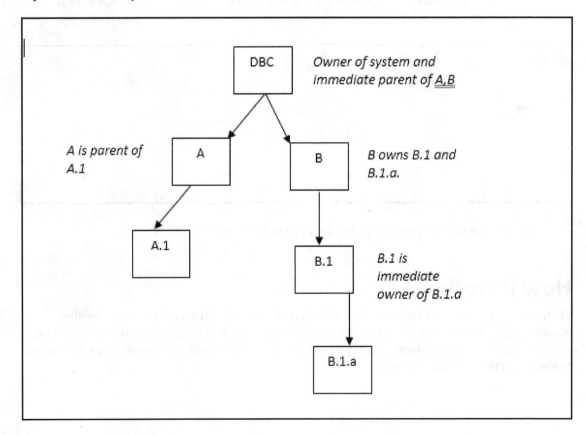

Creating profiles and assigning them to users

Profiles is used to identify and group similar types of user on the system. It has a set of common parameters that are applied. It includes:

- Account IDs
- Default database
- Spool space allocation
- Permanent and temporary space allocation
- Password attributes
- Queryband

As best practice it is beneficial to create different profiles for different user groups, identified based on their application type, business vertical, and other similar properties. Parameter settings in profiles always take precedence over those specified in CREATE or MODIFY USER statements.

Profiles can be modified after creation if required.

Getting ready

To step through this recipe, we will connect to the Teradata database instance and use Teradata Studio to execute the create profile command.

You need to have **admin** access to create a profile on the system.

How to do it...

The following are the steps for creating profiles and assigning them to users:

1. Open Teradata Studio and connect to the Teradata system.

2. In the **Navigator** panel, scroll down to the **Profiles** option, and double-click or left-click to show the **Profiles** option:

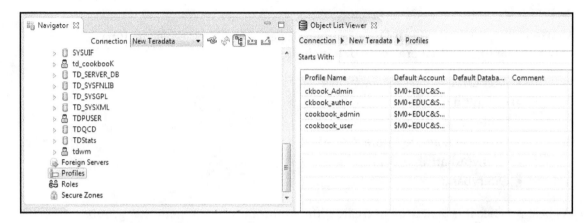

3. If any profiles are on the system they will be shown in the object list viewer.
4. Click on the **Create a new profile** icon, which will open the details form for new profile creation:

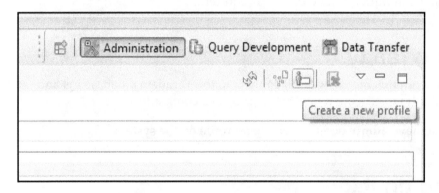

5. Fields marked as * are mandatory.

6. Key in the unique name for the profile. The profile name should identify a group of users, a department, or an application that it's been assigned to:

- **Account**: Assign an account string to the profile; you can assign more than one account string.
- **Default database**: From drop down menu select the database under which profile is to be created.
- **Spool space**: This value limits the amount of results a query can fetch. Users under the same profile share spool space. A higher spool value is recommended if you have high numbers of users in the same profile.
- **Temporary space**: Will be used to create GTT tables.

7. Click on the **Password** option to set the security options for the user password. It is recommended to use high password standards:

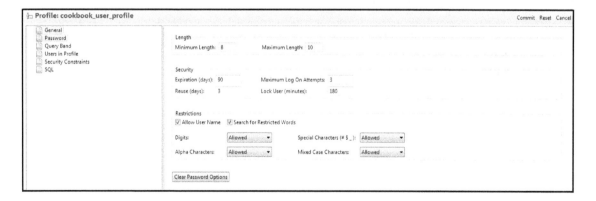

8. Click on the **Query Band** option if you need to bind profiles to a specific query band. **Query Band** is useful in performance optimization activities:

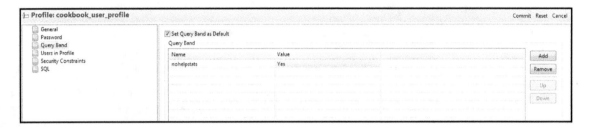

9. Select the list of users that you want to set under this profile from the **Next** option, **User in Profile**:

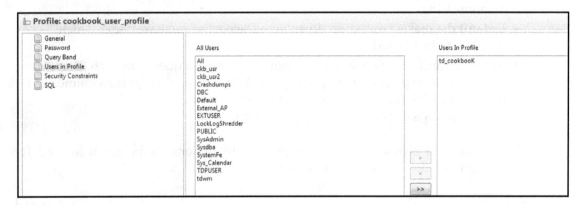

10. To check the **SQL** of the option we selected, click on the **SQL** option. If required, you can modify the **SQL** and copy it to execute it manually from **SQLA** or a **BTEQ**:

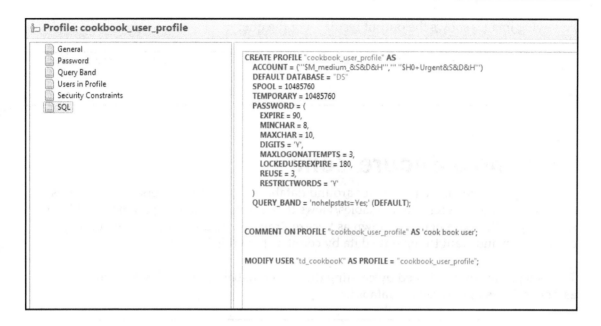

How it works...

Profiles help to cluster users based on similar traits. This gives you an advantage when you want to change parameters for multiple users at once. When a profile is changed for a user, it's applied to a user based on the option changed:

- Spool and perm/temp space allocation are imposed immediately
- Password attributes take effect upon the next logon
- Account IDs and default database are considered at the next logon

There's more...

DBC.ProfileInfo is the related view for profile. You can also query dbc.dbase, where user info is stored:

```
sel * from dbc.profileinfo;
```

Following images shows the output result set of the query:

ProfileName	DefaultAccount	DefaultDB	SpoolSpace	TempSpace	ExpirePassword	PasswordMinChar	PasswordMaxC...	PasswordDigits	PasswordSpecC...	PasswordRestric...	MaxLogonAtte...
ckbook_author	$M0+EDUC&S&D&H	null	5.0E8	1.0E8	null	6	15	Y	I	null	3
cookbook_user	$M0+EDUC&S&D&H	null	5.0E8	1.0E8	null	6	15	Y	I	null	3
cookbook_admin	$M0+EDUC&S&D&H	null	1.0E9	1.0E9	null	6	15	Y	I	null	3
ckbook_Admin	$M0+EDUC&S&D&H	null	1.0E9	1.0E9	null	6	15	Y	I	null	3

Creating a Secure Zone

Ever thought of creating a parameter around database objects? The users defined in this parameter can only access data in tables/views that are also set in this parameter. This setting up of this parameter is known as **Secure Zone**. If you are from a multi-country organization and want to separate data by country, then this is for you.

This is typically accomplished by creating different database hierarchies, known as **Zones**, in a single Teradata database:

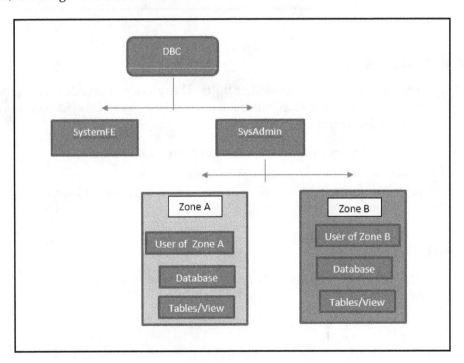

Getting ready

To step through this recipe, we will connect to the Teradata database instance and use Teradata Studio to execute the `create profile` command. Secure Zone is only available from Teradata 15.11 onwards.

You should have admin rights to perform zone creation.

How to do it...

The following are the steps for creating a Secure Zone:

1. Open Teradata Studio and connect to the Teradata system.
2. Open the **Administrator** window.
3. Scroll down to the **Secure Zone** option.
4. Double-click or left-click to show **Secure Zone**. This will display existing Secure Zones on the system:

5. Click on the **lock** icon at the upper right side to open the option to **Create a new Secure Zone**:

6. This will open the **Secure Zone** panel.

7. Fill in the required name, and select the **Root Name**. The root must not have any objects, descendants, roles, or profiles assigned to it:

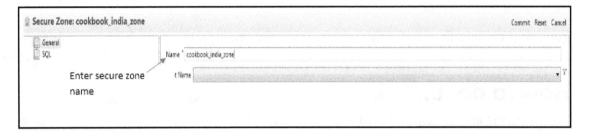

8. Get the SQL if required, or else hit **Commit**.

9. It will open up the options page for the newly created Secure Zone.

10. Enter the zone admin name. First user added to Secure Zone becomes admin of zone automatically:

11. From the users option, select the user needing to be assigned to the zone.

12. Click **Submit** to create a zone with users.

The SQL for creating and adding `admin` to a Secure Zone is as follows:

```
CREATE ZONE zone_name ROOT root_name ;
CREATE USER DBA_user_name FROM database_name ... ;
GRANT ZONE zone_name_list TO user_name_list ;
```

How it works...

Secure Zones are useful when access to data must be tightly regulated and restricted. You can also use Secure Zones to apply security regulatory compliance requirements for the separation of data access from database administration duties.

Secure Zone users are not aware of each other's zones. Zone one users have no idea that zone two exists and vice versa. Even if Secure Zone users execute a query on DBC views, they won't be able to get the details of any secure views. But if they access DBC tables directly, they would be able to see other zone details.

That's why it is important to revoke any SELECT privileges granted directly on DBC tables and to grant access to DBC tables through views only.

There's more...

When doing backup and restore, zone users are only allowed to archive and restore databases in the zone assigned to them.

DBC.ZONES and DBC.Zoneguets are the system tables to get details on zones:

```
Sel * from dbc.zones
```

Following the result set of the query:

ZoneId	ZoneNameI	CreateUID	CreateTimeStamp	ZoneRootId	RootType	ZoneDBAId	CommentString
00-00-1b-04	COOKBOOK_IN...	00-00-01-00	2017-10-16 11:38...	00-00-17-04	D	null	null

Creating user accounts

When creating a new user, the user may be assigned to one or more account ID. The **ACCOUNT** option in **CREATE USER** is used to assign the account. Account is used to analyze the system performance under CPU/IO and space usage, to plan capacity, and for charge back billing. The account string is limited to 128 characters.

When no account ID is specified in the CREATE or MODIFY user statement, it defaults to the database owner's.

Account IDs may begin with $L, $M, $H, or $R. They show different performance groups. General guidelines on performance groups are:

- $L: Low
- $M: Medium
- $H: High
- $R: Rush

ASE (Account String Expansion): Substitution variables can be used in the account ID portion of a user's logon string. ASE is a mechanism to provide more detailed utilization reports and user accounting data. Valid ASE variables are:

- &: An ampersand designates an account string expansion. Can be used with the other variables listed here.
- L: Logon timestamp.
- D: Date.
- T: Time.
- H: Hour.
- I: Logon host/session number/request number.
- S: Session number.

Getting ready

To step through this recipe, we will connect to the Teradata database instance and use Teradata Studio to execute the `create` or `modify account` string command. You should have admin rights to create an account string.

How to do it...

The following are the steps for creating user accounts:

1. Open Teradata Studio and connect to the Teradata system.
2. Open the **Administrator** window.

3. Open the **SQL Editor** and write a CREATE USER query:

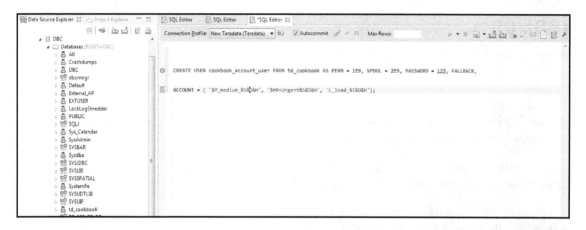

4. Click on the **Execute** button to create a user with an account string.

How it works...

Once the user is assigned to an account string, the usage of groups of users under similar account strings can be tracked and monitored. **Account string** is also used to map to workloads so that priorities for the user are assigned.

If your account starts with a $M, then you are running at a medium priority. $L is low and $H is high. To identify display account string of the current session execute the following query:

```
Select account;
```

Tables **AccountInfo** and **AMPUsage** under **DBC store** data regarding information at account level.

Investigating phantom and leftover spool issues

Spool space is the total amount of space on the system that has not been allocated. The primary reason for the spool space is to store intermediate results or queries that are being processed in Teradata. For example, when executing a conditional query all the qualifying rows that satisfy the given conditions will be stored in the spool space for further processing by the query. Any permanent space on the system that is currently unassigned is available as spool space for the queries.

Each user on the system is assigned certain spool space to complete and execute queries. Spool space can be assigned to users individually or can be enforced by the profile.

An intermediate spool is created while executing queries are released by the system automatically once the step is completed, and in the case of volatile tables it is released once the session is disconnected.

Sometimes, these work tables are not dropped and the spool is not released.

Getting ready

To step through this recipe, we will connect to the Teradata database instance and use Teradata Studio to check spool issues.

How to do it...

The following are the steps for investigating phantom and leftover spool issues:

1. Open Teradata Studio and connect to the Teradata system.
2. Open the **Administrator** window.
3. Open the **SQL Editor** and write a `create user` query:

```
SELECT DATABASENAME, VPROC, CURRENTSPOOL
FROM DBC.DISKSPACE
WHERE DATABASENAME NOT IN (SEL USERNAME FROM DBC.SESSIONINFO)
AND CURRENTSPOOL > 0
ORDER BY 1,2
WITH SUM(currentspool);
```

4. Check for the users whose sessions are not active or in responding mode. The previous query will look for the user who is not logged on to the system but is holding the spool.

5. If the query returns rows, run the **Update space** (updatespace) utility to update the spool space accounting in DBC.DatabaseSpace for each of the databases.

6. Execute updatespace when the system has low user activity.

7. Connect to the **PDN** Teradata node.

8. Type cnsterm 6.

9. In the new window, type start updatespace.

10. This command starts the updatespace utility and gives you back a window number (we started updatespace in window three).

11. Press *Ctrl* + *C* to exit the windows.

12. Type cnsterm 3.

13. Type update spool space for DBname; (where DBname is the database name you got from the query); end it with ;.

14. If no rows are returned, leftover spool issue if not there.

How it works...

Like all tables, spool tables also have table IDs. There are a range of table IDs exclusively reserved for spool tables (C000 0001 through FFFF FFFF) and the system cycles through them. If a table is incorrectly dropped, it remains in existence. Eventually, the system will cycle through all the table IDs and reassign the table IDs which are in use by the leftover spool table.

A user, having been left with leftover spool issues, can face frequent spool failure even if a query is efficient and using limited spool. This needs to be checked with the DBA; update the spool if required.

There's more...

There is a difference between perm space and spool space. Perm space is allocated to an owner or parent; when a child is created from that parent, perm space from that parent is given to the child. This is not the case for spool space. The child with the spool space is as large as its immediate parent.

Unlocking archive HUT locks

HUT locks are placed on tables or databases by Teradata when archive/restore operations are being performed on tables/databases. Sometimes, backup or archive jobs fail, leaving locks on the tables/databases on which the operation is occurring. Ideally the archive/restore/copy script incorporates a `release lock` command in the script to release the lock once the operation is complete. But in case of failure, locks need to be released manually.

Tables/databases with active locks can't be accessed, hence removing locks on them becomes a priority.

Getting ready

To step through this recipe, we will connect to the Teradata database instance and use Teradata Studio or SLQA to release locks. The Teradata Viewpoint portlet remote console will be used to identify locks.

You need to have admin access to the remote console to execute the **Show Locks** utility from the remote console.

How to do it...

1. Connect to the Teradata database using Teradata Studio or SQLA.
2. Log in to Viewpoint on the Teradata system that you have identified.
3. Open the remote console.
4. Browse to the **Show Locks** utility:

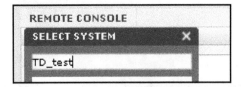

5. The utility will execute and display current locks on tables:

6. You need to make sure locks you have identified are from an ARC job that is not on the system. To verify, check in the query monitor portlet that no ARC job is active on this table. If a job is active, it is not recommended to release the lock. If there is no session, please proceed to the next step:

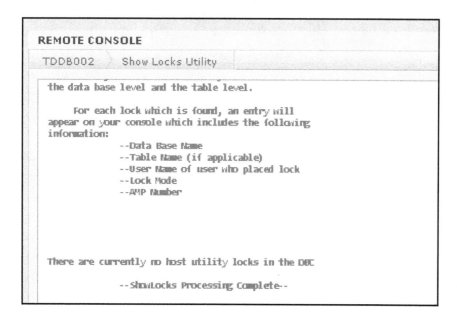

7. Log on via the same account that created the lock to SLQA or Teradata Studio and in the **Query Editor** execute the following statement:

```
Release lock <databasename>.<tablename>;  -- Table levelRelease
lock <databasename>; -- Database level
```

8. If you are not logged on using an ARC user, you can execute:

```
Release lock <databasename>.<tablename>, override;
```

9. Run the **Show Locks** utility again to check if the required table or database is lock free.

How it works...

If **Host Utility (HUT)** locks is not released or ARC jobs got aborted in between, then this may interfere with other job application processing. The thing to note is that the Hut lock is different from transaction locks. Unlike HUT locks, transaction locks have a life of a session from which the command is executed and exist only for the duration of transaction as per its name:

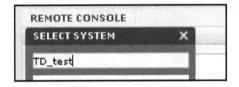

There's more...

RELEASE LOCK removes a utility (HUT) lock from the identified databases or tables:

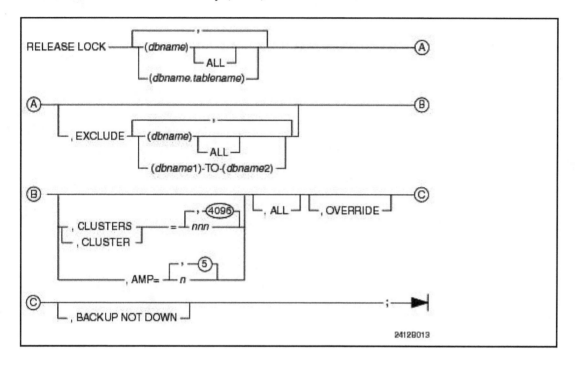

11
Performance Tuning

In this chapter, we will cover:

- Resolving a slow or hung system
- Monitoring slow queries
- Aborting a session from the supervisor window
- Resolving AWT saturation
- Identifying suspect queries
- Managing the DBC space
- Optimizing queries

Introduction

It is important to keep the Teradata database system running in optimal condition so it can be available at 100% capacity and cater to all the work in an optimal fashion. But sometimes a wrong user query or the concurrency of work increases and degrades system performance. DBA should be ready for this unexpected situation and should have tools of the trade ready to overcome this situation.

Teradata performance features and recommended practices are difficult to capture in one document.

The following recipes will guide you through setup processes and monitoring day-to-day performance. They will also help you to identify and act upon system problems, enabling database admins to identify the cause of poor performing queries quickly and accurately. This will help to improve system response times and allow you to manage available resources optimally.

In performance tuning, we have to look at these parameters to improve system performance:

- Minimize IO
- Reduce CPU utilization
- Optimize query execution
- Utilize Teradata features

Resolving a slow or hung system

Teradata system can be so overburdened by workload and user work that the system becomes completely saturated and brought to a standstill. However, a slow system is different from a hung system. It may be difficult to tell whether the system is truly hung or just so busy that it cannot service any more requests until it works through the load. In a true Teradata system hang situation, the system itself will not be busy at the CPU level, because generally a process is unable to complete for whatever reason but may be holding some resources (for example, the CPU or monitor task); other processes are waiting behind it. If the system is very busy, CPU will be high and AMP worker tasks may be completely in use or exhausted, but the system will still be processing user work.

Getting ready

You need to connect to the Teradata system via SLQA/Teradata Studio. Supervisor/remote console via viewpoint also needs to be connected:

```
login as: root
Using keyboard-interactive authentication.
Password:


TDExpress15.10_sles11:~ # cnsterm 6
Attempting to connect to CNS...Completed.

Input Supervisor Command:
```

How to do it...

The following are the steps for resolving a slow or hung system:

1. Log on to your database via SQLA/Teradata Studio or a remote console.
2. If step 1 succeeds, then the database is not hung.
3. Execute the following query and check the response time. These query runs with a minimum response time when the system is performing optimally:

```
**ALL AMP Query**
Sel * from dbc.dbcinfo;

**Single AMP Query**
select time;
```

4. Check on **viewpoint, system health portlet**; if it shows down, check the number of sessions in the query monitor window:

System health portlet

5. If the health portlet shows down and the number of sessions is not zero then the system is up and running but could be hung. At this time it could be that the viewpoint itself is not refreshing. Check the date and time on the portlet; see if it refreshes.
6. If the health portlet shows down and the number of session is zero, then the system is down and not hung:

7. If the answer is *no* in step 1, the database is probably hung, but at this point we need to do steps 8 to 10 to verify.

8. We will check CPU utilization by executing the following command:

```
psh sar -uq 5 5 **Execute command 5 times in 5 second interval**
```

The `sar` (system activity reporter) command can be used to look at CPU and memory usage. The following figure depicts the memory usage:

```
dbs1:~ # sar 5 5

Linux 11.6.5-7.244-smp (dbs1)

1:16:35     CPU    %user    %nice   %system   %iowait     %idle

1:16:38     all     0.0      0.0     0.17      0.00        99.83

1:16:41     all     0.0      0.0     0.17      0.0         99.83

1:16:44     all     0.00     0.0     0.0       0.0         100.00

Average:    all     0.0      0.0     0.1       0.0         99.89


dbs18:~ #
```

9. **If the CPU is 100% busy**, then something is running. That alone does not determine if the system is moving.
10. If any nodes show higher WAIT I/O, this could be the start of a slow lun/disk problem.
11. **If the CPU is not 100% busy:** Are maybe only some nodes showing as 100% CPU busy? The resource contention may be at **AWT (AMP worker tasks)** level.
12. The next step would be to check AWT count and to do this we will execute the awtmon command:

```
awtmon
awtmon -s **display in summary format for all nodes**
awtmon -s -t 50 **display in summary format where Inuse awt > n
specified**
awtmon -s -t 50 2 2 **shows 2 samples taken in 2 second intervals
of all AMPs with n or more AWT's in use**
```

13. The count of AWT from this is equal to ~62 (normal system with 80 AWT) on some or most all AMPS, the system is saturated. The maximum number of AWT here depends on your system configuration.

14. Execute this command few times to check if the count is moving. If it is then work is getting done and the system is slow.

15. If AWTs are high on some AMPs then check for skew query from viewpoints that are on the system. The following output shows one AMP, 29 being out of AWTs, and also shows the worktypes that are using the AWTs:

```
dbs_001-9t:~ # awtmon -s
====> Sat Nov 4 1:5:28 2017 <====
byn001-9:  Amp 0   : Inuse:  4:   FOUR:  1 THREE:   3
byn001-10: Amp 1   : Inuse:  3:   THREE:  3
byn001-11: Amp 29:Inuse: 68:ABORT: 5 NEW:57 THREE: 3 TWO:  3
byn002-12: Amp 89  : Inuse:  5:   NEW:
```

16. Once you have established that the system is slow and not hung, proceed to viewpoint to catch high impacting queries and take necessary actions.

17. If no work is getting done, the system CPU is idle, and you are not able to log in to the system by any means, you need to engage with Teradata system engineers.

How it works...

By using multiple tools only we can identify the exact root cause of the system, hung or slow. Steps to resolve system bottlenecks should be carried out and analyzed carefully. System slowness symptom or a hung system are two totally different things, different procedures need to be applied based on the scenarios.

After catching the culprit query it is necessary to act upon it immediately, otherwise it can have a cascading effect on the system and it is possible that system slowness will turn into a system hung issue.

It is advisable to limit the amount of work when the system is under stress; new work not only won't be able to complete, but it will also hamper the existing work on the system. Workload management is very important in such scenarios.

Monitoring slow queries

It sometimes becomes necessary to abort running jobs on the system. Before aborting any job, it should be identified and problematic steps (on which it is currently executing) need to be captured and analyzed so that this can be corrected before the next run.

Teradata provides many methods/tools to identify these problematic jobs, but sometimes when a system is unresponsive or has high usage it is difficult to identify the exact query or job that is causing the issue. In these cases we need to check the system with multiple tools so that a confirmed result is drawn.

We can monitor system resources from:

- Viewpoint
- SQL queries
- PCMC queries
- Various tools running from the supervisor window/remote console

Getting ready

To execute the next recipe you need to connect to the Teradata database via SQL/Studio. Log on to the viewpoint and remote console.

How to do it...

1. Connect to the Teradata database and log on to viewpoint.
2. On viewpoint, check the high resource consumption query/session. Concerned session depends on your requirements. You can sort sessions by high CPU or IO.
3. Click on **Session**.
4. Check the step the query is currently executing on.
5. Once you have identified the session from viewpoint, we need to check it from the database side also.
6. Log on to `qrysessn` from the remote console portlet on viewpoint:

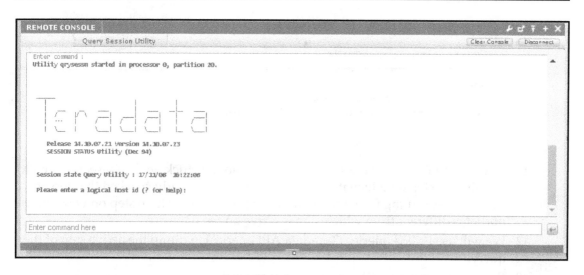

7. Enter the appropriate host ID. Type * to specify all host IDs.

8. Enter the session number (the same as in viewpoint) for which you need information.

9. Specify Y for yes if detailed information is required for HUT/FASTLOAD/MLOAD/EXPORT sessions.

10. Click enter to terminate the `qrysessn` utility.

    The following code block will give you a better idea of the query that is to be run:

```
# cnsterm 6
> start qrysessn
# cnsterm 1
 Please enter a logical host id (? for help):
> *
*
Please enter session ids (? for help):
> 101239
101239
Please enter session ids (? for help):
>
Is detail information needed if the session is involved in
HUT/FASTLOAD/MLOAD/EXPORT?
y-yes, n-no
> n
n
QUERYSESSION will run in Perf Group: default
Session state query results : 11/04/17  18:30:03
  Host    Session  PE      DBC User ID
  -----   -------  -----   ----------------------------------
```

```
     1        101239  1  DBC sysdba

State details : ACTIVE
================================================================
=====
End of session state report
Please enter a logical host id (? for help):
>
QrySession has terminated
```

11. Once we establish that the session is active and not stuck on database, we need to identify the step on which it is executing. We have already checked the step on which it is executing from viewpoint in step 4. But some time step on viewpoint portlet is different from which step is active on the database.

12. We will use PMPC queries (Teradata API queries) to dump the active step of the query.

13. Execute all sessions with an active amp request:

```
**Active sessions**
SEL HostId (TITLE 'Host',FORMAT 'ZZZ9'),
 UserName (TITLE 'Active Users'),
 SessionNo (TITLE 'Session'),
 LogonPENo (TITLE 'IFP')
FROM TABLE (SYSLIB.MonitorSession(-1,'*',0)) AS t1
WHERE AmpState='ACTIVE'
ORDER BY 1,2;
```

14. Extract the `IFP` number of the session we are interested in from step 13:

Host	Active Users	Session	IFP
1	sysdba	101239	16383

15. Next, we need to identify the current step the session is on and match it to the viewpoint one:

```
SELECT *
FROM
TABLE(syslib.MonitorSQLCurrentStep(1, 128988, 16383)) as t1;
```

HostId	SessionNo	NumOfSteps	CurLvl1StepNo	CurLvl2StepNo
1	101239	5	4	4

16. The previous session is active on step 4 of a total of 5 steps in a query. This the actual step on which query is still active on.

17. Execute this query multiple times to check the progress of the session; if it is on the same step it means the query has been active on that step for a long time.

18. We will now get more details about this step by comparing estimated rows vs actual rows of previous steps:

```
SELECT t2.StepNum (FORMAT 'ZZZ9'),
  t2.EstRowCount (FORMAT 'ZZZ,ZZZ,ZZZ,ZZ9'),
  t2.ActRowCount (FORMAT 'ZZZ,ZZZ,ZZZ,ZZ9'),
  t2.EstElapsedTime (FORMAT 'ZZZ,ZZZ,ZZ9'),
  t2.ActElapsedTime (FORMAT 'ZZZ,ZZZ,ZZ9'),
  SUBSTRING(t2.SQLStep FROM 1 FOR 50) (TITLE 'SQLStep')
FROM
TABLE (syslib.MonitorSQLSteps(1, 101239, 16383)) AS t2;
```

Following is the output from the query:

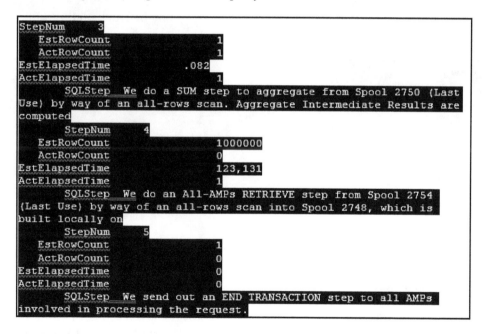

19. Estimated and actual step from explain needs to be reviewed; if estimation seems to be extensively high and join processing not right, you might proceed to abort this session.

How it works...

You would need to monitor a session if the current request in that session is progressing very slowly and taking much longer than expected to complete. The session in that case needs to be investigated before the request may in turn use more resources (CPU, IO, Spool) than it should and possibly degrade the performance of other sessions on the system.

In these cases you would need to monitor and identify the session in order to get more information about the session. What is the session doing? Why is it behaving that way?

Viewpoint, SQLA, or other performance monitoring applications are used to establish common ground and improve the analysis if any of the tools. We might not have access to one tool and might use another to identify and resolve the bottleneck.

There's more...

If a session is stuck but not active on the database side, it may be stuck on the client/gateway/network side:

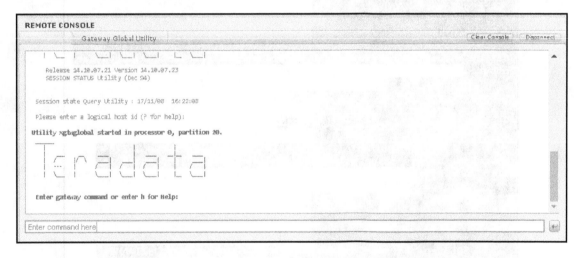

In order to get more information about the session state, we can use `xgtwglobal` to get more information about the status of a session. This can be invoked from the viewpoint portlet remote console:

```
> se ho <host_id>  -- Get the hostid from qrysessn
> di se <ses_no> -- input the stuck session_no
> di se <ses_no> lon
```

Aborting a session from the supervisor window

Sometimes, it becomes a requirement to abort a session from the supervisor window. We can also abort a user from viewpoint, but when sessions are not able to abort from viewpoint, in some cases you need to abort them from the supervisor window.

Caution needs to be taken while executing commands from supervisor windows, as they execute from the node and, if not executed properly, can abort or restart the system.

Getting ready

Connect to the Teradata database using viewpoint and the open portlet remote console.

How to do it...

The following are the steps for aborting the session from the supervisor window:

1. Log on to viewpoint.
2. Open the remote console portlet.
3. Log in to abort the host utility:

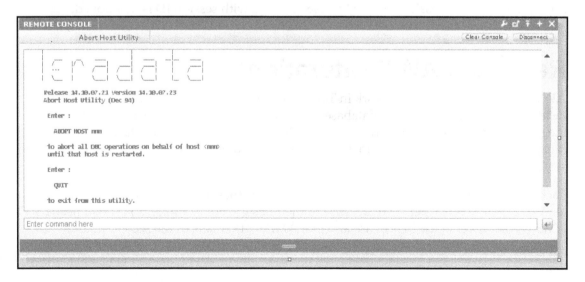

4. Execute abort session command `* . <username>`.

5. You can abort the session via `username` or using the session ID.

6. A group of session IDs can be clubbed together to abort sessions:

```
                <hostid>:<sessionno>
                <hostid>.<username>
abort session *.<username> [logoff] [list] [override]
                <hostid>.*
                *.*
```

How it works...

The `ABORT SESSION` command allows the user to abort a group of sessions and optionally log them off. `<hostid>` is a value within the range of 0 to 32,767. Multiple `<sessionno>` can be used to abort sessions all together. `<username>` is character data with a maximum length of 30 characters.

There's more...

You can also abort user queries using SQLA which executes using PMPC monitor table:

```
SELECT AbortSessions (1, 'sysdba', <sessionid>, 'Y', 'Y');
```

Log off and abort all sessions where the user `sysdba` with session ID is mentioned.

Resolving AWT saturation

AWTs are the smallest unit of work in Teradata. These are the tasks or execution threads inside of each AMP that get the database work done, such as executing a query step once the step is dispatched to the AMP. Each AMP has up to 80 AMP worker tasks available to them. AWTs can be increased from 80 if required, based on requirements and the size of the system.

Each request executing on a system may require more than 1 AWT to complete. Utilities tend to use more AWT per AMP because of their design. For example, a Fastload needs 3 AMP worker tasks in the first phase and one AMP worker task in the second phase.

AWT, are very critical and are always in demand, below is the break up of 80 AMP worker tasks:

- 24 AWTs are reserved for a special purpose
- 56 AWTs are general purpose
- A maximum of 50 AWTs can be used for Dispatched steps
- The normal case is 62 AWTs used for Dispatched steps and the first level of spawned work

It is important to understand what happens when AMP worker tasks are exhausted and what makes these AWT run out:

1. SQL request sent from a host to Teradata is processed by a PE:
   - PE: Parses request, does syntax checks and generates join plan.
   - Dispatcher sends join plan steps to AMP via BYNET driver.
   - BYNET driver broadcasts all-AMP steps to all AMPs or sends a single point to point message to a single AMP.
2. BYNET driver, upon receiving the AMP, puts a request in a Message Queue (mailbox).
3. When AWT is available, the scheduler takes a request out of the Message Queue and assigns it to an AWT step.
4. When AWTs are not available, requests remain queued up in the Message Queue.
5. When the Message Queue for a given message type reaches the limit of its configuration, additional messages of the same type sent to the AMP are rejected by the AMP and are queued into the sending node's BYNET retry queue. For all-AMP messages, if one AMP's Message Queue is full, then the message is rejected by all AMPs. When messages go into the BYNET retry queue, the system is under flow control or AWT are not available for new work.

This so-called flow control or AMP worker task saturation needs to be checked using a different monitoring tool.

Getting ready

You need to connect to the Teradata database and log on to Viewpoint.

How to do it...

The following are the steps for resolving AWT saturation:

1. Log on to viewpoint.
2. Open the remote console portlet on viewpoint.
3. Connect to any node using the ssh terminal.
4. Execute puma -c to display the resource control information for each worktype in Vprocs. The information includes the minimum, maximum, currently in-use, and the peak number of AMP worker tasks assigned for each worktype:

```
puma -c
```

5. With all default AMP numbers, if the total in-use count for the MSGWORKNEW and MSGWORKONE worktypes of a VPROC is = 62, it indicates a congested AMP. This means more new work is coming to the system and existing work is not getting completed. Can be seen in figure as INSUE column is at 62.

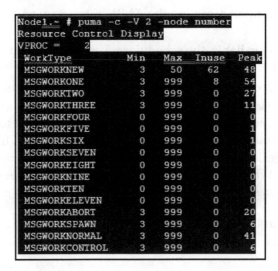

6. Execute this command a couple of times to see if the in-use values change, and to see if current work progressing on system.
7. Next is to execute puma -m, which will display message count details to analyze flow control on AMP:

```
Node 1-6:~ # puma -m
```

```
<---------------- byn001-6 ---------------->
```

MbxId	Part	Vproc	Owner	MsgCount		MsgDQCount
171909067		81	25345	20		446
171912845		81	13971	19		88
171913303		81	983	19		1
171909144		81	31078	20		624
171913255		81	32250	4		6
171912043		81	32347	20		1708
171913067		81	32640	18		37
171911532		81	17786	20		5467
171911342		81	31670	20		6142
171913011		81	32348	20		2661
171907316		81	23003	19		1237
171908597	11	81	30710	21	Work	481087
171913213		81	31229	11		10
170691363		82	1014	6		14
170379523		83	31845	13		7

8. `Vproc 81` seems to have a high number of messages; this could mean either very skewed work is executing on this AMP or high resource intensive work is currently executing on this AMP. It might also be because of hardware issues such as a slow disk attaching to this AMP.

9. To verify this we will execute the following query via SQLA or Studio. to see if we get the exact same AMP number as we got from the puma command:

```
locking row for access
SELECT NodeId
,VprId
,SUM(MsgChnLastDone)    (TITLE 'LastDone' )
FROM DBC.ResUsageSVPR
WHERE VprType LIKE 'AM%' AND TheDate = date
GROUP BY 1,2
ORDER BY 3 desc;
```

Following is the output from the query:

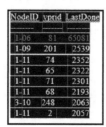

NodeID	vprid	LastDone
1-06	81	65081
1-09	201	2539
1-11	74	2352
1-11	65	2322
1-11	71	2301
1-11	68	2193
3-10	248	2063
1-11	2	2057

10. Once we have established that one of the AMPs is in flow control and the AWT are exhausted, we need to monitor the system very closely and repeat these steps again until we see that the system is in a stable condition.

11. Monitoring in such cases is extremely important because, if not monitored properly, the system can run into a hung state.

12. Once we get the AMP number we can query DBQL and check the associated users, or CPU and IO, done on that AMP:

```
LOCKING ROW FOR ACCESS
SELECT * FROM DBC.DBQLOGTBL
WHERE MaxIOAmpNumber = 81
OR MaxCPUAmpNumber = 81;
```

13. Sessions which are running with skewed resources need to be terminated and tuned before their next execution.

How it works...

It needs to be understood that, on a very busy system, there are probably always some processes in flow control. This in itself is not necessarily a bad thing, after all we need a Teradata database to perform with 100% efficiency. It becomes bad when processes are stuck in flow control and there are no or few messages that are being processed on a mailbox. All the information and context needed to perform the database work is contained within the query step. Once the step is complete, the AWT is returned to the pool.

Workload management helps in controlling flow control and excessive use of AWT at the same time. User work needs to be allowed on the system in an effective way, and bad jobs should be aborted before they can take over the system. But sometimes, due to hardware failure or bad user queries, system starve of resources.

Calculation of threshold of AWT to get exhausted is complicated, but we can put them in range to represent the maximum number of AWTs that can service user work without any issue. Generally, the value of the threshold is equal to the total number of AWTs per AMP (recorded in the `AwtLimit` variable) minus 18, though this formula is based on some assumptions that do not always hold true.

For a typical system with 80 AWTs per AMP, an AMP is:

- Approaching exhaustion if `InuseMax` is in the range of 50 to 58
- Starting to exhausted if `InuseMax` is between 62 and 68
- Exhausted if `InuseMax` is greater than 68

There's more...

The system automatically records AWT usage in the `ResUsageSAWT` table. There are several columns in the table that help to analyze and plot graphs against AWT and flow control usage over a period of time.

Table carries both history values and point in time snapshots, carrying two sets of information:

- AMP worker task usage. In-use counts as well as maximum in-use count of each message work type on each AMP.
- Message Queue depth.
- Flow control metrics.

Following code gives details from resusage table.

```
***ResUsageSAWT**
SELECT
extract(hour from thetime),
extract(minute from thetime),
VprID
,FlowControlled (decimal (8,0))---flowcontrol indicator
,FlowCtlCnt (decimal (8,0)) --number of time system went into flowcontrol
in 10 min
,MailboxDepth (decimal (8,0))
FROM DBC.ResusageSAWT
WHERE TheDate = 'YYYY-MM-DD'
ORDER BY TheTime,VprID;
```

Identifying suspect queries

Daily, thousands of queries execute on a Teradata database. Some queries' execution is under milliseconds; these are quick and not visible in the monitoring portlet called viewpoint. Some queries have a tendency to execute over minutes, some execute over hours. Whatever the queries are, they need to consume resources on the system. Queries that consume resources such as CPU and IO in their threshold values are classified as good or optimal queries.

Queries that over consume the resources are called suspected queries. Analysis of these queries is necessary from time to time. If these are not inspected over time it can cause the system to under perform.

Definition of and classification of these suspect queries depends on the system. A Teradata database with high configurations such as a large number of nodes can withstand high resource queries for some time, but still these queries—irrespective of the system—are bad in nature and need to captured and tuned.

Getting ready

You need to connect to the Teradata database system using SQLA or Studio.

How to do it...

The following are the steps for identifying suspect queries:

1. Connect to the Teradata system using SQLA or Studio.
2. Execute the following query:

```
SEL Logdate , Hr (TITLE 'Hour'), Wrkld as WorkloadName, SUM(CPU) as
TotalCPU
FROM
(
SEL logdate , EXTRACT(HOUR FROM LogonDateTime) AS Hr , b.RuleName
AS Wrkld ,
CASE WHEN TotalIOCount = 0 THEN 0
ELSE ((AMPCPUTime+Parsercputime) * 1000)/TotalIOCount
END AS "PJI",
CASE WHEN (AMPCPUTime + Parsercputime) =0 THEN 0
   ELSE (TotalIOCount) / ((AMPCPUTime + Parsercputime) * 1000)
END AS "UII",
```

```
CASE WHEN ((AMPCPUTime+Parsercputime) / (HASHAMP()+1)) =0 THEN 0
ELSE ( 1 - (AmpCPUTime / (HASHAMP()+1))/NULLIFZERO(MaxAmpCPUTime))
END AS "CPU_skew" ,
CASE WHEN (TotalIOCount / (HASHAMP()+1)) =0 THEN 0
ELSE (1-(TotalIOCount / (HASHAMP()+1))/NULLIFZERO(MaxAmpIO))
END AS "IO_skew", MaxAMPCPUTime * (HASHAMP()+1) /*no. of Amps*/ AS
ImpactCPU,
SUM(AMPCPUTime + Parsercputime) AS CPU
FROM pdcrinfo.dbqlogtbl_hst a INNER JOIN (
sel RuleId, RuleName
from tdwm.RuleDefs
group by 1, 2) b ON b.RuleId = a.wdid
WHERE AMPCPUTime > 1
            AND logdate BETWEEN date-30
            AND date-1
            GROUP BY 1,2,3,4,5,6,7,8
            HAVING (PJI > 3
            OR UII> 3
            OR CPU_skew >0.5
            OR IO_skew >0.5
) )a
GROUP BY 1,2,3
order by 1,2,3;
```

3. Copy the result of this query to Excel and classify the query based on **PJ** (**product join**), **UII** (**unnecessary I/O**), CPU skew, and IO Skew.

4. Analyze queries based on output.

How it works...

The metrics are used to get an idea of query efficiency when consuming CPU and I/O resources.

PJI is the measure of how CPU intensive your query is. If PJI is relatively high for a query, then the query takes many CPU cycles for the given number of I/Os; PJI stands for **product join indicator**. This can also be seen in explain when you see a product join keyword. But sometimes it is not necessary for a query to do a product join when a value is high, as it can also mean that the query is doing a full table scan or high scan of a table which is causing more IO cycles than the CPU. Hence the name of the metric. PJI values of up to three can be acceptable and can't be avoided because of the nature of queries; anything above three indicates that you have to review your query and check that you are not doing unwanted product joins or scanning a large row table.

If UII is relatively high for a query, then it could mean that many I/O blocks are read, meaning how IO intensive your query is, but a relatively low number of rows is actually processed. UII is a ratio of IO to CPUTIME. If it is a full table scan with only a few rows qualifying, then an index could reduce the I/O consumption in this case.

Both metrics are available in Viewpoint's Query Monitor portlet, and every individual query has these values displayed when you click on the session ID.

Managing DBC space

A system user named **DBC** (**database computer**) is the owner of all disk space on a system. When the system is initially set up, spaces for child databases are derived from DBC itself. DBC's space includes dictionary tables, databases, views, and all the child databases:

```
**DBC database space**
    Select sum(MaxPerm) from DBC.DiskSpace where DatabaseName = 'DBC';
```

It is very important to understand space in DBC itself. Why is it important and what it is used for?

Once you allocate space from DBC to other databases, it is important that you keep adequate space in the DBC database to accommodate the growth of system tables and logs, and the transient journal. Also, if you are not using a separate database for the spool, space in DBC can also be used for spool purposes (all the empty space in the system is used as the spool).

The main reason to keep an eye on DBC is because of **TJ** (**transient journal**). It maintains snapshots of rows that are going to be processed or are getting processed. Let's take an example to understand transient journal; let's say you are withdrawing Rs. 1000 from an ATM. If all goes *ok* your back account will be depleted by Rs. 1000. But what if the transaction cancels in between? Do you still want your account to show less than Rs 1000? No, right? This is the scenario in which TJ comes into picture. By returning data to its original state after failure, transient journal helps in maintaining the integrity of transactions.

The following recipe will help to resolve the DBC space issue if occurring; there is also a proposed solution to alert admin when this occurs. First we will check the space on the overall system, and if you find that space on production databases are under control, you will move to the TJ table.

Getting ready

You need to connect to the Teradata database using SQLA or Studio. Log on also to viewpoint.

How to do it...

The steps for managing DBC space are as follows:

1. Log in to the Teradata database using SQLA or Studio.

2. Identify the tables in the database that have grown significantly:

```
**Table Space**
LOCK dbc.tablesize ACCESS
SELECT tablename, SUM(cur rentperm)
FROM dbc.tablesize
WHERE databasename ='<databasename>' -- if require to filter
specific databases
GROUP BY 1 ORDER BY 2 DESC;
```

3. If the tables from step 2 do not show any abnormal growth, we will check on another possibility. The DBC maxperm limit is exceeded on just one AMP, but there is still enough free space on other AMPs:

```
**Space per AMP/VPROC to check skewness**
LOCK ROW FOR ACCESS
SELECT
vproc,
SUM(currentperm),
SUM(maxperm)
FROM dbc.diskspace
WHERE databasename = '<databasename>'
GROUP BY 1 ORDER BY 2 DESC;
```

4. We will now check the space in TJ to check if we have run into a large TJ:

```
**To check space and skewness in TJ table**
SELECT DatabaseName,Tablename,MAX(CurrentPerm) AS MaxPerm,
MIN(CurrentPerm) AS MinPerm ,
(100 - (AVG(CurrentPerm)/NULLIFZERO(MAX(CurrentPerm))*100)) (FORMAT
'Z9.99') AS SkewFactor
FROM dbc.TableSize
WHERE databasename IN ('dbc')
AND     tablename IN ('TransientJournal' )
GROUP BY 1,2
```

5. If DBC space is filling up fast, user logons will be refused to secure the database.

6. Using your existing session, check for large insert, update, or delete which is abort state from viewpoint. Aborting session takes 3 times the original session to finish.

7. Try to modify space from other databases that is owned by DBC. The GIVE command won't work when DBC is full.

8. DBQL tables from DBC may require immediate cleaning.

9. You can turn off DBQL logging temporarily while doing this procedure so that no new rows are added; we'll turn it back on in step 12.

10. Create an empty table in a database other than DBC and run an insert/select for all of the DBQL data from the original table into the new empty table. (You can insert data based on date range if required, if space is low in the overall system.)

11. Run a Delete ALL (fastpath delete) on the DBQL tables in DBC. Running a Delete ALL uses something called fastpath which avoids using the transient journal and makes the delete complete without any issues:

```
**Fastpath Delete**
Delete from dbc.dbqlogtbl ALL;
```

12. Turn ON DBQL logging which was switched OFF in step 9.

13. If you are not able to log on to the system due to DBC refusing sessions, it is advisable to call Teradata GSC.

How it works...

When DBC is running dangerously low on space and refusing to insert a row into one of the resource logging tables, the database will eventually stop functioning, as in new logins will be refused and queries running on the system will spool out.

Regular space checks needs to be performed on a system to maintain the system performance. CPU lost can be gained again, but if a system has exhausted space, one way out is to delete some data from that system. So, it is of utmost important that critical tables are regularly backed up, so such space crunch data can be deleted without any implications. When space issues happen, there are only two ways to counter this. First, obviously, is the more time and money-consuming:

- Add space to the system by adding nodes
- Delete data

There are many other space checks that need to be done regularly on a system so that space is maintained adequately for data growth in tables:

- MVC on tables
- Skew analysis of tables
- Identifying unused, duplicated tables

There's more...

Transient journal can be avoided if using following method:

- Insert into an empty table (fastpath insert)
- Fastpath delete (using all)
- Avoid UPDATE on large skew tables with INSERT INTO .. SELECT
- Using ; before the second INSERT

As we have seen, space can become a performance issue if it is lacking, because processes are not able to complete. Other than DBC running out of space, there are a few more phenomena that can occur because of low disk space:

- Frequent cylinder migration
- Min-cylpacks
- De-fragmentation execution

See also

- Viewpoint alter of TJ

Optimizing queries

In this recipe, we will show you the basic steps that you can follow to optimize or tune a query. Please be aware that a query can be tuned via multiple methods. This recipe will provide some fundamental steps that can be applied to any query to optimize it as per its identified issue.

A query can show the following issues:

- A product join
- A skewed join
- High CPU/IO steps
- Skewed PI
- Other factors such as using function in joins, joining unmatched columns, and many more

Getting ready

You need to connect to the Teradata system via SQLA or Studio. Identify the query that needs to be optimized.

How to do it...

The following are the steps for optimizing the query:

1. List the data objects involved in the query. Do a show on query. Using the SHOW command before the query will display all the objects (tables, views, procs, macros) involved in the query:

   ```
   **To get all the object in a query**

   SHOW
   SELECT USERNAME , tbl.queryid , AcctStringDate , startTime , CAST(
   (EXTRACT ( HOUR FROM ( ( FirstRespTime - StartTime ) HOUR( 3 ) TO
   ```

```
SECOND ( 2 ) ) ) (TITLE 'Hour')) * 3600 + (EXTRACT ( MINUTE FROM ( (
FirstRespTime - StartTime ) HOUR( 3 ) TO SECOND( 2 ) ) ) (TITLE
'Minute')) * 60 + (EXTRACT ( SECOND FROM ( ( FirstRespTime -
StartTime ) HOUR( 3 ) TO SECOND( 2 ) ) ) (TITLE 'Second')) AS DEC (
10 ,
 2 ) ) AS response_secs , CAST( (EXTRACT ( HOUR FROM ( (
Firststeptime - StartTime ) HOUR( 3 ) TO SECOND( 2 ) ) ) (TITLE
'Hour')) * 3600 + (EXTRACT ( MINUTE FROM ( ( Firststeptime -
StartTime ) HOUR( 3 ) TO SECOND( 2 ) ) ) (TITLE 'Minute')) * 60 +
(EXTRACT ( SECOND FROM ( ( Firststeptime - StartTime ) HOUR( 3 ) TO
SECOND( 2 ) ) ) (TITLE 'Second')) AS DEC ( 10 ,
 2 ) ) AS delay_secs , appid , sessionid , MaxAmpCPUTime * HASHAMP
( ) + 1 ( NAMED myEffectiveCPU ) ,
 AMPCPUTime ( NAMED myTotalCPUTime ) , myEffectiveCPU -
myTotalCPUTime ( NAMED mySkewOverhead ) ,
 ( myTotalCPUTime / ( myEffectiveCPU + 1 ) * 100 ) ( NAMED
myParallelEfficiency ) , MaxAmpIO * HASHAMP ( ) + 1 ( NAMED
myEffectiveIO ) , TotalIOCount( NAMED myTotalIOCount ) ,
myEffectiveIO - myTotalIOCount( NAMED SkewIO ) , spoolusage ,
 ERRORCODE , errortext , querytext , queryband
FROM dbc.QryLog tbl ,
 (
SELECT procid , queryid
FROM dbc.QryLogObjects
WHERE objectdatabasename = 'pdcrinfo'
 AND objecttablename = 'Accesslog'
 AND CAST( CollectTimeStamp AS DATE ) = CURRENT_DATE
GROUP BY 1 , 2 ) obj
WHERE CAST( tbl.CollectTimeStamp AS DATE ) = CURRENT_DATE
 AND obj.queryid = tbl.queryid
```

2. Run `DIAGNOSTIC HELPSTATS ON FOR SESSION`. This will help you to see recommended stats in the `EXPLAIN` plan that you will generate in step 3.

3. Before executing any query it is always recommended to check the `EXPLAIN` plan of the query. A know query can also have a bad explain on any given day, if the stats are not proper on it. Do an `EXPLAIN` of query.

4. In the explain plan generated in step 3, look for (these are high-level problem that can be seen via the naked eye):
   - Product join
   - Extremely high or low row estimates
   - The translate function

5. At the end of explain plan you will also get the recommended statistics that you might need to collect. Do not collect them blindly; we need to check which ones will help us.

6. On the objects derived in step 1 (by using the SHOW command), check the statistics of the underlying tables:

```
Help stats DBC.DBQLobjtbl;
Help stats DBC.DBQLogtbl;
```

7. Now we need to compare the stats from these tables to the stats we got in explain plan; look for stats on columns that were collected no later than 1 week (in some cases, 2 day stats are also considered stale). Mark those stats from recommendations that are stale. If you find some extra stats that are stale, mark them too.

8. From the derived object list, check for tables that have PPI, Primary Partition Index, applied. Check in the query if these columns are used. If not, try to put them in the where clause. Using PPI helps in avoiding a full table scan; also, joining two PPI tables on similar PPI columns helps in effective join creation.

9. Check for common errors, if PI/PPI missing from join.

10. In explain plan check for translate keyword, this implies an unwanted translation between data type is occurring .

11. The most basic and easy method is to break a query into multi-step processes using volatile or global temp tables to match the data type in the join:

```
("(TRANS_DT <= ETS_DT) AND ((TRANSLATE((ACCT_New )USING
LATIN_TO_UNICODE)(FLOAT, FORMAT '-9.99999999999999E-999'))
(ACCOUNT_NUMBER ))").
```

12. Check if distinct is used. Can it be converted to GROUP BY (if the data is more skewed)?

13. If explain plan show more estimated times in the **MERGE** step can lead to skewed PI. Also, you might want to check if a table can be moved from **SET** to **MULTISET**.

How it works...

To begin with query optimization, you first need to identify queries that are impacting and are under performing on system. Tuning efforts can be rewarding when the right queries are identified and captured. Choosing the queries with the greatest work impact is an integral part of performance tuning. You want to spend your time and effort on those queries which have the most return on the time you invest and to make system more stable for others.

The explain plan is the most effective way to optimize any query without its execution. If you are able to read the explain plan correctly and effectively, you can tune your query without any issues. Your business outcome should be in line with explain; if estimated rows are too low or too high, you should be able to identify that. The flow for optimizing a query is explained in the following figure:

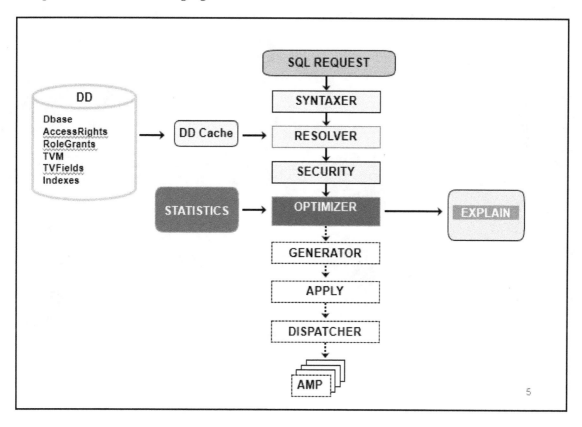

See also

Identifying suspect queries.

12
Troubleshooting

In this chapter, we will cover the following topics:

- Restarting the Teradata system
- Insufficient memory to parse this request
- Recovering AMP down
- Performing scandisk on the system
- Unlocking the DBC
- Managing the FSG cache

Introduction

Teradata Database provides system-based utilities that help users to change system parameters or to check the system's status.

You can start the utilities either via the command line or the graphical user interfaces. These utilities have similar behavior to other utilities you will have used in other systems. You need to choose from the given options and the result will be displayed based on the options you chose. To execute these utilities, you must have the appropriate access provided.

Executing command-line utilities should be done with care, as they can bring down the system if they are not executed properly.

Utility files are copied to all nodes by PDE software. This is done when your TD engineers configure/build Teradata Database.

These tools are also available from the Viewpoint remote console page as well, as shown in the following screenshot:

Some of the utilities that help in maintaining system health are as follows:

Utility Name	Used For
DBS control	Lists and changes system parameters
Packdisk	Recovers cylinder space
Defragment	Defrags cylinder on AMPs
Scandisk	Checks file system consistency
Checktable	Internal data consistency; should be executed after scandisk
Table rebuild	Recovers inconsistent data output from scandisk or checktable
Recovery manager	Checks rollback tables on the system
Showlocks	Displays locks on objects held by backup and recovery
Updatespace	Overcomes phantom spool space issues
Vproc manager	Manages Vproc and restarts the system

Restarting the TD system

In this recipe, we will look at how we can use the Teradata utility to restart the Teradata system. Please take care when executing these commands. You should execute the restart command only in extreme conditions; moreover, before executing this you must contact the Teradata engineers for your site. They can give you the best advice if you need to execute these commands.

There are two kinds of TPA reset:

- Intentional or scheduled restart using a command
- Unintentional or unscheduled restart due to a malfunction

An unscheduled restart causes jobs to abort in between and can cause other ill effects, whereas scheduled ones are better as they allow jobs on the system to complete and provide notifications to users before the system is restarted.

Getting ready

You need to connect to the Teradata Database console. As we will be performing the restart on the VMware machine, you need to make sure that the `bin` directory is added to the session path. If the following command gives you an error, follow the next step:

```
tpareset
bash: tpareset: command not found
```

For Linux, execute `tdatcmd`—this adds the directories to the path to execute command-line utilities.

For Windows, go to **Start** | **Programs** | **Teradata Database** | **Database Window**:

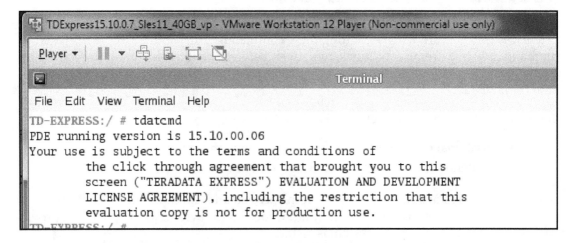

How to do it...

1. Open the **Teradata Database** console on VMware:

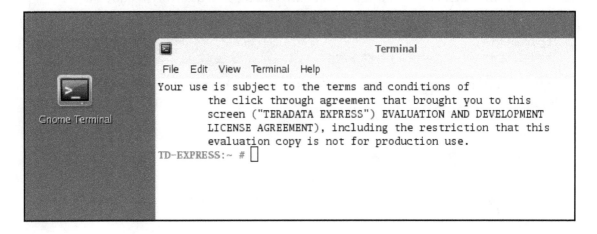

2. Execute the `tpareset` command:

```
File  Edit  View  Terminal  Help
Your use is subject to the terms and conditions of
        the click through agreement that brought you to this
        screen ("TERADATA EXPRESS") EVALUATION AND DEVELOPMENT
        LICENSE AGREEMENT), including the restriction that this
        evaluation copy is not for production use.
TD-EXPRESS:~ # tpareset

tpareset: Error, Reason for the reset must be specified.

Usage: tpareset [ -force ] [ -dump | -panic [-nodump] ]
        [ -stop [-keephgpgs] | -xit [-keephgpgs] | -exit [-keephgpgs]]
        [ -yes ] [ -help ] reason

TD-EXPRESS:~ #
```

Screen on execution of the tparest command

3. You need to provide an option and a reason with the command; now execute the following command as shown in code block:

```
tpareset -f testing the restart command
```

4. Press y to complete the reset and it will reboot all the nodes:

```
TD-EXPRESS:~ # tpareset -f testing the restart command

            You are about to restart the database
                    on the system
                      'localhost'
            Do you wish to continue (default: n) [y,n] ^Ct
```

tparest reboot prompt for reboot

5. The system is restarted. Check the status of the system using the following command to make sure the system is up and has all its nodes functioning after the restart:

```
pdestate -a
```

Can be seen in following figure:

```
TD-EXPRESS:~ # pdestate -a
PDE state is RUN/STARTED.
DBS state is 5: Logons are enabled - The system is quiescent
TD-EXPRESS:~ #
```

How it works...

You might need to restart the system to kill an unwanted process, after making changes to the system, or even after a version upgrade. TPA reset is done using using various options, as shown in the following table:

Option	Meaning
-f	Forces full reboot of all nodes. No Linux restart occurs.
-x	Shuts down the database.
-y	Auto confirmation, silent restart.
-d	To take dump before restart.
-l	Restarts with delay.
-p	Node panic before dump is taken.
-q	Silent mode, no user confirmation is asked for.

There's more...

Teradata Database also saves restart information in the `Software_Event_LogV` DBC table. You can query this table to check when and for what reason the restart occurred on the system. It will be stored as a plain text document on your desktop:

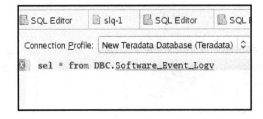

Query for Software_Event_LogV

This can also be checked from Linux. Restart messages are stored under the following path on a Linux machine:

`/var/log/messages`

Once you are at the required path, do a read of the messages file using `more` or `cat`. You need to search for `restart` to check when the restart is registered in the log:

```
Jan  2 05:33:29 TD-EXPRESS gnome-session[4769]: WARNING: Unable to determine session: Unable to lookup session information for process '4
Jan  2 05:34:41 TD-EXPRESS gnome-session[4769]: WARNING: Unable to determine session: Unable to lookup session information for process '4
Jan  2 05:39:19 TD-EXPRESS Teradata[4994]: INFO: Teradata: 13895 #PDE: TPA restart initiated by this node, 001-01, for event 10198.
Jan  2 05:39:19 TD-EXPRESS Teradata[4994]: INFO: Teradata: 13895 #PDE: TPA restart requested by node 001-01 for event 10198.
Jan  2 05:39:19 TD-EXPRESS kernel: tdmeter: meter_mode Set To 0.
Jan  2 05:39:19 TD-EXPRESS Teradata[10803]: DEGRADED: Teradata: 10198●#Force a TPA restart.●
Jan  2 05:39:19 TD-EXPRESS Teradata[10803]: Restart reason is: testing the restart command
Jan  2 05:39:27 TD-EXPRESS recond[10815]: INFO: TdatTools: 29001 #tuning change: /usr/pde/etc/recondTunables.txt
Jan  2 05:39:27 TD-EXPRESS recond[10815]:   Before:     t11_current_soft_resource_limit  = 0
Jan  2 05:39:27 TD-EXPRESS recond[10815]:   After:      t11_current_soft_resource_limit  = 0xffffffff(-1)
Jan  2 05:39:27 TD-EXPRESS recond[10815]: INFO: TdatTools: 29001 #tuning change: /usr/pde/etc/recondTunables.txt
Jan  2 05:39:27 TD-EXPRESS recond[10815]:   Before:     t12_maximum_hard_resource_limit  = 0
Jan  2 05:39:27 TD-EXPRESS recond[10815]:   After:      t12_maximum_hard_resource_limit  = 0xffffffff(-1)
Jan  2 05:39:27 TD-EXPRESS recond[10815]: INFO: TdatTools: 29001 #Current Working Directory set: /var/opt/teradata/tdtemp
Jan  2 05:39:28 TD-EXPRESS recond[10815]: INFO: TdatTools: 29001 #pdeMain has started recond -r
```

It is also critical to look for this in your logs when an unscheduled restart has occurred on the system or when you are running out of AWTs.

Insufficient memory to parse this request

One of the most important utilities in the Teradata regime is `dbscontrol`. Failure 3710 occurs when there is insufficient memory to parse this request, during the optimizer phase.

This happens when the query you are executing crosses the max parser memory size limit defined in `dbscontrol`. Current values for MaxParseTreeSegs stored in `dbccontrol` record fields do not allocate enough parser memory to process the request. In this recipe, we will use the `dbscontrol` parameter to display and change the MaxParseTreeSegs database parameters.

Changing their values without consulting Teradata engineers is not recommended. Each database is designed with these unique values based on the configuration and software version, so, take precautions when you change these values.

Some of the parameters, when changed, require a system restart, but MaxParseTreeSegs does not.

Getting ready

You need to connect to the Teradata Database console. As we will be performing the change on a VMware machine, you need to make sure the `bin` directory is added to the session path. If the following command gives you an error, follow the next step:

```
dbscontrol
bash: dbccontrol: command not found
```

For Linux, execute `tdat cmd`—it adds the directories to the path to execute the command-line utilities.

For Windows, go to **Start** I **Programs** I **Teradata Database** I **Database Window**:

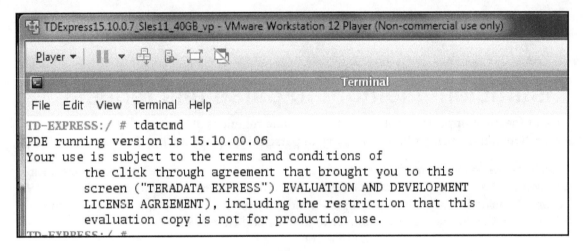

How to do it...

1. Open the Teradata Database console on VMware, as shown in the following screenshot:

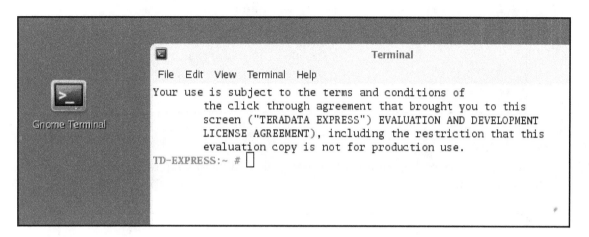

2. Execute the dbscontrol command, and the screen will look something like this:

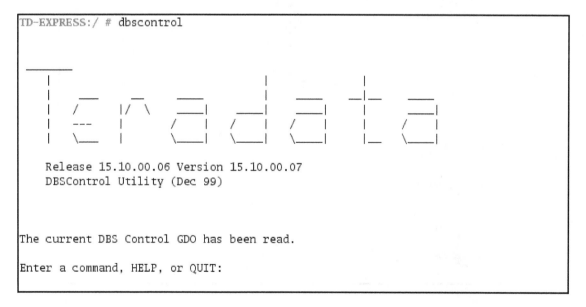

Screen on execution of dbscontrol command

3. Next, execute `display` to display the current values; copy these values in a separate file, in case you need to revert back to them:

```
DBS Control Record - Optimizer Statistics Fields:

    1.  DefaultTimeThreshold         = 0 (Disabled; Default value)
    2.  DefaultUserChangeThreshold   = 0 (Disabled; Default value)
    3.  SysChangeThresholdOption     = 0 (Enabled with DBQL ObjectUsage; Default value)
    4.  SysSampleOption              = 0 (Enabled; Default value)
    5.  BLCStats                     = 0 (Enabled; Default value)


Enter a command, HELP, or QUIT:
display
```

The current values on execution on display command

4. Run the following command to change this value to `4000` or the desired number you want to set to `modify perf 4=6,000`:

```
DBS Control Record - Performance Fields:

    1.  DictionaryCacheSize        = 8192      (KB; Default value)
    2.  DBSCacheCtrl               = TRUE      (Enabled)
    3.  DBSCacheThr                = 10        (Percent; Default value)
    4. •MaxParseTreeSegs•         •= 4000 •
    5.  ReadAhead                  = TRUE      (Enabled)
    6.  StepsSegmentSize           = 1024      (KB; Default value)
    7.  RedistBufSize              = 3832      (Bytes; Default value)
    8.  DisableSyncScan            = FALSE     (Enabled)
    9.  SyncScanCacheThr           = 10        (Percent; Default value)
   10.  HTMemAlloc                 = 10        (Percent; Default value)
   11.  SkewAllowance              = 75        (Percent; Default value)
   12.  Read Ahead Count           = 1         (Data block; Default value)
   13.  PPICacheThrP               = 10        (PPI cache per AMP = 1.0% of 100.00MB: 1.00MB)
   14.  ReadLockOnly               = FALSE
   15.  IAMaxWorkloadCache         = 64        (MB)
   16.  MaxRequestsSaved           = 600
   17.  UtilityReadAheadCount      = 10        (Blocks; Default value)
   18.  StandAloneReadAheadCount   = 20        (Blocks; Default value)
   19.  DisablePeekUsing           = FALSE     (Enabled)
   20.  IVMaxWorkloadCache         = 1         (MB; Default value)
   21.  RevertJoinPlanning         = FALSE     (Default value)
   22.  MaxJoinTables              = 128
   23.  DBQLXMLPlanMemLimit        = 64000     (KB; Default value)
   24.  LimitInlistCVal            = 1048576
   25.  NumStatisticsCacheSegs     = 5         (SizeofSegment is 1024KB)
   26.  SHOW IN XML Memory Limit   = 64000     (KB; Default value)
   27.  DictionaryCacheSegmentSize = 16        ( * 64 KBs; Default value)
   28.  PRPDMaxSkewedVals          = 50        (Default value)
   29.  PRPDSkewPct                = 80        (Percent; Default value)
   30.  DBQLLOBCacheSize           = 2         (MB; Default:2, Min:2, Max:16)
   31.  HJ2IMHJ                    = FALSE
```

5. Execute the Write command; this change will become effective after the DBS Control Record has been written.

6. If a restart is required, it will be displayed in the dbscontrol field. Some settings will be displayed after they are changed, but may not be changed internally unless a restart takes place.

7. Use QUIT to execute the utility.

How it works...

dbscontrol record fields are logically grouped based on how the Teradata Database uses them. The physical position of the field in the record is not significant. The group names are defined as follows.

The dbscontrol utility program provides a means to display and modify the fields of the DBS Control Record, which is stored on the system as a **globally distributed object** (**GDO**). The general command syntax is as follows:

```
<Command> [ <GroupName> ]
```

This is a command followed by a group name (if any). The valid commands are DISPLAY, MODIFY, WRITE, HELP, and QUIT.

The valid group names are GENERAL, FILESYS, PERFORMANCE, CHECKSUM, STORAGE, INTERNAL, STATISTICS, and COMPRESSION.

Note that all commands and groups may be abbreviated to their first unique character.

Execute the following to the display general parameters related to dbscontrol:

```
Enter a command, HELP, or QUIT:
dis g

DBS Control Record - General Fields:

    1. Version                      = 10
    2. SysInit                      = TRUE          (2015-10-17 23:42)
    3. DeadLockTimeout              = 240           (Seconds)
    4. (Reserved for future use)
    5. HashFuncDBC                  = 6             (Universal)
    6. (Reserved for future use)
    7. (Reserved for future use)
    8. SessionMode                  = 0             (Teradata mode)
    9. LockLogger                   = FALSE         (Disabled)
   10. RollbackPriority             = FALSE         (Disabled)
   11. MaxLoadTasks                 = 5
   12. RollForwardLock              = FALSE         (Disabled)
   13. MaxDecimal                   = 15
   14. CenturyBreak                 = 0
   15. DateForm                     = 0             (IntegerDate)
   16. System TimeZone Hour         = 0
   17. System TimeZone Minute       = 0
   18. System TimeZone String       = Not Set
   19. (Reserved for future use)
   20. RoundHalfwayMagUp            = FALSE
   21. (Reserved for future use)
   22. Target Level Emulation       = FALSE
   23. Export Width Table ID        = 0             (Expected Defaults)
   24. DBQL Log Last Resp           = FALSE
   25. DBQL Options                 = 0             (No options)
   26. ExternalAuthentication       = 0             (On)
   27. IdCol Batch Size             = 10000
   28. LockLogger Delay Filter      = FALSE
   29. LockLogger Delay Filter Time = 0             (Seconds; Default value)
```

There's more...

You can access the `dbscontrol` utility via the following steps:

1. The command line `dbscontrol`.
2. Viewpoint **Remote Console** (select DBS Control) as shown in the following screenshot:

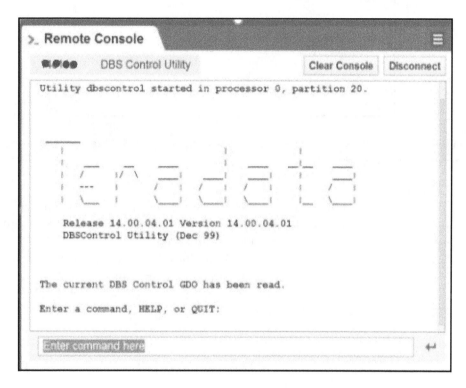

Viewpoint **Remote Console**

3. Supervisor start `dbscontrol`, as shown in the following screenshot:

```
TD-EXPRESS:/ # cnsterm 6
Attempting to connect to CNS...Completed.
Hello

Input Supervisor Command:
> start dbscontrol
start dbscontrol

Started 'dbscontrol' in window 1
 at Tue Jan  2 08:01:13 2018


Input Supervisor Command:
> dis perf
```

As we saw, there are eight valid fields in the `dbscontrol` record. Here, we list some of the important fields and their purposes:

- **General fields**:
    - **DeadLockTimeout**: This field is used by the dispatcher to determine the interval, in seconds, between deadlock time-out detection cycles. The default value is 240.
    - **SessionMode**: This field defines the system default transaction mode, case sensitivity, and character truncation rule for a session. The setting is either 0 (Teradata) or 1 (ANSI). The default is Teradata. The ANSI setting defaults SQL sessions to ANSI transaction semantics.
    - **LockLogger**: This allows you to log the delays caused by database locks to help in identifying lock conflict. To enable this feature, set the field to TRUE.
    - **MaxLoadTasks**: The maximum combined number of FastLoad, MultiLoad, and possibly FastExport. This field works differently depending on the value of MaxLoadAWT. The maximum value can be 15.
    - **CenturyBreak**: This field defines which Teradata Dates are specific to the 21st century.
    - **IdColBatchSize**: This is used for identity tables. Indicates the size of the pool of numbers to be reserved for generating numbers for a batch of rows, to be bulk-inserted into a table with an identity column.

- **Performance fields**:
  - **MaxParseTreeSegs**: These fields define the maximum number of tree segments that the parser will allocate while parsing a request. The valid range of values is 12 to 12,000. The default value is 2,000.
  - **ReadAhead**: This field is used to enable or disable the performance enhancements associated with the read ahead sequential file access workload for database 15.10.
  - **HTMemAlloc**: This field specifies the percentage of memory to be allocated to a hash table for a hash join. A value of 0 turns off hash joins.
  - **SkewAllowance**: This field specifies a percentage factor used by the optimizer in deciding on the size of each hash join partition. It makes allowances for data skewed in the build relation. The valid range is 20 to 80.

- **Filesystem fields**:
  - **FreeSpacePercent**: Used to determine the percentage of free space on cylinders during bulk load.
  - **MiniCylPackLowCylProd**: Falling below this number will generate a `miniclypack` on the system. Setting a higher value can hamper system performance.
  - **DefragLowCylProd**: Falling below this number will generate cylinder defragmentation on the system. Setting a higher value can hamper system performance.

- **Statistics**:
  - **DefaultTimeThreshold**: Value in days which indicates threshold values after which statistics recollection will be performed.
  - **DefaultUserChangeThreshold**: Value of data percentage changes after which statistics recollection will be performed. *If USING THRESHOLD PERCENT* is used then it will supersede this option.
  - **SysSampleOption**: Sample option for statistics recollection.
  - **BLCStats**: To collect block level statistics information. 0(default), 1 will enable, 2 will disable.

Recovering AMP down

Teradata is mainly made of nodes, access module processors known as AMPs, a Parsing Engine, and BYNET.

Every database machine is composed of hardware and software. Teradata is a powerful database that comes with high-end processing hardware and secure and fast analytical software.

Teradata hardware components are:

- Teradata TPA or database nodes (Trusted Parallel Application)
- BYNET nodes
- Non-TPA nodes (used for applications, loading, connecting to the mainframe system, and so on); not common to every customer
- Ethernet or other connectivity hardware

The Teradata software components are:

- Virtual processors:
    - Access module processors
    - Parsing Engines
- BYNET software
- Database software

Figure shows how SMP and MPP systems are made of:

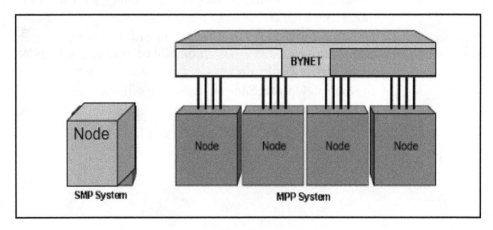

In this recipe, we will look at how we can make the AMPs in our VMware online and offline. This is used in situations when you need to recover a down AMP on a system. It is advised that you get in touch with your Teradata site engineer before performing any of the steps mentioned here on your production system.

Teradata engineers assigned to your site have better knowledge and tools to make informed decisions regarding system restart.

We will use the Vproc Manager utility in this recipe for troubleshooting the AMP down situation.

Getting ready

You need to connect to the Teradata Database console. As we will be performing the change on a VMware machine, you need to make sure the `bin` directory is added to the session path. If the following command gives you an error, follow the next step:

```
Vprocmanager
bash: Vprocmanager: command not found
```

For Linux, execute `tdatcmd`—it adds the directories to the path to execute command-line utilities.

For Windows, go to **Start** | **Programs** | **Teradata Database** | **Database Window**:

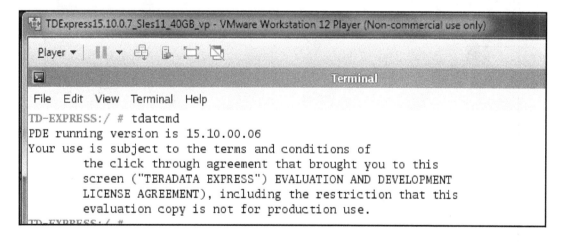

How to do it...

1. Open the Teradata Database console on VMware, as shown in the following screenshot:

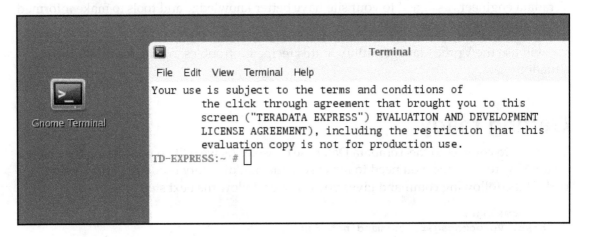

2. Execute the `vprocmanager` command:

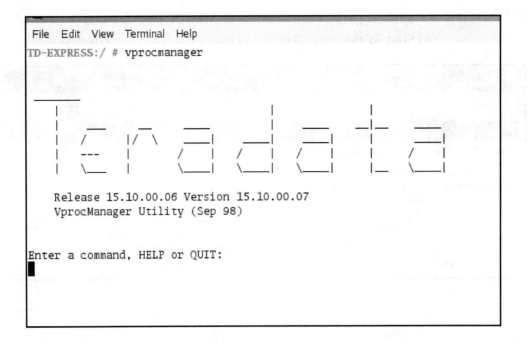

3. Let's first check the status of Vprocs and the overall system health. Execute the `status` command as follows:

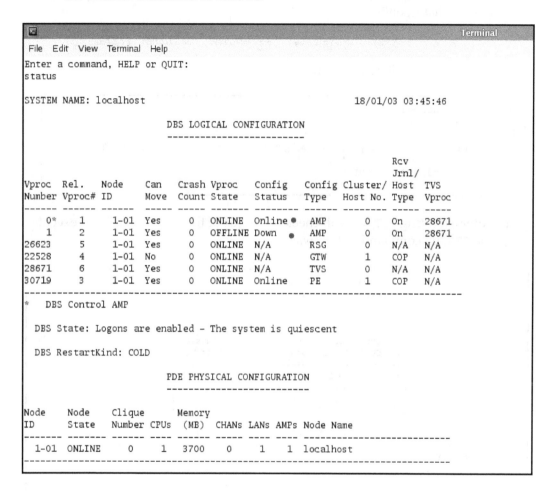

```
                                                                    Terminal
 File  Edit  View  Terminal  Help
Enter a command, HELP or QUIT:
status

SYSTEM NAME: localhost                              18/01/03 03:45:46


                      DBS LOGICAL CONFIGURATION
                      -------------------------


                                                          Rcv
                                                          Jrnl/
Vproc  Rel.   Node    Can   Crash Vproc   Config  Config Cluster/ Host  TVS
Number Vproc# ID      Move  Count State   Status  Type   Host No. Type  Vproc
------ ------ ------  ----- ----- ------- -------- ------ -------- ----- -----
    0*   1    1-01    Yes     0   ONLINE  Online   AMP      0      On    28671
    1    2    1-01    Yes     0   OFFLINE Down     AMP      0      On    28671
26623    5    1-01    Yes     0   ONLINE  N/A      RSG      0      N/A   N/A
22528    4    1-01    No      0   ONLINE  N/A      GTW      1      COP   N/A
28671    6    1-01    Yes     0   ONLINE  N/A      TVS      0      N/A   N/A
30719    3    1-01    Yes     0   ONLINE  Online   PE       1      COP   N/A
-----------------------------------------------------------------------------
*   DBS Control AMP

  DBS State: Logons are enabled - The system is quiescent

  DBS RestartKind: COLD


                      PDE PHYSICAL CONFIGURATION
                      --------------------------

Node    Node    Clique      Memory
ID      State   Number CPUs (MB)   CHANs LANs AMPs Node Name
------- ------- ------ ---- ------ ----- ---- ---- -------------------------
 1-01   ONLINE     0     1   3700    0    1    1   localhost
-----------------------------------------------------------------------------
```

4. As seen in the output, one of the AMPs has an offline status and the other is online. Note that we have only two AMP systems on VMware, AMP 0, and AMP 1.

5. Next, to bring AMP 1 online, we will execute the SET command. This needs to be accompanied by an AMP number, followed by the status indicating that we require that is, online:

```
SET <AMP NUMBER > = <STATUS> -- ONLINE, OFFLINE, FATAL
```

Can be seen in following figure:

```
Enter a command, HELP or QUIT:
SET 1 = online

Vproc 1 will begin recovery in the background via the Recovery Control Task

Enter a command, HELP or QUIT:
```

6. After executing SET, we will check the status of the system again. Re-execute the STATUS command as follows:

```
                     DBS LOGICAL CONFIGURATION
                     -------------------------

                                                     Rcv
                                                     Jrnl/
Vproc  Rel.   Node   Can   Crash Vproc   Config   Config Cluster/ Host  TVS
Number Vproc# ID     Move  Count State   Status   Type   Host No. Type  Vproc
------ ------ ------ ----- ----- ------- -------- ------ -------- ----- -----
    0*    1    1-01  Yes     0   ONLINE  Online   AMP      0      On    28671
    1     2    1-01  Yes     0   UTILITY Catchup  AMP      0      On    28671
26623     5    1-01  Yes     0   ONLINE  N/A      RSG      0      N/A   N/A
22528     4    1-01  No      0   ONLINE  N/A      GTW      1      COP   N/A
28671     6    1-01  Yes     0   ONLINE  N/A      TVS      0      N/A   N/A
30719     3    1-01  Yes     0   ONLINE  Online   PE       1      COP   N/A
-------------------------------------------------------------------------
*   DBS Control AMP

  DBS State: Logons are enabled - The system is quiescent

  DBS RestartKind: COLD


                     PDE PHYSICAL CONFIGURATION
                     --------------------------

Node   Node   Clique    Memory
ID     State  Number CPUs (MB)  CHANs LANs AMPs Node Name
------ ------ ------ ---- ------ ----- ---- ---- -------------------------
 1-01  ONLINE    0    1   3700    0     1    1   localhost
-------------------------------------------------------------------------
```

```
Enter a command, HELP or QUIT:
restart


Are you sure you want to Restart the DBS now (Y/N)?
Y█
```

8. Let's execute the STATUS command again, as shown in the following screenshot. AMP 1 is now online:

```
File  Edit  View  Terminal  Help
                        DBS LOGICAL CONFIGURATION
                        -------------------------


                                                    Rcv
                                                    Jrnl/
Vproc  Rel.   Node   Can   Crash Vproc   Config   Config Cluster/ Host  TVS
Number Vproc# ID     Move  Count State   Status   Type   Host No. Type  Vproc
------ ------ ------ ----- ----- ------- -------- ------ -------- ----- -----
    0*    1    1-01  Yes     0   ONLINE  Online   AMP       0     On    28671
    1     2    1-01  Yes     0   ONLINE  Online   AMP       0     On    28671
26623    5    1-01  Yes     0   ONLINE  N/A      RSG       0     N/A   N/A
22528    4    1-01  No      0   ONLINE  N/A      GTW       1     COP   N/A
28671    6    1-01  Yes     0   ONLINE  N/A      TVS       0     N/A   N/A
30719    3    1-01  Yes     0   ONLINE  Online   PE        1     COP   N/A
------------------------------------------------------------------------------
*   DBS Control AMP

  DBS State: Logons are enabled - The system is quiescent

  DBS RestartKind: COLD

                        PDE PHYSICAL CONFIGURATION
                        -------------------------

Node   Node   Clique    Memory
ID     State  Number CPUs (MB)  CHANs LANs AMPs Node Name
------ ------ ------ ---- ------ ----- ---- ---- -------------------------
 1-01  ONLINE   0     1   3700    0     1    2  localhost
------------------------------------------------------------------------------


  PDE State: RUN/STARTED
```

How it works...

The `Vprocmanager` utility program provides the means to manage/change Vproc attributes. The general command syntax is as follows:

```
<COMMAND> <Options> <Arguments> [ ; ]
```

A command is followed by its specific arguments. All commands, options, and arguments may be abbreviated to the shortest unique string.

Some of the commands are `BOOT`, `HELP`, `INITVDISK`, `QUIT`, `RESTART`, `SET`, `CLEARMVAMP`, and `STATUS`.

To get help regarding any command, enter the following:

```
HELP <COMMAND NAME>
```

Let's check how it works on the `SET` command:

```
Enter a command, HELP or QUIT:
help set

SET [/V] <VprocList> [=] <VprocState> [[,] <VprocList> [=] <VprocState>]...

SET RESTART [=] <RestartKind>

     o The first format of this command is used to change the state
       of a vproc or a list of vprocs. A maximum of 30720 vprocs
       can be specified. Any state change becomes effective immediately,
       although *no* changes are made regarding the Message Group(s)
       the vproc is in and whether it is the Control vproc or not.
       These changes are deferred until after the next DBS restart.
       The slash "V" option enables verbose mode if specified.
     o A VprocList is composed of one or more VprocIds or a range
       of VprocIds as seen below:

            <VProcList>  ::= VprocRange [ [,] VprocRange ]...
            <VprocRange> ::= [ VprocId | VprocId TO VprocId ]

     Examples:
          0 1 2 3
          0, 1, 1022 to 1023
          0 to 10, 1021, 1022
     o Valid VprocStates  are ONLINE, OFFLINE, UTILITY, NEWPROC,
       or FATAL. Enter "HELP <VprocState>"  for additional
       information.
     o The second format of this commands is used to define the Restart-
       Kind to use during the next DBS restart. It does not force an
       immediate restart.
     o Valid RestartKinds are COLD or COLDWAIT. Enter
       "HELP <RestartKind>" for additional information.
```

The following is the syntax for executing the SET command:

```
SET [/V] <VprocList> [=] <VprocState> [[,] <VprocList> [=] <VprocState>]...
SET RESTART [=] <RestartKind>
```

There's more...

Vproc manager (Vprocmanager) can be used for the following functions:

- Checking the status of the specific Vproc or Vprocs
- Altering the state of a Vproc or a series of Vprocs
- Initializing and starting the specific AMP Vproc
- Initializing the file subsystem on the vdisk associated with a certain AMP Vproc
- Forcefully restarting the database

Performing scandisk on the system

Teradata Database, as we know, provides a layer of security to your data, and to maintain its integrity it provides various tools for our disposal. One such utility is scandisk, which helps in checking filesystem errors on the cylinder.

Let's understand it as a Windows defragment tool provided on any Windows machine. It runs through the system data file structure and finds inconsistencies within it. In this figure (only for representation purposes), the highlighted squares are the sector are being scanned and the unhighlighted ones are getting ready to be scanned:

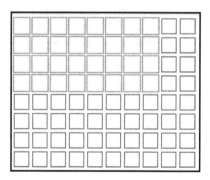

Any table or sector reported to have inconsistencies should be rebuilt using the table rebuild utility, and Teradata site engineers should be notified.

Getting ready

You need to connect to the Teradata Database console. As we will be performing the change on a VMware machine, you need to make sure the `bin` directory is added to the session path. If the following command gives you an error, follow the next step:

```
cnsterm
bash: cnsterm: command not found
```

For Linux, execute `tdatcmd`—this adds the directories to the path to execute command-line utilities.

For Windows, go to **Start** I **Programs** I **Teradata Database** I **Database Window**:

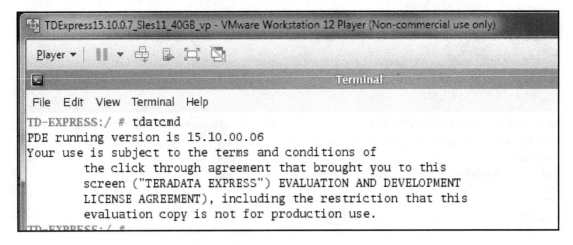

How to do it...

1. Open the Teradata Database console on VMware as shown in the following screenshot:

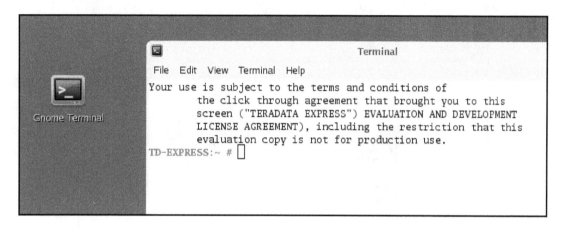

2. Start the `cnsterm` supervisor screen (or window) `cnsterm 6`. Ferret needs to be started first in the supervisor window before executing `scandisk`. Make note of the window in which `ferret` is started:

```
TD-EXPRESS:/ # cnsterm 6
Attempting to connect to CNS...Completed.
Hello

Input Supervisor Command:
```

3. Next, execute `ferret` and make note of the window in which `ferret` is started. To start `ferret`, execute the command that follows:

```
start ferret
```

```
Input Supervisor Command:
start > ferret
start ferret

Started 'ferret' in window 2
 at Wed Jan  3 05:52:41 2018


Input Supervisor Command:
>
```

4. Now exit the `cnsterm` `6` window by pressing *Ctrl + C*.

5. We will now enter the window in which the `ferret` utility was started in step 3, which is window 2 in our case.

6. Execute `cnsterm` `2`. You will see in the following screenshot that `ferret` is already started in window 2:

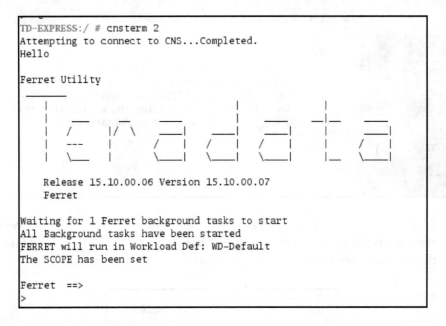

```
TD-EXPRESS:/ # cnsterm 2
Attempting to connect to CNS...Completed.
Hello

Ferret Utility


Release 15.10.00.06 Version 15.10.00.07
Ferret

Waiting for 1 Ferret background tasks to start
All Background tasks have been started
FERRET will run in Workload Def: WD-Default
The SCOPE has been set

Ferret  ==>
>
```

The workload in which `ferret` operates is the default. Check on the viewpoint for this workload.

7. Next, we will execute `scandisk` in the `ferret` window, as shown in the screenshot:

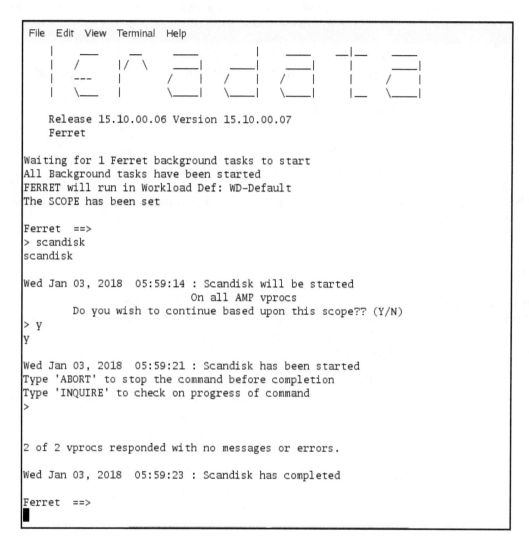

```
File  Edit  View  Terminal  Help

         |    __     __       |     __     _|_    __
         |   /     |/ \    __|    __|    __|   |     __|
         |   ---    |      /    |   /    |   /    |     |    /    |
         |   \__    |      \__|   \__|   \__|    |_    \__|


     Release 15.10.00.06 Version 15.10.00.07
     Ferret

Waiting for 1 Ferret background tasks to start
All Background tasks have been started
FERRET will run in Workload Def: WD-Default
The SCOPE has been set

Ferret  ==>
> scandisk
scandisk

Wed Jan 03, 2018  05:59:14 : Scandisk will be started
                    On all AMP vprocs
      Do you wish to continue based upon this scope?? (Y/N)
> y
y

Wed Jan 03, 2018  05:59:21 : Scandisk has been started
Type 'ABORT' to stop the command before completion
Type 'INQUIRE' to check on progress of command
>


2 of 2 vprocs responded with no messages or errors.

Wed Jan 03, 2018  05:59:23 : Scandisk has completed

Ferret  ==>
█
```

8. Use the ABORT or INQUIRE commands to cancel and check the progress of `scandisk` respectively.

How it works...

It is recommended to have the system in quiescent mode before executing `scandisk`. The `scandisk` command performs the following tasks in the background:

- It verifies data block content and matches the data descriptor
- Checks that all sectors in the cylinders are allocated to one and only one of the following:
    - Bad sector list
    - Free list
    - A data block
- It ensures that continuation bits are flagged correctly

Although scandisk does not restart your database, it is recommended to execute scandisk before checktable and before rebuilding any table.

There's more...

Teradata offers many other tools for checking consistency in data over the disk and cylinders. The checking of data and sectors is recommended as maintenance task on system. These utilities not only help in maintaining data integrity, but some of the tools such as `packdisk`, help restore system space when cylinders are low in space:

- **Checktable utility**: Checktable is a diagnostic and validation tool; it checks for inconsistencies, corruption in internal data structures such as table headers, row identifiers, and secondary indexes. It can be executed in three levels.
- **Table rebuild utility**: It repairs data corruption identified from `scandisk` and `checktable`.
- **Packdisk utility**: Packdisk helps to pack/free up/combine cylinders in AMP, making space for more data. To avoid mini-cylpacks on the system, `packdisk` is the recommended activity to be performed on the system.

Unlocking the DBC

Like every system, Teradata has a super user, and this super user is called **DBC**. DBC is the super parent in the database hierarchy, and subsequent database/user are children or inherit from it only.

Teradata introduced its first system, named DBC/1012, in the early 1980s. Teradata in its early release only used to connect to mainframe systems, but with subsequent advancements, it started to connect to a whole lot of applications and databases.

As seen in the following screenshot, DBC sits at the top of the pyramid:

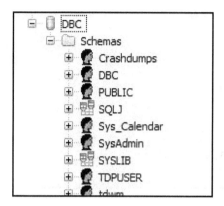

Teradata recommends not using this user; instead, create an admin user under DBC and use that. But in certain cases, you might need a DBC user, for example, if you want to grant access to other super users. Like other users, the DBC user can also be locked if multiple wrong attempts are made to log in.

 DBC stands for **database computer**.

A super user is of the utmost importance, and for that reason, DBC credentials need to be secured in the best way possible. If your DBC account is locked for some reason, it is important to contact a Teradata site engineer and resolve the issue via the service desk.

Getting ready

You need to connect to the console utility on the gateway node using the root user.

How to do it...

1. Log in to the gateway node as root.
2. Open `cnsterm 6` and execute the command shown in the screenshot:

```
TD-EXPRESS:/ # cnsterm 6
Attempting to connect to CNS...Completed.
Hello

Input Supervisor Command:
 > start tstsql

Start tstsql

Started 'tstql' in window 1

at Tue 16  Jan  2018  09:01:18 2018

 . .
```

3. Exit the window using *Ctrl + D* and enter `cnsterm 1`. In this window, the `tstsql` utility will have already been started.
4. Execute the following login statement in the `tstsql` window:

   ```
   .logon dbc/dbc
   ***Logon successfully completed.
   MODIFY USER dbc AS RELEASE PASSWORD LOCK;
   .logoff
   .quit
   ```

5. Exit the supervisor window.

How it works...

Teradata Database has many layers of security. The following table shows some ways to secure your database:

Method	Parameters
Authentication	User credentials Logon encryption Multiple type login mechanism, such as LDAP IP filters

Access control	Security roles Secure zones Query banding
Data protection	Network traffic encryption View Data encryption

To enable data encryption from SQLA, check the following fields in the advanced setting of ODBC:

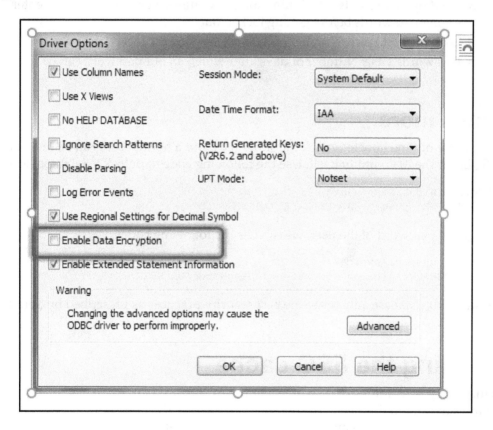

Teradata Database records and manages security settings in system tables. These tables can be audited as and when required. The following are the table and column values of `DBC.SyssecDefaults`:

- **ExpirePassword**: After how many days password will expire
- **PasswordMinChar**: Minimum number of characters that passwords should have
- **PasswordMaxChar**: Maximum number of characters that passwords can have
- **Password Digits**: Digits allowed in the passwords if the value is set to R
- **PasswordSpecChar**: Special characters allowed in passwords if value is set to 'R'
- **MaxLogonAttempts**: Maximum number of times a user is allowed to enter wrong passwords before getting locked out
- **LockedUserExpire**: Number of days after which the locked user will expire
- **PasswordReuse**: Number of days after which an old password can be reused

There's more...

The steps here outline how to unlock the super user, but a normal user can be unlocked from SQLA or the BTEQ utility itself. Use the following code to unlock a database user:

```
/*Unlock a database user*/
MODIFY USER  <user>  AS RELEASE PASSWORD LOCK;
```

To change the password of the user, we can use the following code:

```
/*Modify user password*/
MODIFY USER <username> as password=password FOR USER;
```

Make sure your database adheres to the best security practices as prescribed by Teradata.

Managing the FSG cache

With increasing need for faster responses of queries, Teradata Database has come up with many ways to cater to this need. The file segment cache, FSG subsystem, manages database files. It is the memory that is managed by PDE. The Teradata file system, FSYS, uses FSG services to access database segments on disk. AMPs are the basic entity that consumes the FSG cache as part of database segments residing in memory.

Understand FSG cache as a simple cache mechanism that stores parts of data rows in memory so AMPs, when reading data, do not have to go to the physical disk but can read rows from the memory itself. As we know, reading from memory is way faster than from the physical disk.

FSG provides an interface that allows the FSYS logic to merely access and release segments in memory. FSG takes care of the details of getting the data to and from permanent disk storage.

The FSG subsystem handles low-level database disk access. It typically manages database disks as raw devices, although it can also manage data in files on some platforms. FSG is responsible for caching recently used data, reading data from the disk into its cache, and writing updated segments out to the disk.

This memory is set up based on your hardware configuration and the nature of the request executing on the system. Any changes to FSG first need to be discussed with the Teradata site engineer.

In this recipe, we will check the FSG cache allocation for our VM machine and change the value accordingly.

Getting ready

You need to connect to the Teradata node using the `root user`.

How to do it...

1. Connect to the Teradata node using the remote console utility. Log in as a `root` user, as can be seen in the following screenshot:

2. Connect to the `ctl` utility and execute the following command, as shown in the following screenshot. It will show the amount of FSG cache available to a node:

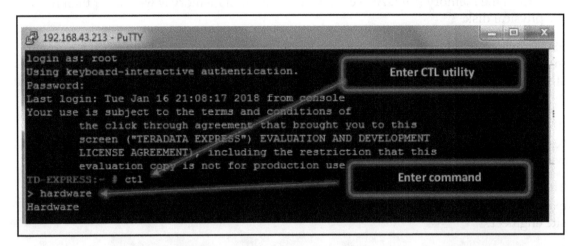

3. The following output would be generated, with maximum, minimum, and average values. This shows that AMP does not use all the memory but only a portion of it as per its needs:

```
TD-EXPRESS:~ # ctl
> hardware
Hardware

Node                                    min   max   avg              min   max   avg

#nodes              1            cpus/node    1     1     1   nodes/clique   1     1
1
nodes w/AMPS        1            mips/cpu   359   359   359   arrays/clique  0     0
0
                    segmem/vproc(mb) 1109  1109  1109

VPROCS
Type   Name         ##                                       Min     Max     AVG
 1     AMP          2 vprocs/node  2     2     2   kmem/vproc 440320  440320  440320
 2     PE           1 vprocs/node  1     1     1   kmem/vproc      0       0       0
 3     GTW          1 vprocs/node  1     1     1   kmem/vproc      0       0       0
 4     RSG          1 vprocs/node  1     1     1   kmem/vproc      0       0       0
 5     TVS          1 vprocs/node  1     1     1   kmem/vproc      0       0       0
 6                  0 vprocs/node  0     0     0   kmem/vproc      0       0       0
```

4. Now check the percentage of memory allocated to the system using the following command. It shows 30% of FSG allocated to the VM:

```
> screen dbs                                        Command
(0) Minimum Node Action:          Clique-Down
(1) Minimum Nodes Per Clique:     1                 (2) FSG cache Percent:   30
(3) Clique Failure:               Clique-Down       (4) Cylinder Read:       On
(5) Restart After DAPowerFail:    On                (6) Cylinder Read Ageing Thresho
ld:  0
(7) Maximum Fatal AMPs:           0
```

5. Now, to reduce it and free up some RAM, you can use the following command:

```
/*changing FSG cache*/
FSG cache Percent=20
```

6. To check the memory allocation per AMP, quit the ctl utility using the quit command, and at the root level, execute the following command:

```
/*check memory per AMP*/
pdeglobal fsg| more
```

7. The following would be the output:

```
CTB. DBS changes not written.
TD-EXPRESS:~ # pdeglobal fsg |more

-------- /var/opt/teradata/tdtemp/pdeglobal.dat --------

FSG:
  Cache: 1e (30%)
  VH Cache: 0 (0%)
  VH Cache Version: 1
  TotalPages: e0738  AvailPages: 35de4  TVSadj:
  Vprocs: 6 (6)  AMPs: 2 (2)  MemPerAmp: 1ae0000   Decimal value would be 450887680
  OneMegsPerAmp: 1ae  PdisksPerAmp: 1
  Depot: ON  HashAge: OFF  RWLockUpgrd: ON
  slotqsortthold: 1
  Pre-write: ON  Pw_iothreshold: a  Pw_max_io: 3  Oom_max_io: a  Pw_ahead_oom: 78 (120
)
  Pcache_oom: 60 (96%)  Pcache_pw: 5c (92%)
  Vcache_oom: 60 (96%)  Vcache_pw: 5c (92%)
```

How it works...

As we saw, the FSG cache is distributed randomly between AMPs, which shows that each AMP holds only certain amounts of data. This cache contains as many of the most recently used data rows as will fit in it. When Teradata Database tries to read a database block, it checks the cache first to minimize the I/O and improve the response time of queries. The following figure shows how requests flow for the disk and FAG cache:

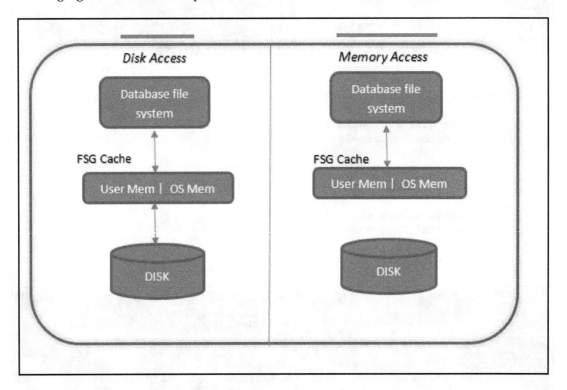

As there are other programs existing on memory, like database programs and OS modules, it is necessary that FSG cache size needs to be optimized. Objects or rows in FSG cache are freed up as per the ageing process.

You can monitor FSG cache using reusage macros, such as `ResUsageSpma` and `ResUsageSvpr`.

There's more...

A new feature in Teradata 14.10 was introduced called **Teradata Intelligent Memory** (**TIM**). It works in accordance with the FSG cache by keeping the *hottest* data on the system in memory automatically. The hottest data is the data that is accessed by requests/queries more often than others. And if a table is partitioned, it helps in keeping more the frequently used partition of the table in memory.

The TIM cache data is based on its temperature, and doesn't need to determine what is kept in the FSG cache based on an LRU algorithm. The most frequently accessed data on the system is placed into the FSG cache and then marked as *very hot* by the database, and this data is eligible to remain in memory where traditional aging techniques would have otherwise aged the data out of the cache.

Other Books You May Enjoy

If you enjoyed this book, you may be interested in these other books by Packt:

Learning Pentaho Data Integration 8 CE - Third Edition
María Carina Roldán

ISBN: 978-1-78829-243-6

- Explore the features and capabilities of Pentaho Data Integration 8 Community Edition
- Install and get started with PDI
- Learn the ins and outs of Spoon, the graphical designer tool
- Learn to get data from all kind of data sources, such as plain files, Excel spreadsheets, databases, and XML files
- Use Pentaho Data Integration to perform CRUD (create, read, update, and delete) operations on relational databases
- Populate a data mart with Pentaho Data Integration
- Use Pentaho Data Integration to organize files and folders, run daily processes, deal with errors, and more

Microsoft Power BI Cookbook
Brett Powell

ISBN: 978-1-78829-014-2

- Cleanse, stage, and integrate your data sources with Power BI
- Abstract data complexities and provide users with intuitive, self-service BI capabilities
- Build business logic and analysis into your solutions via the DAX programming language and dynamic, dashboard-ready calculations
- Take advantage of the analytics and predictive capabilities of Power BI
- Make your solutions more dynamic and user specific and/or defined including use cases of parameters, functions, and row level security
- Understand the differences and implications of DirectQuery, Live Connections, and
- Import-Mode Power BI datasets and how to deploy content to the Power BI Service and schedule refreshes
- Integrate other Microsoft data tools such as Excel and SQL Server Reporting Services into your Power BI solution

Leave a review - let other readers know what you think

Please share your thoughts on this book with others by leaving a review on the site that you bought it from. If you purchased the book from Amazon, please leave us an honest review on this book's Amazon page. This is vital so that other potential readers can see and use your unbiased opinion to make purchasing decisions, we can understand what our customers think about our products, and our authors can see your feedback on the title that they have worked with Packt to create. It will only take a few minutes of your time, but is valuable to other potential customers, our authors, and Packt. Thank you!

Index